Plain Stories
and Other Parables

Steven Schafer

Copyright © 2013 by Steven Schafer

ISBN: 978-1-304-55044-6

You may freely use any or all of the content of this book to tell your own stories. Proper credit is appreciated. Sale of the book or reproduction if any part in any form for personal profit is prohibited.

Contents

PREFACE 5
Redeeming Spit 7
Love Always Wins – Sometimes 13
The Wadi House 18
Old Hickory and Rev. Bill 23
Miracle at the UAW 28
The Hills on the Hill 35
The Little House 40
Of Rocks and Ants 45
The Son 50
Bill is Bored 56
A Lot to Remember 61
Prophet Nancy Gill 67
Jeffrey Goes to Heaven 72
The Story of Jerubal and the War 78
The Home Run 85
The Monarch and the Eagle 92
The Sisyphus Solution 97

THE PLAIN STORIES
    Arthur 101
    The Buzzard Buzz 107
    Father Jesús 115
    Mayor Jake 122

The Lourdes House	128
The Him Sing	134
Hazlet Pond	140
Prom '07	148

THE KRISTOFF YERUSHALIIM SERIES

Kristoff Yerushaliim	155
The Grand Opening	163
Out on a Limb	170
Crazy Louie	178
The Mt. Eremos Sermons	184
Trouble in Sea Gull Harbor	191
The Mayor's Daughter	198
They Who Have Ears	203
Sunrise Over Lake Huron	210
The End of the Beginning	217
The Funeral	224

Preface

Jesus never stood at a pulpit. So far as we know he never even preached a sermon in the way we think of sermons. He told stories. He told stories that made people think, that challenged them and their life styles. He told stories about God and the Kingdom. He told stories about life and faith and hope. He told stories that people could relate to in their own lives and culture. And, quite significantly, he let the stories stand on their own. He didn't explain them – so much so that the disciples questioned him about it. "Why do you speak to people in parables?" (John 13: 10).

Jesus told stories because stories stick in people's minds and memories far longer than sermons. He wanted people to ask themselves and one another: "What is he trying to say?" He wanted people to wrestle with his words for then the lesson is personalized and internalized and evaluated and applied.

The creativity of story making and the art of telling got lost somewhere along the way in the church in favor of men or women standing at a pulpit and simply telling their listeners what Jesus meant and how it applies. And that has worked well for two millennia and it continues to be quite effective even today.

But something happened to me a few years ago that changed my perspective on sermonizing. I attended an annual minister's convocation. I've attended dozens of these. The speakers are usually quite good, the fellowship pretty great. But this particular year the speaker didn't speak - at least in the same way others had. He sat on a stool and told stories. I was fascinated and inspired and suddenly knew that THIS is how Jesus must have taught - with simplicity and imagination and verbal imagery that made me take notice and to "see" the lessons being taught - sometimes to wonder just what the lesson was. That day I bought every one of the CDs Ed Kilbourne had available (http://www.edkilbourne.com/) and, over the course of the next few weeks listened to them repeatedly. I bought books of "narrative sermons." I tried to soak up as much information on story/sermon telling as I could find. Then, one Sunday morning, I stepped away from the pulpit and told a story. And I liked it. So did my congregation.

This book is a collection of what I have come to call "story sermons" that I've written and told. Most of them were written as story sermons but a few of the earlier ones were written as sermons that were mostly already stories before I even knew such a thing existed. I believe each one to be wholly original except where noted but must admit that ideas and concepts and phraseology may have inadvertently been borrowed from some of the volumes I've read. For any unintentional plagiarism that may be contained here, I sincerely apologize to the author(s) - and thank them.

Every story sermon has a spiritual point (often more than one) that may or may not be quickly discernible. If you cannot find it/them, please enjoy the story simply as a story. I didn't intend to be quite so obtuse that one can't figure out my "lesson" but sometimes that is the nature of story telling.

As you read the stories, please keep in mind they were written for telling aloud so may not be, in some ways, grammatically correct in structure as a story written for reading must be. Such is the nature of the art.

I must thank the people of my church - Mt. Hope Congregational - for being so open to creativity and putting up with the unusual from me from time to time. They have embraced and look forward (so they say) to summer Sundays where story sermons have emerged in these years. They are great people serving a great God.

And, of course, I must thank my wife Sue and my daughters Rachel and Abi for always being the inspiration of my life. They don't appear too often in my story sermons, but they have frequently from the pulpit in traditional sermons, by name and/or by allusion and they have always handled that part of their public lives with wondrous grace.

REDEEMING SPIT
Mark 7: 31-36 and Mark 8: 22-25

In the beginning God created the heavens and the earth.
Now the earth was formless and empty, darkness was over the surface of the deep, and the Spirit of God was hovering over the waters....

Thus begins the greatest drama of the universe. It's set in poetic form there in the book of Genesis. Two sets of three, then a finale. First, God created the three great kingdoms:
Day 1: The Kingdom of light and darkness.
Day 2 The Kingdom of land and sea.
Day 3: The Kingdom of vegetation and trees and plants and the seed that replenishes them.
Then, in the second set of triplets, he made the rulers over the three kingdoms:
To rule over the kingdom of light and darkness (the first kingdom) God made the sun and moon. These would make sure it wasn't perpetually daylight nor perpetually darkness. They would provide seasons and tides and sustain life.
Then God made the rulers over the kingdom of land and sea - fish and whales and huge sea creatures, dinosaurs and birds and insects and all sorts of predatory animals.
And, finally, God made the rulers over the plant life on earth – livestock and non-carnivorous animals of all kinds – plant eaters – animals of peace... and then, late in the day, God made humans to be the caretakers over all of it...
It is a wonderful story. God made some truly awesome things. At the end of each day he surveyed all He made and saw that it was good... (I hope you won't mind me referring to God as "He." I don't really think God has a gender, and for us to refer to God as male may do a bit of disservice and certainly may be misleading... God is God and there is none like... him/her/it... I like the pronoun "he" even though that isn't very accurate. Please indulge me.
God made some truly beautiful creatures. He made the gazelle and the panda and the cute little puppy dog next door and the butterfly and the squirrel.... But God must have had a sense of humor too, back during those super-creative eons. He made the funny looking giraffe and the ape and the kangaroo and the platypus... And he made some ugly – even rather disgusting – animals too (at least from our perspective – I'm sure each one thinks itself quite handsome).

Saint Paul looks at creation in a more personal way and says that, even within a given creature – a human – there are "presentable" and "unpresentable" parts. Not that any are less important – just less attractive from some kind of subjective view... You can figure out what those might be in yourself... But I'd like, this morning to redeem just one of them – and not just a body part but a bodily function... Spit.

Spit is such a useful part of who we are. Little boys love to spit – on the ground, at one another, while playing baseball so they can emulate their heroes who spit that disgusting tobacco juice...

Whether we actually do it or not, some people find themselves using the phrase, "I spit on his grave" to express a deep resentment against someone who is dead. The phrase "spit in his face" is used half a dozen times in the Bible (Numbers 12: 14; Deuteronomy 25: 9; Job 17: 6, 30:10; Matthew 26: 67) – an ancient tradition, spitting in the face.... Every generation knows exactly how insulting it is. There is probably, really, nothing wrong with one's saliva but it is better not to have someone else's in your face...

"She makes me so mad I could spit" – don't know exactly what that means other than that you are REALLY mad at someone...

Someone told me last week that they took a trip to China and were rather disgusted with the fact that Chinese people are constantly spitting everywhere – the pollution in some of their cities is so bad that it fouls their sinuses and coats their throats so they are constantly spitting to get it out of their systems... A little habit the government tried desperately to break before the Olympic games there in 2008.

Believe it or not Jesus was a spitter... Really – He was. Oh, I don't think he would do it in any kind of uncouth way, but spit he did... (and it all came back on him during his trial and crucifixion as they hit him and spit on him in a most uncouth way...)

I can see it now. Jesus is walking through the streets of some small town out on the plains of Galilee. His disciples are with him – Peter and James and John and Judas [spit]. They are chatting among themselves... talking about how nice the weather has been, reviewing the response of some of the folks back in the last village... laughing – joking (they weren't always serious, you know)... I like to think Jesus was laughing right along with them. "Did you hear the one about..." All of them, Jesus included, anticipating their next adventure – enjoying one another's company. They all knew that whatever would happen next would happen soon no matter what it was. Jesus was gaining in popularity and wherever he went there were people with problems and people who wanted something – people who knew (or suspected) that Jesus could help them...

Have you ever been to a magic show? I love magic. I've never actually seen the real thing, of course – REAL magic I mean. That might be rather frightening... But I've seen illusionists who make us believe that that beautiful girl who we clearly saw being sawn in half and put back together without a scratch really happened (even though we know it is impossible and didn't REALLY happen)... I've seen an illusionist make a live elephant disappear. No idea how they do those things but love to see it done... I actually know how some tricks are done. I wish I didn't. Knowing spoils the fun...

But what Jesus was doing was nothing short of magic – the real thing – not an illusion (we soften the word and call what he did "miracles" but essentially it's the same thing – really DOING the impossible).

So Jesus walks through town. Everyone knows he is there. You can see their faces peeking out from behind the curtains. They know that what he does is the real thing and not just entertainment and they are rather frightened of him. If he can do what they've heard he can do, there is no telling what he is capable of...

A man named Jubal was one of the onlookers. He has heard of Jesus for quite some time now. Well, not actually heard of him literally. Jubal was deaf. And, like many deaf who have never heard a sound, he made none with his own mouth either other than some groaning and grunts when he wanted to get someone's attention. But he was happy. He had family and friends who loved him. He had never heard sound so he didn't really miss it all that much – for him it was normal (although he knew that SOMETHING was different about him – it was just hard to know exactly what that missing something was like – what did "sound" sound like?)...

On the day Jesus and his men walked through town, Jubal's friends kidnapped him. Really quite against his will, they dragged him to Jesus to see if the magician could work his wonders for their friend. "Jesus – Jesus!! Here is a man who has never heard the sound of a bird singing. He has never heard the toll of a bell. He has never heard the lapping of the water onto the seashore... And he has never uttered an intelligible word. What can you do for him?"

Well, you know, don't you, even before I tell you? Jesus healed him. But Jesus isn't a sideshow performer, so he takes Jubal aside, into a nearby storefront, to get away from the crowd that had gathered. Jubal is more than a little anxious. He doesn't know what Jesus is going to do (well, he does, just like you and I know – he KNOWS Jesus is going to heal him – but he doesn't know HOW it all works – will it hurt? Will I even LIKE sound?). So he stands there trembling, all alone with Jesus. And Jesus does something most extraordinary. He takes his two index fingers and sticks them in Jubal's ears. He pushes them in hard (it does kind of hurt) then suddenly pulls them out with a POP! A pop? Jubal had never heard a pop before. A pop! A most wonderful and most peculiar sound! And he could hear Jesus breathing – he could hear his own breath for the first time in his life. Jubal didn't know you COULD hear breathing! He could hear the people outside, although he couldn't tell what they were saying – he understood no words – he had never heard one – he had never heard the vowels or consonants others so easily make... But there was one thing certain... he could hear! It was really quite wonderful - sound...

Jesus hadn't said a word yet. Jubal wondered what Jesus' voice sounded like. Rather, Jesus took Jubal's chin and gently pried his mouth open. He knew wanted him to do. He stuck out his tongue... Then Jesus spit on his fingers and touched Jubal's tongue with the spit and looked toward the ceiling and said some kind of magic word, *Ephphatha!* to God and Jubal felt something happen to him that he could never, after that instant, describe... and he could speak! I don't know if the first sounds from his new voice were actual words or not - up until a few seconds ago he had never even HEARD actual words, but there was no doubt that words could be formed! Jubal was the happiest man on earth!

"Jubal," Jesus says, (Jubal though that voice must surely be the sweetest voice in the universe) "Jubal - if you don't mind, keep what happened here to yourself."

I have a feeling that was an impossible request, but whether Jubal did or not, his friends were so blown away that they told the story to everyone they knew and to everyone they met for the rest of their lives...

I like to call this little tour of Jesus' through the small towns of the Galilee region the "Tour of Spit" because he did it again a few days later. This time it was with a man named Gaius. Gaius was blind. He lived in the town of Bethsaida. Gaius was a doubter. He had heard the stories. He just didn't believe them. Think about it. It's been 2000 years since Jesus and we STILL can't heal a person born deaf or born blind or born with some kind of deformity. We aren't even close with all our technology and know-how. Even today if someone told you that there is a guy out there who is able to heal congenital defects you wouldn't believe it. Gaius' doubt was based in reason and experience...

But for some people faith comes easier. Some of the city fathers of Bethsaida came to Jesus. "Jesus, there is this really fine man in our city who is blind. Would you touch him?"

Jesus gets his address and goes for a visit. He rings the doorbell and hears Gaius inside, making his way to the door. "Gaius, I'm Jesus – from Nazareth – perhaps you've heard of me. Let's take a walk and have a chat."

"I've heard of you. You're that religious guy. I've heard people talk about what you can do. Frankly, I don't believe a word of it. Anyway, what is it you want with me?"

"Let's take a walk," Jesus says. And he takes hold of his elbow and guides him to the edge of town and a bit beyond. When they are just beyond the city limit sign, they stop under a shade tree.

"Hold still a moment Gaius." And he takes hold of both of his shoulders and leans close to his face and spits right into each of Gaius' eyes.

"What are you doing!!!" Gaius exclaims.

"Open your eyes. What do you see, Gaius?"

"I see nothing. I'm blind... wait... I do see something. I see shapes and shadows – are those men over there? They look like trees... I can see! I can't see very clearly, but I can see!"

Jesus reaches out and touches Gaius' eyes again and when Gaius opens them his whole world opens up. Now he can see clearly. He can see colors and faces and textures and – and he can see the wonderful smile on Jesus' face...

"Gaius, don't go back just yet. Take a walk through the countryside and see all that is to see before you become the talk of the town and people begin asking you all sorts of "impossible to answer" questions... Enjoy your vision. Never take it for granted.

Jesus didn't have to say much about God to the people he healed or to the people who saw his healings. It seems that the whole world was pretty God-conscious at that point in time. But they were no fools. They knew that there was no human way possible to do the things Jesus was doing. He was either the devil incarnate or God – and his obvious goodness made it clear that he wasn't the devil...

One last spit story...

Jesus is sitting with a group of men discussing spiritual matters. Many had experienced, themselves, a non-publicly obvious miracle Jesus was doing. It seemed that every time he opened his mouth, something profound came out. You simply couldn't be around Jesus without feeling that you had learned something – that you had been mentally stimulated – that, somehow, you had grown closer to God... It was, really, quite an extraordinary thing.

While they were talking, a blind man walks by – not Gaius – this is a different town. Gaius was last week. Simon was born blind, too. "So, Jesus," says one of the men in the discussion group, "Simon there was born blind. Who caused it? Was it his parent's sins or some sin he would yet commit and God was punishing him in advance?"

"Well, Rufus, you're asking the wrong question. God's punishment of sin has nothing to do with blindness or lameness (although sometimes our sins or our parent's sins do cause some of those problems). God is not vindictive. God's punishments are more of a spiritual nature. We are in error when we attribute our ills to God. Simon (was that his name?) didn't sin, nor his parents – or, even if they did, his blindness is not God's punishment for those sins... But all things work together for good. One of those goods is so you might witness what is about to happen..."

"Simon," he calls. "Simon – come over here."

When Simon approaches, Jesus gathers some saliva in his mouth and spits on the ground. Then he bends down and starts mixing his spit with the dirt and making a little mud ball. (I'll bet you've never seen anyone playing with their spit have you?)... He picks up the ball and divides it in two and forms it onto Simon's eyes.

"Simon," he says. You've got mud and spit on your eyes! Go over to the pool of Siloam and wash yourself..."

I don't know what was going through Simon's mind, probably that here is a real kook – until he came back. He was glowing! He wasn't doing the blind shuffle. He was walking like a whole man. He could see! ... He was so transformed that he had to convince his friends and family that it was really him...He literally LOOKED different.

Spit – what a wonderful, useful thing – at least as Jesus could use it... And I have a feeling that ANYTHING – anyONE, in Jesus hands, can be used in amazing, wondrous ways. You – me – anyone!

LOVE ALWAYS WINS – SOMETIMES
Luke 15: 11-32

If you live long enough and observe enough different people and see different situations, it's not so uncommon to be able to see some actual Biblical stories come to life. They probably won't be exact, but close enough. I've seen, in real time, the stories of Cain and Abel – two brothers in conflict because one was jealous of the other. I've not experienced one actually killing the other, but I've seen in their eyes that that might be considered as a good option… I've seen David and Goliath where the underdog wins against all odds. That's always fun to see. Not to mention the common occurrence of someone saving animals – in a flood or for some other reason – like Noah. I've seen people, in anger, doing something rash, like Moses throwing down the tablets of the ten commandments. …Talk about having to apologize – can you imagine Moses going back up Mt. Sinai to ask God for another set because he smashed the first ones in a rage? There is such a thing as going "hat in hand" but telling the Lord God – the Almighty – the maker of the heavens and the earth – the God of all power and authority… "Yahweh… I, um, I've broken all your commandments. Literally - I've broken them. I need another set. Sorry?…" I've even seen real asses talk like in 2 Samuel (well, OK, mine weren't literally asses and Samuel's were, but sometimes an ass is an ass)...

So it won't be surprising to you if I tell you a story that might just have a ring of familiarity to it… There won't be any big surprise ending, I'm afraid. At every point you will know what's coming. The surprise is in the story itself. It's true (maybe with a few embellishments and certainly a changing of names)…

Pastor's kids are noted for being hellions. I suppose that, from their earliest days they are taught to not do anything to embarrass their father, the minister. It wouldn't look good if the minister's family is out of control. And, I suppose, most ministers really are quite conscious of that. "If my kid isn't 'good,' then how can I possibly preach goodness and kindness and gentleness and self-control to others…" And there is a certain validity to that. Congregations EXPECT the pastor's kids to be good (except here at Mt. Hope during my tenure – you've expected my kids to be kids – thank you very much for that – I really can't thank you enough for loving my girls and allowing them to grow up more or less 'normal' in an on-display family). But it is that EXPECTATION to be good that is overwhelming to so many PK's (preacher's kids) and drives them in the other direction. They KNOW they can't meet what is expected of them so they give up on any kind of goal even in that general direction...

My best friend growing up was a PK. I loved him for his adventurous spirit but, as I look back on it, he was trouble. He didn't even TRY to be good. Fortunately he was two years older than I was, so by the time I was a High School junior he had graduated and, since it was during the Viet Nam war, he signed on with the Air Force to avoid getting drafted... So long John Willis... ...I'm pretty sure the Air Force saved my life - or at least my reputation.

I have a minister friend whom I will call Adam. His wife I'll call Sarah. They are in the Methodist church. They are great people. Adam tends to be rather more formal as a minister than I am but he's brilliant and, so far as I can tell, an excellent minister. I have little doubt that his sermons are of the highest quality and that people in his congregations have always grown in their Biblical knowledge in the few years the Methodists allow their ministers to be in one place... But he's not nearly as brilliant as his wife, Sarah. She may be the most intelligent person I know... and talented – she is a wonderful writer and when she speaks her words are just a joy to hear, so good is her expression... Sarah had wanted, earlier in life, to become a minister herself, but that was in the day when women ministers were not well accepted and she was strongly advised against it. So she became a teacher. From all accounts a very good one - maybe the best her school systems had ever had.

Sarah and Adam have two sons: Calvin and Alvin. Yes, I agree. It seems cruel to have such alliteration of their son's names – Calvin and Alvin – why would parents do such a thing? But I suppose parents do worse things. Al was a couple of years older than Cal. They got along – or didn't – about as much as any two brothers. At one point they went away to college – way over in Montana. First Al then, a couple of years later Cal started. There was a denominational college there that offered minister's children a substantial discount on tuition. Adam, as pastor, was not a rich man and Sarah, a teacher, didn't quite ring the bell with her salary either, but they were doing alright... Nevertheless, two in college at the same time was more than they could handle – especially if there was discounted tuition in Montana. Discounts they could afford. Obviously the two brothers didn't get home often. Montana is a long way from anywhere...

Alvin took his brotherly seniority seriously and watched out for his kid-brother Cal during his first two years. He took him under his wing, so to speak, and tried his best to make sure he did well. And he did. But then Al graduated and headed for the job market. He ended up taking a job about a mile from where he grew up – right back where mom and dad lived. He even started going to dad's church. Eventually he would become a deacon.

But young men in Montana, especially younger brothers – youngest children – all on their own for the first time – out of sight of mom and dad – out from under the protection of an older sibling – don't always handle their new life very wisely – especially if they've been PK's...

Cal stopped going to class. He stopped studying. He started to drink. He began to use language that wasn't becoming to anyone, let alone a PK. He stopped writing to his parents – didn't even email them... From time to time he would post on Facebook and those little tidbits were all Adam and Sarah knew of their son's life.

After the first semester there without Al watching over his shoulder he flunked out. He went home in disgrace. He was embarrassed and humiliated... Adam and Sarah tried to be supportive but they were VERY disappointed. Cal continued to drink and even started doing some drugs – right there in the parsonage. Sarah couldn't handle it (neither could Adam, of course), so one day she confronted him. "Cal – your life is in the gutter. You need to get it together. I detest the drinking and the drugs. I will not allow them to be in my house."

You can't blame her, of course. Minister's home or not, no parent wants those things around - especially as they watch their child on a downward spiral... But what do you do once they are legal adults? You can't FORCE them to stop. You can't kick them out...

Two days later Cal disappeared. He took whatever cash he could find in the house and one of the cars and he left. Not even a note.

I don't know which is worse – having a child die or having one who is heading for the worst kind of troubles life offers – one who disappears and you don't even know where to start looking – knowing that unless something happens, that son could easily get into a lifestyle in which he ends up dead – and you'd never even know it... and if not dead, in some kind of skid-row life - and again not know...

Adam and Sarah had more tears and sadness than you can imagine. There was no more happiness in their lives. Christmas came and went. Then Easter... ...No Christmas wonder. No Easter joy... Their son was missing – maybe laying in some gutter somewhere – maybe drugged out in some flop-house – maybe dead... In those kinds of situations you can only think of the worst... Cal never wrote nor emailed now - not to anyone. He had stopped posting or commenting on Facebook...

Life would never be normal again for Adam and Sarah, of course, but eventually it resumes some semblance of normality. Adam's sermons weren't so filled with angst – at least not every Sunday. Sarah's children saw their teacher smile now, once in a while... But at home Cal's absence never went unnoticed... Not for a minute did they stop worrying and wondering - day after day - week after week - month after month...

A year later Cal emailed his brother. "Al, I'm still alive, in case anyone was wondering. I'd like to come home but don't know if I dare. Mom and Dad must hate me. What do you think?"

Cal had gone to a college friend's home in Iowa. But after a few weeks the friend's family got tired of having a druggie around and asked him to leave. He couldn't hold a job in his condition, although several employers had given him a chance for a few weeks or a couple months... But eventually he had sunk so low that he even stopped looking for a job. He was homeless – penniless... He ended up literally sleeping on a park bench at night and panhandling during the day. He was losing weight. His hair was getting matted. He had constant headaches. Even the drugs didn't seem to help – although they were the only friend he had so he spent as much time in a stupor as he could... One night in early fall it was getting dark and the rain had started. Cal was about as miserable as he had ever been in his life. He was seriously considering suicide but was afraid of hell. He wasn't sure it really existed, but what if it did??? He wasn't sure God existed, either, but what if He does???

Then, almost as if to prove his own existence, God sent someone to Cal. A fellow about his own age, hood pulled over his head to keep the rain from running down his neck, was walking through the park and saw him. He saw that he was in a bad way and, for some unknown reason, couldn't bring himself to just pass by. He, himself, had been a drug user, and knew what Cal was going through. He invited Cal to come to his house. Cal did and, this angel of God and his wife, cared for Cal. They dried him off and gave him a place to rest and food to eat – no drugs – that was a part of their past lives that they could no longer tolerate... They found him a job. He stayed with this amazing couple for several weeks. And, after hearing his story – and knowing some things about life that he had never realized, they encouraged him to call his parents.

All Cal could do though, was to send an email to his brother telling him where he was...

The next day Cal's father arrived in Iowa to bring his son home... His parent's love had overcome all of Cal's sins and all of the pain he had caused. Their love offered complete and unconditional forgiveness. He was their son and NOTHING could change that...They were so glad to have their son back – the classic Prodigal Son story come to life.

But all of that is just the beginning of the story. Alcohol or Drugs or Sex or Theft or Debauchery of any kind is not so easily eradicated from one's life. Over the course of the next several years Cal fell off the wagon several times. It was as though he couldn't help it. Some of those things had gotten so much into his psyche and soul... And somehow that subculture seeks out those who are weak and pulls them back down... But he never left home again. Even when the darkness plagued him again and again, he was wise enough to know that love could help him pick himself up again and start over and over and over and over... until he was victorious... (That's the way it is with all sin and all sinners. We are addicted. We cannot stop. We can only cling to the love of our Heavenly Father which is steadfast and never ending nor ever changing).

I am pleased to report that Cal did overcome – at least for now. He joined the Navy. He found a new life. He has started to attend a little church in the town in which he is stationed. He's the youngest person in the congregation and, because of that, he sort of stands out. The older people minister to him in wonderful ways. They don't know his past and I'm not sure it would make any difference if they did. They simply love him with the love of God... And he loves them. He's still not sure if there is a hell, but he is most certain that there is a God and he is most certain that love is one of the most potent forces on earth...

And if you talk to Adam and Sarah, they would tell you that their own faith is stronger now but that it was sorely tested during those dark days. Their love never wavered, but love's gentle, patient ways seemed, so often, ineffectual. But, as Adam says, "If God believes in love so much, it's obviously worth trying. We did. It does work!"

Love always wins – sometimes. Or should I say "some time." If doing the loving thing doesn't work, wait. Perhaps it will down the road. It may take time. But, in thinking about Adam and Sarah's story – Cal's story – I realize that the outcome might have been so much different. Addictions are very powerful. Love might have lost this one. But here is the thing. We love (God loves) not necessarily because we believe love always wins (although it does – if not in this life then the next) – we love because it is right. And from time to time we can see, even in this life, that love wins magnificently.

THE WADI HOUSE
James 1:22-25

When we were kids – you and I – our parents made it pretty clear what was right and what was wrong. We grew up with a set of values that were pretty clear-cut. Most of us had what we needed to live quite well in those early years – not wealthy by any stretch of the imagination – but we never went hungry – we never felt "poor" – we always had what we needed. I look at some of those little 4"x4" pictures with the white border on them that were taken back in the time I was growing up and I see something I never realized at the time – we had very little. I see a farm wife and her stick thin husband and somewhat raggedy little kids and I realize that we were probably living a bit on the edge. My father had to get a factory job to support us. The farm wouldn't do it… He literally had to work 60 hour weeks every week for us to survive… We just thought he liked to work. And I never suspected that we ever had any financial problems. But, thinking back, I realize we probably had plenty of them. I was just oblivious to them - as children ought to be.

I was born shortly after World War II. That makes me one of those famous "baby boomers." The soldiers came home from fighting to preserve freedom for the world and started families – and nine months later along comes Steve and several million other babies…

Maybe the most important and sometimes least realized thing about us Baby Boomers is the fact that we sprung from that generation now dubbed "The Greatest Generation." We liked to think of ourselves as somehow great, too, but we have thus far not measured up… Our parents had an amazing work ethic. They had a deep-seated and well tested patriotism. They had a belief, for the most part, that God exists and is watching out for those who trust Him. They knew that life is difficult and lived with that fact without dwelling on it nor feeling sorry for themselves.

Some of us Baby Boomers grew into adulthood with some pretty good examples to follow. We had our own children and tried to pass those values on to them. We grew up to be pretty responsible, respectable, reliable, really pretty nice people. At least WE think so.

But there were others of us Baby Boomers who rebelled against some of those old values - antiquated values - and began to teach their children that things once considered wrong are actually right and maybe even good – that, in fact, there may not BE such a thing as right and wrong / good and bad except within them - whatever they "think" or "feel" is good is good. Whatever they "think" or "feel" is bad is bad… It's all in "me."

But it's a bell curve, really. On one side you've got people who have retained their values intact without any wiggle room. On the other end you have people who have thrown out traditional values entirely. But in the big hump in the center (where our salvation as a nation is) are most of us who have retained SOME or MOST of the values from our childhood but have tried to think them through and allowed for the evolution of society…

I'm a big "middle" section person. I wasn't spoiled as a child and I tried not to spoil my girls, but probably did. I tried to teach right and wrong as I was taught it, but haven't always practiced what I preach… For the most part my girls learned the lessons but I find that they haven't clung to as many legalisms as I had – thinking I was quite liberated from those but finding that I have plenty in comparison to them… But they've grown up into fine young women, so we must have struck some kind of balance that worked. Being a parent is SO hard in today's world… It's a world of compromise and consideration and making decisions on an individual basis' instead of having so many hard and fast rules.

I wonder what kind of a father Jesus would have been. Certainly loving. Certainly forgiving. Certainly understanding of human frailties. Certainly aware of the sin nature we carry around in our psyches… But Jesus was a pretty black and white kind of guy. I think he would have been a tough guy to have to call "dad."

"If you have ears," he said, "you'll hear…" He said, "Those who act on my teachings, are wise. But those who don't, are foolish." Now, our parents said that sort of thing, but most not so bluntly.

I was so overwhelmed a few weeks ago when all the flooding was going on in Iowa. I just couldn't believe some of the things they showed on TV. I saw a house – intact – floating down the river. I guess I didn't know a house could float… And not a small house, either. It will be years before some of those places are back to normal…

Israel is almost a desert land – one of those places where it is dry for six to nine months of the year – not a drop of water… Then the rainy season comes. It is mountainous, so when the rains do come, all the rain that falls on the mountains rushes down into the lowlands to join with the rain that is going on there – all of it traveling as fast as it can to the Jordan River, swelling that gentle, narrow, slow moving river into a frightening torrent with super powerful currents…

The water from the mountains hits the dry and parched land and literally makes instant rivers. It washes gullies throughout the land as gravity rushes it to low ground. In Israel those gullies are called "wadis." A wadi is just a dry ravine winding it's way over the land most of the year, but with the spring rains a wadi is a raging river washing out anything in it's path. A wadi can go from dry to raging in a matter of minutes...

It's summertime. It's a weekend so people are out enjoying the beautiful weather. It's early in the season, so the heat isn't too oppressive yet. There isn't a cloud in the sky and Jesus and a small group of people are sitting in the shade of a wadi's wall, just talking. They talk about some of the goings on in their small village – "Did you hear that Hester, the seamstress has been divorced by her husband? It's a terrible thing. I don't know what she did to bring about his wrath, but she's in trouble. Fortunately she does have some marketable skills..." "Baruch, down at the butcher shop got caught selling meat that isn't kosher – what a scandal he's caused. My sister bought some of it and served it to her family. They just don't know what to do now. They've never had non-kosher food before. The Rabbi is advising them..." "My uncle Saul – you know – the carpenter – had to let a couple of people go because he just wasn't getting enough work in this economy..." You know how it goes. When people get together they tend to talk about people. Sometimes it's gossip and sometimes it's just local news or color...

Someone once suggested that small minds talk about people, good minds talk about things, but great minds talk about ideas. I don't know whether that is always true or not, but I imagine Jesus was one of those people who tended to talk about ideas much more than people or things. He was a pretty sharp fellow, as you might guess. He was pretty much silent when the talk was about Hester or Baruch or Saul or anyone else – but, of course, he always enjoyed listening to people talk and interact. He enjoyed people getting along and bonding with one another... I can see him – smiling, nodding his head in understanding – but not saying much... not much of an opinion about local gossip – but enjoying hearing it as much as the next guy... But he knew and they knew that Jesus wouldn't keep silent for very long. He didn't talk about people or things, but boy could he come up with ideas and talk about those...

Now, some of Jesus' ideas weren't very palatable. They were intriguing, but not really always so practical. The Rabbis demanded a lot from believers. Jesus went way beyond the Rabbis. It somewhat rankled even some of Jesus' supporters when he came out with that "ear" statement (the one I mentioned earlier – "If you have ears on your head and you don't have Ipod buds stuck in them, you ought to be able to understand what I'm saying" – or something like that) then going on to classify those who did as he said as being wise and those who didn't as foolish. "Jesus, you need to temper your statements a bit. This isn't an all or nothing world. There are shades of gray. There are levels of commitment. Everyone's ideas are equally valuable. There is no universal right and wrong."

"Ah, my friends," Jesus says, "Perhaps you are right – in the small matters of life. Perhaps there are differing valuable opinions and positions that people might take. I think Frosted Flakes is the best of all breakfast cereals. You think Cheerios are. I think Michigan State is the best college. You like University of Nebraska. One of us might be right, depending on the criterion. Or both of us might be wrong... It doesn't really matter – these are differing opinions only – they are meaningless... Whatever truth they may contain is inconsequential. But the big issues of life are different. There are very real consequences in being wrong. In the big issues it DOES matter where you hang your hat..."

So the until now silent Jesus has broken his silence and thrown down the gauntlet of serious discussion. And, as might be predicted, what he said wasn't about people. It wasn't about things or events. It was about ideas – concepts – values – truth.

"What are the big issues, Jesus? Terrorism, Morality, Abortion, Different Religions, Heaven and Hell, Taxes, Civil Disobedience, the Economy, Political Parties? None of those are really black and white. All people can do is arrive at a position that satisfies them and hold on to it."

"Right and Wrong – Wise and Foolish. I'm not really sure there is a middle ground on the big issues. You decide..." As he settles in they know one of his stories is coming.

"This is really very pleasant sitting here with you this afternoon. We're out of the sun. The wadi wall is giving great shade. The countryside is really quite pretty. We're close to town. These pomegranates are delicious. I have the feeling I could stay here forever and be happy for the rest of my life. What could be better than shade from the sun and good friends and plenty of food? Maybe I'll do that. I'll build a house right here where we are sitting. I think I could live out the rest of my life sitting on the front porch watching the world go by. In fact, because this wadi is practically a road going all the way up to the mountains, it would be so easy to get building materials in here that the cost would probably be quite reasonable. I could build a little shed right over there for housing my livestock and for storing things. What could be wrong with that?

"There are a few houses up on the bluff, but I've got to tell you, the sun up there is a scorcher in the hot months. No trees – just baking away in the sun... Withering! Why, all you can keep up there are camels. Cattle would wither away and sheep couldn't find a blade of grass to eat. I'll build my house right here. What do you think? Will you join me?"

Jesus had a way with words. They got the point. Unless you were nothing more than a tourist passing through, even *thinking* of building a house in a wadi is the most foolish thing you can do. It wouldn't last a year. The first rain would cause a flash flood and the house would be washed away along with the shed and all the cattle you might have and, if you survived, you'd have gained a reputation for being the most foolish man who ever lived. The people up on the bluff would look over the cliff, down at any rubble that might remain and just shake their heads in wonderment…

"That's the way it is with truth," Jesus says. "There are some things that are embraced only by fools and some things that, even though they might, on first blush, seem foolish, are wise. The choice we make makes all the difference. All I'm saying is that I have demonstrated again and again that following me is wise. The converse is simply foolishness. I'm not trying to be a braggart. It is an observable fact…"

The men sitting there in that wadi were silent for a long time, thinking. They knew he was right. They knew that THEY would never build a house in a wadi. But they knew too that he wasn't really talking about building a house. He was talking about how we handle things in our lives. He was talking about some of the storms that come along. He was talking about losing a job or getting a divorce or the death of a parent or a chronic illness or a friendship betrayed or a stock market crash or that phone call at 3AM from the police… They knew he was talking about the importance of being wise before the spring rains come and not being found to be a fool.

After a few minutes Jesus breaks the silence. He says, "I am the way and the truth and the life. No person comes to the heavenly father but by me. There IS such a thing as truth. You can find it in who I am and in what I say and how I suggest you should live your lives. We only go around once. It's pretty important to get it right the first time. Follow me – follow my ways – adapt my attitudes and values and ideas and you will be wise… The alternative…??? What can I say?…"

Well, the afternoon gave way to evening and the little creatures of the desert night began to appear and Jesus and the small group of friends headed for their homes… up on the bluff, safely out of the wadi and the pleasant afternoon and they never forgot his words and, from that day on, measured just about everything they did and everything they were against the folly of the foolish house in the wadi.

OLD HICKORY AND REV. BILL
Romans 12:9-18.

Are you ready? We're in an election year. Next November we will be electing a new president. Next January that unlucky man elected will inherit all the problems left by Barak Obama. He got quite a load of them from George W. Bush when he walked away from the Oval Office. Bush inherited a few of his from Bill Clinton who inherited some his from the first George Bush – and on and on it goes....

I'd like to make mention of a couple of our presidents this morning. Andrew Jackson... Everyone has heard of him – "Old Hickory" they called him. Our seventh president. He was quite a guy. People couldn't wait for him to finish his term. He was just about the most divisive president we've ever had (although somehow he managed to get his face on the twenty dollar bill). Some people thought he was just wonderful. Others thought he was the Devil. He was so good at dividing the country that BOTH political parties today are attributed to him. When he was elected there was really only one functioning political party. It was called the "Democratic Republican Party." The four presidents before Jackson - John Quincy Adams, James Monroe, James Madison and Thomas Jefferson were all Democratic Republicans. Jackson so divided the party that they split and the Democratic Party AND the Republican Party were born.

If you visit the Capitol building in Washington D. C. one of the guides will tell you a story about Jackson. It seems that, right there in the capitol rotunda an assassination attempt was made on Jackson's life. But Jackson saw it coming and physically disarmed the assassin and practically beat him to death with his cane – the secret service had to pull him off or he would have killed the man.

Jackson was a military man - a great military leader - but not so good at many of the things a president ought to be good at. When he left office, the economy was a shambles. Martin Van Buren – vice president and now president – had to pick up the pieces as best he could but it was already too late and Van Buren is credited with the first great depression of the United States. They called it "The Panic of 1837," but it was a depression regardless of the name they gave it.

Depressions are bad times for most people. Jobs are lost, prices are high, food is sometimes scarce... Not much good comes out of a depression. But even in bad times, the human spirit strives to survive. Back in those days, Detroit was the capitol of Michigan. The people of Detroit suffered along with the rest of the nation. But hope still beat in the human spirit. So much so that the residents of one street in Detroit even renamed their street – what is now known as 25th Street – they renamed "Mt. Hope Avenue," in the hope of better times to come…

That depression didn't last long, but something positive almost always comes out of something bad. One of those was that Churches started. The First Congregational Church started in downtown Detroit – near Shelby and Jefferson. A man named Henry Hammond was the first minister. We don't know much about Rev. Hammond except for the fact that he was there for only three years then he moved on. The First Congregational Church of Detroit was in that location for 45 years. During those 45 years some very good things happened. You see, the church was committed to reaching out into the community. They were committed to teaching children about Jesus. They were committed to, even as adults, learning and growing in faith and wanted to be the best people they could possibly be on this earth… A noble goal… They weren't saints. They were just like you and me. They did their best to be the best they could.

There was one young couple in the congregation that really stood out: Bill and Nellie Mitchell. Well, actually they weren't all that young. Bill was nearly 50 and Nellie – well, it's not nice to tell a woman's age, so we'll keep that confidential.

Bill was kind of an interesting man. He was balding and had the same kind of fly-away hair as Martin Van Buren – surely that wasn't the preferred style for men's hair for 50 years – a big mustache – both hair and 'stash gone white. Not really an attractive style. I hope it doesn't come back any time soon…

Nellie was a plumpish sort of woman. She worked as a school teacher until the kids were born, but wasn't employed publicly any more…

Bill had been to college and had a bit of seminary. Never finished. You know how it is – kids come along and things change...

Bill and Nellie had three kids – all grown up and married by now – starting to have children of their own. Bill worked as a cobbler – good work in those days. Shoes were expensive and fixing them was a high priority for just about everyone. He never lacked work. He didn't have his own shop or anything like that, but he had steady work and that was all that mattered.

Bill was a rather serious fellow. He was as smart as anything. He loved to read. He loved to discuss issues of theology and the politics of the day. I'm pretty sure there were a lot of things he'd rather do than nail the soles on people's shoes. In fact, he had, earlier in his life, felt a call to work with souls – not shoe soles but human souls. Bill thought, at one time, that God was calling him to be a minister. But life got in the way.

That happens to a lot of us doesn't it? Maybe, in some way or another, ALL of us. When we are young and idealistic we have every intention of making our mark on the world – maybe in business or as a civic leader or as a sports hero or a movie star... But eventually reality sets in and we realize that the gifts God gave us may not be the right ones for what we had dreamt of doing or being. We have to set another path for ourselves. Or, and this happens more than you might imagine, life gets in the way – we are too busy earning money to pay the bills to pursue dreams or we fall in love and get married and kids start being born and the dream becomes an impossibility... Not that the wife or husband and the kids aren't cherished beyond measure, their arrival on the scene just changed everything...

That's what happened to Bill. Nothing wrong with being a cobbler... In those days ministers hardly earned enough to live on anyway. "No regrets," he told himself... And he meant it.

Nellie knew. Wives always know. She knew that Bill just wasn't "fulfilled" in his life. And she knew why. It was her and the kids. She knew that Bill had a deep spirituality. He loved the Lord with all his heart. She mourned the fact that his dream – maybe his calling – would never come to be...

There is something about a truly God-given dream that one just can't get out of your system. Bill couldn't be a minister so he did the next best thing. He taught a Sunday School class. Now, in those days Sunday School was a relatively new concept. It was "invented" in England just 50 years before. It was a social experiment by Robert Raikes in England – designed to stem the trend of children in the slums from descending into lives of crime. Quite a success story, really. 1 ¼ million children in England started attending Sunday School - and today every church has one.

I'm not sure when the idea of Sunday School came to America – obviously some time later.... Maybe the idea of Sunday School was only 30 years old in Bills day...

It was adults – volunteers – who were teaching the children but everyone quickly discovered something. The adults didn't know all that much Bible knowledge to teach. So, in America, the Sunday School concept expanded to include the entire family – adults as well as children. That's why, to this very day, we have adult education as well as children's.

So Bill found his niche. He became an outstanding Bible teacher. Often there would be 30 adults in his class. He began by teaching the basics: the stories of Genesis, the parables of Jesus, the sermon on the mount... In subsequent years he taught some of Paul's letters... His students were becoming quite Biblically literate for the first time in their lives. The very idea of missing one of Bill's classes was unthinkable...

First Congregational was growing. A man by the name of William H. Davis, D.Div. was the pastor. He was a man of great vision and charisma but of small ego. One day he called Bill into his study. "Bill," he said, "I've been thinking about the future. We've outgrown the church building we're in and I think it's time for old First Congregational to move. I've found a wonderful new building up Woodward Avenue at Forest. Perhaps you've seen it – a big red stone church. It's for sale and I think we ought to buy it... But here's the thing. I know that when we go up there we are going to lose some members who don't like change – we're going to lose some others who find it simply too far to go. The change-resistors we can't do anything about. Life IS change. But I hate to lose some of our best families because we've moved out of range. I'm wondering if you would be willing to take a few of those families and start a church. I'm thinking, basically, your adult Sunday School class. Just about all of them tend to live over in the Mt. Hope Avenue area..."

Bill was overwhelmed, of course. He didn't know what to say. Could it be that the dream of being a minister was actually going to happen? What would Nellie say? Is this some kind of wondrous working of God?.... "But Rev. Davis – I've not finished seminary and I'm not ordained."

"Don't you worry about that, Bill. You already know more about the Bible than most upstart seminary graduates... Peter and James and John weren't ordained – neither was Jesus, for that matter. They seemed to do pretty well. We'll work at getting you ordained..."

And Bill began to dream again... "What WOULD a new church over in the Mt. Hope area look like? What should I MAKE it look like?"

And, of course, Bill wasn't talking about the physical structure. He was talking about...He was talking about ...US ... 119 years ago.!

So he began to think and he found that his "church mind" came to life. Ideas began to explode in his head... "I want to build a church that, above all else, glorifies God. I want to build a church that believes the Bible. I want to build a church that believes in loving one another. I want to build a church that causes members to talk about it as being 'family.' I want to build a church that reaches out into the community and draws people in to loving Christ..." Bill was very excited (and Bill was anything but an excitable person).

Nellie brought Bill down a bit. Wives almost always tend to do that when their men get too excited about something. She seemed somewhat skeptical that Bill could do it... Starting a church is an enormous undertaking. Bill reminded her that HE wouldn't be doing it. GOD, through Bill's efforts, would be doing it. Nellie had to admit that MAYBE such a thing would work. And as she began to think of which families lived over in the target area, even she began to get excited. Just maybe – just maybe – God could do something over on Mt. Hope...

They set up "church" in a little clapboard building right on Mt. Hope Avenue. You already know what they called the church...

I don't know how long Bill was the minister of the church. But I know that those were some of the best years of his life. The church DID learn to love one another. They did strive to follow Christ. They did always seek to glorify our Lord.... Those were his goals. Those were his dreams. That is where we come from. That is us.

So, thank you Old Hickory. Thank you for providing the climate for a depression that gave rise to hope. Thank you Rev. William Davis D.D. for having the vision to send people out from your church to start others – the First Congregational Church in Royal Oak, North Congregational in the northern part of Detroit and, of course, that little start-up over on Mt. Hope Avenue where Rev. William Mitchell was the first pastor. And thank you, one and all, for loving one another, for seeking to follow Christ, for giving glory to our Lord – for being the church. That's what was always intended.

The facts about Rev. William Mitchell and his wife are all fictional. Rev. William Mitchell was the first minister of Mt. Hope but little is known of his life.

MIRACLE AT THE UAW
Matthew 3:11

Did I ever tell you about my conversion – when I went from being a Pagan to a Child of God? I grew up in a church where there was a specific formula for that "new birth" experience. I figured it out from my earliest days. Our minister majored on sermons we young people, when we became teenagers, fondly referred to as "scaring the hell out of us." He may or may not have been a good preacher - I really couldn't say - but he certainly did have a flare for pointing out to us our tendency to sin and just how serious sin is and especially the eternal consequences if sin isn't dealt with. The idea was that the minister would give one of those pulpit pounding sermons, sinners in the congregation would feel the conviction of sin (that was the Holy Spirit speaking), then he would conclude the sermon with an "altar call" where, in a very long prayer, we were asked to hold up our hands if we knew we were sinners and needed the salvation of God. Then, in an even longer plea/prayer, we were asked to come to the altar and kneel while the rest of the congregation prayed. The prayer would go on until there were the same number kneeling there as hands had been raised. Unless you had actually done that – raised your hand, walked to the front of the church and knelt at the altar, you never really knew exactly what went on with the minister and deacon and the sinner up there on his or her knees. But whatever it was, when they were finished with you, you were declared to be a new person, saved by faith and the whole congregation was happy and went out with the good feeling that God had been at work that day or that evening.

I resisted all that for a long time. I knew that my parents had dedicated me to the Lord when I was a baby and that they wanted nothing more than for me to make that long walk to the front of the church. Their desire for me to do that was the major impetus for me to stay put in the pew. I didn't think it really mattered all that much. I had believed in God from my earliest days of consciousness. It was going to be pretty hard to guilt me into making such a public show of things.

I see some of you grew up just like me… I wasn't baptized as a child. I was dedicated. I grew up in a Baptist-like church (although hit had Congregational roots) and we didn't baptize babies, we dedicated them. Then, when kids were around 13 or 14 we were baptized by immersion. We didn't have confirmation. What's the difference? When the water is applied. For me the early part was dry and the later part wet. For most Congregationalists the first part is wet and the second part dry. Either way it's the same thing. The first time the parents make a promise to God, the second time the young person does. Interestingly, you can find both practices in the Bible. That's why we do both at Mt. Hope.

But something happened one summer in Bible School. I imagine I must have been about 10 years old. We had the typical singing and crafts (I still have two of the crafts I made in VBS all these years later). We had the snacks and lessons and then, of course, at the end of each day we were asked whether anyone wanted to come to the front of the church and receive Jesus as his or her savior. But this is VBS and they had a bit of a twist to their altar call. If you received Jesus today you would be given some kind of little toy... a Hot Wheels or something - although Hot Wheels hadn't been invented yet) . That was all I needed. I was the first one up there... And that was my birth into the Kingdom of God. I guess I'm really quite the materialist at heart.

But I was 10 years old and something really did happen that day. "Born Again?" I don't know. "Saved?" Who can say. "Forgiven?" I was 10. I really didn't have all that much to be forgiven for... But I met Jesus that day. He became my best friend. In the years ahead we would grow up together. Somehow he was always about my age (I wonder if he is like that for everyone). We'd talk to one another. We'd talk about life in the family with a brother I couldn't stand. He had brothers too, so he knew what I was going through. We'd talk about school and we'd talk about homework. We'd talk about feelings of loneliness and a growing internal anger I felt as an adolescent. We'd talk about the future and what I'd become (neither of us have come up with anything yet). We even, fairly often in those teenage years, would talk about girls.

I saw Jesus last weekend. Sue and I went to Ohio for the wedding of one of my cousins (it's a strange thing to have a cousin several years younger than my own daughters – but I actually have two - because I have an aunt three years younger than me). The wedding was in a Congregational church even though neither my cousin nor her husband-to-be are Congregationalists. They were "outsiders" getting married there. Exactly why not in their own churches I have no idea. They were married by a minister who they didn't know (rather than one of their two minister cousins) – it showed. It was the wedding I swore 30 years ago that I would never do – very impersonal – even though my aunt cried appropriately.

Like I said, I first met Jesus in Ohio. Every time I go back I wonder if I am going to see him again. I was disappointed. He wasn't in the Congregational church. Oh, he was probably there, but I didn't see him. The minister mentioned him. The vows included him. The soloist sang about his love. The Bible teaches that where 2 or more believers are gathered he will always be among them, so he was no doubt there. But I couldn't find him in the crowd.

The wedding ended and we moved on to the reception. I was pretty sure I'd see him there - people milling around and such. Jesus loved wedding receptions. Remember – he did his water to wine thing at one. There are few things he likes more than a good party.

The reception was held at the UAW hall. Defiance, Ohio is a big union town. General Motors' Central Foundry is there. It is (or was) the largest foundry in the world. It's a huge place. Much larger than any of the auto plants I've seen in the Detroit area. I worked there two summers during my college years. Nothing motivated me more to stay in school than foundry work in the summer...

The UAW hall is a large cinderblock room. It is at least twice the size of our fellowship hall and twice as high. It was easy to imagine hundreds of angry or anxious union workers meeting to ratify or reject the latest contract proposal. But it was decorated for a wedding on Saturday and looked quite respectable. The one feature of the room that didn't really fit with it's rather austere construction was over in one corner - a very large fountain. It was really rather massive. It was the sort of thing you might find outside in a large park. It was circular and had an outer ring of spouting water and, in the center, two or three jets were shooting the water 8-10 feet into the air. It was, really, quite spectacular.

Weddings and wedding receptions in small towns aren't at all like they are here. Here you spend $20,000 on a wedding – having a sit-down meal for the limited number of people you can afford. In small town America weddings are big deals and everyone invites everyone they want to invite. Then they serve them sandwiches and potato salad and Costco cake... And their marriages last or don't last as long as anyone else's...

It was fun to see relatives I haven't seen for a long time. My cousin Judy has 8 children under age 15 and home schools them. She is amazing. Another cousin, six months younger than me, is retiring at the end of September. How does that happen? My uncle, the painter, tells me he recently landed a contract to rubber-coat a warehouse roof for $180,000... And, of course, there was the typical family gossip flitting from one to the other...

Then I saw him. Jesus was a couple of tables over, chatting and laughing with some people I didn't know. I tried to get his attention, but he was engrossed in conversation and didn't see me. But that was OK. So long as he was there. We'd catch up later...

Well, when you invite everyone you want to invite, you end up with quite a variety of people. There were people like Sue and I dressed in our Sunday best all the way to the other extreme of girls in tank tops and shorts – young men in cut-offs and tee shirts... Sue commented that she was stunned at the amount of cleavage... I didn't notice... How times have changed...

Defiance is a car town. The foundry is the center of everyone's life. If it ever closes, the entire area will dry up. It is THE industry. It is THE source of all livelihood (except for farming, of course, but even the family farm is quickly vanishing). ...GM and the farm and the church – that's where I grew up.

About midway through the reception, a man walked in who had obviously just come from work at the foundry. He was a friend of the groom, someone said. But if you've ever been around a foundry, you know that there are few places on earth quite so dirty. It's a gritty, grimy, black dirt. Every square inch of his exposed skin was covered with it. And, even at a wedding where everybody was invited – where there was clearly no dress code – this young man was out of place. He shouldn't have come – at least as dirty and unkempt as he was. Everyone there looked at him with rather furtive glances. They were embarrassed for him. He didn't seem to know any better. HE, rather than the bride and the groom and the tuxedoed wedding party, had become the center of attention...

There were two people there at the party, however, who didn't seem to mind his coming in in such a state. One was a young woman. It was clear that she was his wife. When he came in she smiled a smile of pride and joy from ear to ear. She was just delighted to see him – she had thought that maybe he wouldn't be able to make it. She didn't even seem to notice that people around her were put off at his presence. In her arms was a little baby. He couldn't have been more than a couple of months old. She quickly got up from her seat and she and their baby boy went to greet her husband – the baby's father. Of course, he knew he was dirty. He probably even knew that he was quite a sight. But he knew that, if he had gone home to clean up he would have entirely missed being with his newly married friend on the biggest day of his life. Given the choice he decided to attend dirty.

When his wife came near, he wouldn't let her give him a hug. She would have gotten her beautiful dress dirty. And, of course, he wouldn't even consider touching his baby. It was his deepest hope that his child would NEVER get as dirty as he was at that moment. He certainly wasn't going to dirty him now.

Now, Samantha and Nathan, the wedding couple, had known Jesus most of their lives and were more than delighted to have him at their wedding. But he WAS the only person they invited that they questioned whether they should. They knew that Jesus had a habit, wherever he went and with whomever he came into contact, to stir things up – to make a scene – to do something totally bizarre – to make for awkward moments. They hoped that he wouldn't actually come even though they HAD to invite him...

Jesus was the other person who was delighted to see John, the factory-worker friend. They had never met, but Jesus had heard of him from Nathan and a few others. He had hoped to meet him one day and it looked like today was the day...

Samantha and Nathan – and many others – saw it happen, and those of us who knew Jesus held our breaths. Jesus got a big grin on his face and arose from his chair and headed for John and John's little family standing so conspicuously near the center of the room. None of us knew exactly what was about to happen but we knew it would be something unique and "Jesus-like" unexpected.

Jesus talked to John and Marcie for a minute. We could see John shaking his head. First from side to side then, eventually, up and down in agreement. John had a smile on his face now, too. We couldn't hear what they were saying even though the entire reception hall, at that point, had gotten so quiet you could hear a pin drop. Jesus took the baby and gave him a little hug and a kiss. Then he gave it back to his mother and opened his arms and embraced John in a giant bear hug. Something happened that none of us expected at that point... Nothing... Jesus and John hugged one another and NONE of the grit and grime from John rubbed off onto Jesus – not on his clothing, not on his hands, not on his cheek. It seemed impossible, but there it was... Every granule of factory dirt stayed on John and none was transferred to Jesus. At that point, even those who didn't know Jesus personally knew that something unusual was going on – but none of us knew exactly what...

I glanced over at Samantha and Nathan. They looked mortified. What was Jesus doing? Was he going to ruin their wedding? Was he going to do something outlandish and embarrass them? They hoped not... They hoped not - but probably...

Jesus lead Nathan and Marcie over to one side of the room, out of the limelight a bit. Most people thought whatever was going on was over – an interesting moment to share with friends. But those of us who knew Jesus knew that nothing is ever that simple with him.

We watched... Jesus took John and Marcie over to the fountain and clearly told John to wash his hands in it (I'm not sure why he couldn't have simply shown him where the men's room was)... John did. The grime, of course, came off and was washed away in the swirl of the fountain. Then Jesus did the unthinkable. He stepped over the wall into the fountain itself. What was he doing? Why would he do such a thing? This was most certainly a social faux pas. Then he reached out his hand to John and encouraged him, too, to get in. We didn't think he would, but he didn't hesitate. John got into the pool with Jesus and the two of them had the most incredible Cheshire-cat grins on their faces. Jesus motions for John to take a step further in, where the water was cascading down. He did. Right there, in front of everyone, John was taking a shower – fully clothed – and Jesus was helping. Jesus directed John's head under a water spout and washed his hair, he washed the grime off his face and out of his ears... And, I've got to say, the transformation was really rather amazing. John had been saturated with dirt but that fountain, with Jesus in it, cleaned him up wonderfully well. And we were all astounded to see, for the first time, what he was wearing. John had on a white shirt and tie, nice slacks and, by now, rather sodden shoes. He had gone to work planning to go to the wedding party all along. His dirty white shirt was now as white and clean as mine is this morning. His face as clean as yours. The smile on his face glowed like the sun. Here was the happiest man at the wedding – except, perhaps for Nathan. Nathan had tears of joy in his eyes and laughter erupted from his lips as he looked over at his friend and at Jesus and the spectacle they were making and the wonder of it all...

Then Jesus reached out to Marcie. Not for her to join them in the pool, but for her to give him her baby. She glanced over at John and he nodded that it would be alright... Jesus took the baby and scooped up some water and said to John, "I prewash this baby, John. May he never get as dirty as you were... See to it that he doesn't." He and Marcie looked at one another and you could tell. Their baby, when he grew up, would one day meet Jesus if they had anything to say about it. He would meet Jesus and fall in love with him as hundreds of millions have for over twenty centuries. He would grow up with Jesus and would talk with him about all kinds of things... He would never remember this first encounter, but he would always know that somehow it had changed his life.

It was a pretty decent wedding. One not soon forgotten - that's for sure. It reminded me of an old hymn we used to sing back when I was a materialistic new convert – when I was a child. Would you sing it with me - just the first and fourth verses: "There is a Fountain" by William Cowper:

There is a fountain filled with blood
drawn from Emmanuel's veins;
and sinners plunged beneath that flood
lose all their guilty stains.
Lose all their guilty stains,
lose all their guilty stains;
and sinners plunged beneath that flood
lose all their guilty stains.
E'er since, by faith, I saw the stream
thy flowing wounds supply,
redeeming love has been my theme,
and shall be till I die.
And shall be till I die,
and shall be till I die;
redeeming love has been my theme,
and shall be till I die.

THE HILLS ON THE HILL
Matthew 19:16-27

Our daughter, Rachel, lives in Washington D.C. She and Brendan bought a house shortly after they got married. It's in a neighborhood I wouldn't have chosen – unless, of course, I were 25 and invincible and newly married and filled with idealism. I'm not sure exactly how to describe the house (and actually, the house isn't important to my story today), but try to visualize this: The house is on a street that is descending fairly steeply for about two blocks. But the houses along that two blocks are all on the same level. That means that the 20-30 feet between the street and the houses all have to have steps. Rachel's house is midway down the second block so the street is, really, quite a lot below where the house is. To get up to her front door, you must go up about 20 steps on a very steep stairs. I hate the climb and I'm fairly physically fit. An older person simply couldn't do it.

Well, moving furniture into their house was not one of those jobs where you call your friends and supply them with case of beer for the day and give them a big "thank you" and that will do. Moving up those stairs is major hard work and my 110 pound daughter and her new husband had no chance at all of doing it alone.

When they arrived at their new house (new? The thing was build in 1921) they arrived a couple of days before their truck from "Pods" arrived and, having made a couple of trips to the local Home Depot, they had noticed something they had never seen before and that we don't often see here in the midwest. There, in the parking lot, from early morning until the setting of the sun, gathered 30-50 illegal aliens. Now, I don't know if they were really illegals or not, but they were all clearly Mexicans. They were waiting there, hoping that someone would need help for the day and would hire them... Day loborers!

So on the day the furniture arrived Brendan pulls up to the curb and rolls down his window and a dozen or more men just about attack the car. He says, "I've got some furniture to move into my house. It's up a steep stairs and will be pretty hard work. I need two of you." A few of the older men back away, but the younger ones all want to take him up on his offer. He selects two who look like they might be strong enough for the work and tells them to get in. They do, and Brendan takes them to the house. When they see the stairs, they both say at the same time: **"Hay caramba!"** And they weren't any more excited when the pod was opened and they saw the heavy furniture.

But they were good workers and they got right to it. But Washington D. C. is one of the hottest and most humid places on earth, I think. Those two poor souls, along with Brendan and Rachel, worked SO hard. By noon they were all just about dead, so Brendan decided to head back to Home Depot and get another guy to help out. Most of the men were still standing around, hoping for work, so he chose one and headed back home. This new man, too, turned out to be a good worker and worked hard all afternoon. But it was starting to look like rain. That might cool things off a bit, but no one wants it to rain when all your possessions are going to get wet. So at about 3:00 in the afternoon, Brendan heads back to Home Depot and picks up a couple more men and, within an hour they are all moved in.

The thing about day-laborers is that you hire them pretty much in the dark. You don't know whether they will be good workers and they don't know how much you're actually going to pay them at the end of the day. The expectation on everyone's part is that everyone will be fair. It doesn't always work that way, I'm sure, but what are you going to do? Such is life….

Rachel and Brendan put their heads together. "How much should we pay them?" Rachel asks. Rachel suggests that Raphael worked much harder than Jose. He ought to get more. But then, Juan only worked for half a day and Jorge and Raul for only a couple of hours, each with differing levels of efficiency. Rachel, the daughter of her mother and wanting to treat everyone generously, suggests that, since they had put away a sum of money for moving and had a fair amount left, they could just divide what they had equally among the five men (the amount they had, even divided 5 ways was far more than any of them ever dreamed of earning on any given day). She argued that these were very poor men and they all needed the money desperately and that, even though they hadn't all worked the entire day, whatever they paid them would BE their day's wage. Even the ones who worked only a few hours needed the money. "We can afford it" she said. Let's give all of them a full days pay. Brendan, the union man, said that such a thing would cause a riot. "You can't pay Jorge and Raul the same as Raphael and Jose. They only worked a couple of hours as opposed to 9 hours." Rachel replied, "That's crazy. None of them earned as much as I want to give them. Why should anyone complain?"

"They just will," said Brendan.

Jesus, the great communicator, had a problem. One of his missions in life was to let people know what the "Kingdom of God" is like. But, apparently, the Kingdom of God is so unlike anything in our experience, it became a major task. All he could do was come up with analogies and hope that those who heard him would get the idea. He said, "It's like a camel going through the eye of a needle – almost impossible to get in (Matt. 19:24) … It's like throwing seed on the ground, hoping it will grow (Matt. 4:26)… It's like a mustard seed – being so small yet producing such a large bush (Mark 4:30)… It's like something that belongs to children in it's simplicity and wonder (Mark 10:14)… It's like something close by but yet far away (Luke 10:11)… It's like yeast in bread dough (Luke 13:20)…It is within you (Luke 17:21). OK – here's the bottom line. If you understand it, you do…but if you don't, I'm not sure you ever can (Mark 4:11). …One last try. The Kingdom of God is like Rachel and Brendan at the end of moving day when it's time to pay the workers…

And you all know the story. It's practically identical to the one I told about my kids. In Jesus' story, the employer pays the one-hour worker first. Everyone sees what he gets. They are impressed. It's far more than any of them expected to get! But then he proceeds to give each one the same amount and, for some reason, what they were enthusiastic about a minute ago isn't quite so exciting. Yes, it's more than they expected for a day's work, but still… "I slaved for 9 hours in this blasted heat and humidity," says Raphael. "What gives? Surely my effort is worth more than Raul's."

"Why should you expect more?" says the employer. "Didn't I give you considerably more than you've ever earned in a single day? It's my money. Can't I do as I please as long as I'm more than generous to you?"

I've got to say, I think they had a point. How would you feel? Let's say you typically earn $100 a day. You work all day long. The guy next to you just showed up. He punched in just an hour ago. The boss is generous and gives each of you $175! How would you feel? Happy for the bonus money but cheated in that your wages ended up being far less per hour than the other guy… Of course…

You're on the school board and you are hiring a new teacher. One male, the other female. Both have practically identical qualifications. But you know that most teachers are female and you'd like to have a male teacher in the position. But money is an issue. "Let's offer the woman less than the man and see if she takes it. We can save some money that way." Even suggesting such a thing will get you into deep, deep trouble… Or make it racial. Can you offer an African American less than a Caucasian American for the same job? You'd better not! You'll never hear the end of it. There will be law suits and threats and you'll likely be fired.

And what's with Jesus' employer? Is he stupid? He pays the one-hour worker first while everyone watches. What did he expect to happen? Did he think the 9 hour guys were going to be happy? ...And why – why did Jesus take the side of the employer? Isn't Jesus into doing what's right and fair?...

I remember back in my college days when the "Jesus Movement" was afoot. The campus was awash with hippies and war protestors and free-love advocates and pot smokers... and "Jesus Freaks." I looked a bit askance at the hippies. I admired the war protestors. I was pretty sure the free-lovers would end up pregnant or with some STD. The pot smokers baffled me. But the Jesus Freaks – I was envious of the Jesus Freaks. I had been a Christian all my life. I met Jesus one year in VBS and never looked back. I had been following him ever since. I had never let a curse word cross my lips. I had never had pre-marital sex. I had never stolen anything. I had never, really, done anything "wrong" or even anything that smacked of being wrong. I had made some real sacrifices to follow Christ. Then along come these "Jesus Freaks." They came from the pot smokers and the sexual revolution and anti –war activists. They had been hippies... and they found Jesus and were getting on the cover of Newsweek and their witness seemed to have so much power because of what they came out of... and there was Steve – not likely to ever get on a magazine cover for his 19 year faith... and I resented it.

And it was to me that Jesus told this parable. When we read it we almost always do so with a business model in mind. The unfairness of it all!!! But we forget the first line – the most important line of the whole story: "The Kingdom of God is like..." The Kingdom of God has little to do with fairness or the amount of time and energy we put in. It has to do with God's generosity and grace. If you've just shown up you are on an equal plane with the saint of saints in your midst.

You've got three children, ages 3, 6 and 12. You've obviously loved the 12 year old twice as long as the 6 year old and the 6 year old twice as long as the 3 year old. But do you love the 3 year old so much less than the 12 year old? Of course not. ALL of your love is poured out on each one as lavishly as it can be poured out. And, if you are a parent, you know that the extent of your love for each child is far more than you can ever express... And so it is with God. Whether a person is fortunate enough to spend his/her lifetime in the joys of faith or if one comes to faith after a life of searching and uncertainty, trying all kinds of things that don't satisfy along the way (even though they look glamorous), God welcomes each fully as His beloved children.

The Kingdom of God is like... you and me – doing whatever we can – sometimes failing – sometimes succeeding – and at the end of the day, God rewarding each and every one of us in a way far in abundance to what we have ever dreamed and certainly far more than we could expect. God's children – loved completely – both those old and new.

THE LITTLE HOUSE
Matthew 7:24-29

I have a photograph here of my grandfather. Actually he isn't just my grandfather. He is my grandfather's grandfather. I suppose that would make him my great great grandfather, if genealogies mean anything. If you look very closely, you might be able to see a bit of my eyes in his or maybe my nose or ears. Certainly some dominant gene has passed from generation to generation and landed on me. I always like to hope that the things that are passed on from father to son to son to son to son are good things and that, somehow, the bad genes are filtered out or are, somehow recessive and die out. I'm not sure if that is true or not – I suppose it isn't. My physical characteristics were my father's and his father's before him. My strengths and my weaknesses I inherited from my parents for better or for worse…I can be no other than I am. My heritage dictates my present – dictates my daughter's and possible grandchildren's futures…

I once heard it said that a student can't be any better than his teacher. That makes sense. How can you learn what you haven't been taught? And yet that can't be true, really. If a student can only be 99% as good as his teacher and that student's student only 99% as good as him, logically, in about 100 generations, we'd reach a place where the student wouldn't be any good at all. It is my hope that you will ALL be better than me as it was my father's hope that I'd be better than him… I may be some day, but not yet.

A very long time ago, on this very land where our church stands, there was a farm. In fact, all the land around us was farm land. For as far as the eye could see there were fields of corn and grain. Horses pulling plows and dust blowing the loosened soil were common sights… Where we now see a busy freeway there was a rough dirt path – maybe first made by the Indians who roamed this region 200 years ago – the Shawnee or the Algonquin. The path – later to become a road and later still a freeway – divided one farm from the other. Birds flew in the sky and you could hear them singing in the trees. They still sing, I suppose, but the traffic drowns them out. But that's progress. In a generation or so from now the noise will die down as hydrogen powered cars come into being and all that engine noise is reduced to just the sound of tires rolling along on the pavement.

The farm that was on this land was owned by a family named Swanson. Doris and Dean, I believe were their names. Doris grew up here. Dean was a small town boy from out near Adrian who had come to the big city to try to better his life. He found out that you can take the boy out of the country but you can't take the country out of the boy. He didn't like Detroit. There was plenty of excitement, of course. Henry Ford was in the process of changing the world forever with his assembly lines. Dean worked, for a while in one of the factories. But how can you live life inside when God gave the great out-of-doors. Dean found that he wanted to farm.

Dean had been attending the Immanuel Lutheran Church in Redford where he met Doris. She was really something. She had all the charm of a big city girl but the down-to-earth common sense of a country girl. It was because she was. Dean didn't know it at first, but Doris lived on a farm just a few miles away – came to the city for church because there were no good Lutheran churches out where she lived.

You know how it goes. They fell in love and got married. Dean worked in the factory for a short time longer, but Doris' dad knew a good thing when he saw it and, before long, the young couple were living in a little house dad had built just for them out on the edge of one of the fields and Dean quit the factory and began taking over more and more of the farm responsibilities. Life was good and the future looked bright.

Years passed. Not much changed except that mom and dad died and Dean and Doris now owned the farm. They had a couple of children – Harold and Millie. They moved, of course, into the larger, more comfortable, farm house and left their little starter home sit vacant for quite some time. But that little house meant a lot to them. It was their first home. It was the place where their children were conceived and born. They didn't know what would become of the little house, but were certain that its memories would not end with them. Things once begun take on a life of their own and histories always beget futures filled with memories…

People started moving into the area. Before long it was incorporated. 57 years ago it all took on the name "Livonia."

But Dean and Doris were growing old. They really couldn't farm any more and, besides, the area was becoming so "citified" that farms seemed out of place. They were people who had witnessed the big change – people moving from the city to places called "suburbs" – that's what they called "here" now.

They began to sell off their land. Some to developers (one named Henry Ruff – his name is still quite prominent in the area today). One chunk to a church moving out of Detroit. It happened to be the piece of property that contained their little house – filled with memories – now no longer theirs – but the memories were and always would be....

A few years later both Dean and Doris, now quite old, died. Millie had married and moved away. Harold got the big farm house and would live next door to the new church.

In later years, Harold would see so many changes next door that they almost overwhelmed him. He saw a series of young couples living in his parents "memory house" and wondered how many little ones were conceived there, like he was – a place filled with love and passion and memories. He saw the church go up. Shortly after, he saw an addition being built as, obviously, they were having great success.

Harold always had a sense of ownership of the church's property. He often would roam the seven acres, picking up any trash that was around and sticks. It ought to look good. He was always curious about the church itself, but he had never been inside. He grew up Lutheran and this congregation probably wouldn't accept him. He would sometimes look in the windows when there were no cars in the parking lot to see what it was like inside. To his dying day he would wonder what the basement looked like. There were no windows! Must be dark down there. When he thought he wouldn't be seen he would peek into the windows of the little house and was always gratified to know it was still generating memories...

Harold had no idea how many more residents might live in that little house and how a young youth minister would come along one day and have designs on it as a "youth house" and have the shower removed from the bathroom so that it could never be taken away from him and used as a residence again...

About 15 years ago, Harold got a nickname around here. We called him "Weird Harold." He would flee if he saw you seeing him. He didn't really want to talk to anyone. I once cornered him and brought him in to see, first hand, what the inside of the church looked like. I couldn't convince him that there was no basement. He called me a liar. He KNEW there was a basement. At the time we were raising money to have the parking lot resurfaced and he sent the church a check for $2000. I went over to his house and thanked him and told him he certainly didn't need to do that, but he didn't understand. Of course he did. This was his parent's land and if we were making improvements, he should pay his fair share...

We had an attractive blond secretary at the time. He rather enjoyed standing outside her window, watching her work. It freaked her out a bit, but if she looked at him, he would go away... Until one day he stood outside the office window watching her and she wasn't aware of it. He must have been watching for quite some time and felt he had to go but couldn't until she acknowledged and thus dismissed him, so he gave the window a good sound rap several times, startled her half to death. She quit the next week... A short while later, Harold was committed to a mental facility and his niece moved into the house and became our next church secretary...

I imagine that, if a house could do so, it would weep for poor old Harold. But all a house can do is hold its memories in profound confidentiality and silence.

I've had the opportunity to visit Ernie Liebold's mother in the past couple of weeks. Ernie tells me that she is dying. She has some kind of inoperable condition that will be her demise. We all die. That's not a tragedy. It's a fact of life. But, I've got to say, when I first met Marion I was impressed with her. Ernie had told me that she hadn't long to live but I couldn't help get the impression that she was more alive in our few minutes together than I've been in most of my own 58 years. She remembered, with crystal clarity, where she came from. She was completely aware of her condition and that the end of her life was approaching. It didn't seem to bother her all that much. And I know why. It's because she had learned the lesson of the little house out behind the church. She has learned that where we've come from is terribly important. How we've played the game of life – how we've touched others – how we've tried and sometimes failed and sometimes succeeded, really does matter. But she has learned perhaps the most important thing any of us can learn – that life goes on. Never like it was in the past – not even like it is in the present – but in some other form... Better? Who knows. Just different and, in some way, eternal.

Marion expressed a desire to join our church last Wednesday. She has never set foot inside the building. The only members she had ever met were Ernie and Debbie and me...and God. So on Thursday we took in our newest and oldest member all in an instant. It was a great honor and a compliment to us who are nurturing her son and daughter-in-law well enough that she wants to be a part of it too – even in her dying days....

I don't even know the name of my grandfather's grandfather. I don't know what he did for a living or what kinds of pains he might have suffered in his life. I don't know if he was kind or gruff or whether he was a conservative or a visionary. I don't know if he loved God or was an atheist. But I know that what he began years and years ago, after generations have gone by and after many different paths taken, has arrived at this place in this time for God's purpose – and I am humbled...

Jesus once told a story about two houses being built. I doubt that the literal houses actually existed, but everyone got the point. One was built on the sand and the other on the rock. One fell because it was without a firm foundation – the other stood because it was solidly based. ... I can't help but marvel at those houses. They may or may not have actually, physically existed, but they have influenced every generation for two thousand years.

The future is a pretty powerful force in our world. We live for it. We long for it. We work toward it. But where does it all come from? It comes from the past...lest we forget.

The little house did, in fact exist as did Harold and the parts of the story about him are true. The history of the house is fiction.

OF ROCKS AND ANTS
Proverbs 6:6

Economic downturns, terrorist fears, the housing crisis, healthcare costs out of control, job losses everywhere, even 117 banks defaulting and closing… Bleak times in America in many ways. Here in Michigan all of those seem to be magnified. Whether the rest of the nation is in a recession or not, we most certainly are. Probably the worst of all time in any of our lives. I can imagine that George Bush will be as glad to get out of the White House as we are to see him go (at least 70% of us, from the most recent approval rating poll). But maybe you're over 80 and you remember "The Great Depression." From all accounts, those terrible years make whatever we are going through now look like a cake walk.

One man who was fortunate enough to be born about 50 years before the depression was named Frank Austin. Frank was born on a little farm just outside of Hanover, New Hampshire, home of the famous Dartmouth College[1]. Frank was a precocious boy. He didn't mind feeding the chickens or helping to milk the cows or even making hay out in the fields on the hottest of summer days. From his youngest years he knew what it meant to work and to work hard and to feel the satisfaction of doing a job well. His father was a very intelligent man, even though he hadn't gone beyond eighth grade in his formal education. He was a kind man. He was a man of faith and made sure the entire family – Frank and his younger sister and older brother – were in church every Sunday. Unless you were sick or dying, being in the Lord's house on a Sunday morning was the only option for the Austin family. Frank's mother had finished high school and had hoped to go on to college before she met Frank's father, but love and marriage and, too soon, children, changed her plans. She would now be simply the best mother and wife she could possibly be.

As I said, Frank never minded the numerous farm chores farm boys and girls are required to do, but the chore he most liked was working in his mother's garden. There was something magical about digging a little hole or a little trough and putting tiny seeds in, covering them up, watering them and waiting for them to sprout and grow. He loved to go out and check on them every day and follow their progress. Every morning, right after the milking was finished, he would go to the garden and gently dig down where he knew a bean or a pea or a carrot was planted. When he would see the little white sprout bursting through the seed hull, he was filled with awe. A few days later it would break through the surface of the ground again and

Frank would know that God had, once again, done something marvelous.

But Frank was a typical boy. When he was tending the garden he did more than pick the peas and dig the potatoes. He watched the grasshoppers sitting on the leaves up close. He saw their bulging eyes and their skinny bent legs that could somehow propel them 10 feet in a single jump. He examined the caterpillars and wondered just why they had all those hairs that looked like fur. He saw the grubs on the tomatoes and the crickets in the shadows of the string bean leaves… But his most favorite of creatures was the little ant. The ant fascinated him. It was so tiny but so terribly industrious. Ants never stop working. They build and they gather and they prepare and they burrow and they search for food. Somehow they seemed able to even communicate with one another as to where food is located and who knows what else. And their strength! It wasn't uncommon to see a little ant carrying a crumb that was 5 times his size and probably weighing at least twice as much. And Frank thought of that verse in the Bible: (Proverbs 6:6) *"Go to the ant, thou sluggard, consider her ways, and be wise."* He wasn't sure exactly what that meant, but since it was addressed to a "sluggard" it must mean we ought to emulate the ant's industriousness – it's work ethic – it's never ending passion to achieve…

In his spare time (farm boys don't have much)… In the little spare time he had, Frank liked to tinker. He enjoyed inventing things. He would put a screw driver in a vice and bend it to see if one might get a bit more torque on a screw by doing so. He would hammer nails lightly into pieces of different kinds of wood to see if the sound they made when struck was of different tones. He would take a magnifying glass outside on a sunny day and burn patterns onto blocks of wood with light. Frank was an up and coming inventor.

As always happens to young boys, they become young men and the things they learned along the way serve them in some, often quite different, capacity. Frank went to the local college – Dartmouth. His parents were intensely proud of him, of course.

Frank majored in electrical engineering. He was a good student. He worked hard and studied hard and had a wonderful mind. Frank was rather shy and enjoyed being around books and science and out in his mother's garden on weekends more than he liked bering around people… His friends thought him somewhat peculiar. Frank was a geek before "geek" was a word.

Frank found a girl who would become his wife after they graduated. She, like him, was a bit on the shy side and a bit "geeky," too, so they got along just fine...

Frank graduated from Dartmouth in 1895 and began working right there at the college. One of the highlights of his life was working with Gilman and Edwin Frost in that first year out of school and being a part of the first team to x-ray the human body. A young boy in Hanover had fallen while ice skating and broken his hand. The invention was new, but they gave it a try. The rest is history.

Frank taught electrical engineering at his alma mater for twenty years. It was a bit early to be retiring, but he and Anna[2] had been frugal. They had never had children so that expense wasn't on them. They had saved enough to retire young. Frank, being the sharp guy that he was, invested well. He studied the markets and invested in stocks that were solid. He didn't invest all he had, of course. That would be foolish. He kept a stash in their savings account for rainy days. His calculations clearly showed that he and Anna could live out their lives in modest comfort.

But eight years into their retirement something catastrophic happened. The Great Depression hit. Overnight the Austins lost almost all of their investments. The bank where they had their rainy day fund closed and none of their deposits were insured. The Austins, despite good planning and wise investing and hard work, were suddenly penniless... If it hadn't been for Frank's garden and the goodness of merchants and neighbors who were in the same predicament, there is no telling what would have become of Frank and Anna.

Fretting and hand-wringing do no good. Frank knew that. Frank knew that hard work is a good thing but even hard work doesn't always work in hard times. There are no guarantees in life. Frank turned to God. "Lord, we, like so many others, are hurting. But we trust in you... we trust in you. May your name be glorified in all we are and do."[3]

Frank had to keep busy. That is the best thing to do when depression (the great one or just internal ones) is on the doorstep. But how do you keep busy when you are retired or laid off and have no money to go anywhere or do anything – when you are a rather introverted sort of guy and hanging out at the local coffee shop or on the street corner would be the worst thing you could imagine?

Frank started a boy's club. He had always gotten along well with children - it was adults that made him uncomfortable... He let it be known that his workshop was open all day long to any boy in town who wanted to hang out and work on little projects. It wasn't wildly successful. Only a handful of boys showed up. But that was enough. He taught them how to work with tools. He showed them how to make a boat from a piece of scrap wood. He demonstrated how to make doll furniture for their sisters or cousins. He kept them busy working and learning and enjoying both work and education... Not bad lessons for children of any generation. Not bad lessons for you and me – work is good – learning is good. Never stop doing either one.

If you are old enough to remember 1974, you remember a phenomena that occurred that year for about six months that made a man named Gary Dahl a millionaire. He "invented" something that took the country by storm. Do your remember what it was? Gary Dahl was an advertising executive in California who went to a builder's supply store and picked up some nice stones. He took them home and pasted plastic eyes on them, boxed them up in miniature cardboard crates as you might ship an animal in, and sold "Pet Rocks" for $3.95 each. Who would buy a rock with eyes in a little crate? In 1974 millions did. To this day no one can figure out why...

One of the boys in Frank Austin's boys club was, like Frank as a boy, fascinated with insects. He watched them out in Frank's garden, but even in the workshop there were a few spiders and ants. He watched the spiders spinning their webs and trying to trap their dinner. And he watched the ants, ever searching for food and then carrying it off. In the dirt floor of the workshop, the boy watched them burrow in. But then, he lost interest as they disappeared into the ground...

Did you know that there are more ants on earth than any other living creature? In fact, and this may disturb you a bit, ants make up 15%-20% of all biomass on earth (not counting sea creatures and plants). That means that if you took the universe's largest scale and put all human beings on one side and all 14,000 species of ants on the other, the weight of the ants would far outweigh the people...

Frank was an inventor and, at this point, invented something so simple that it had to be a smashing success. It made the "Pet Rock" episode look like amateur hour... He took four scraps of wood and routed parallel channels in each one, joined them together around two pieces of glass (making a double framed picture frame kind of contraption). He put sand between the pieces of glass and several dozen ants and the "ant farm" was invented. His little friend could now see BELOW the ground and observe what the ants were doing... "Austin's Ant Farms" became a post depression fad and Austin was selling up to 400 ant farms per day... He would pay local boys and girls $4 for a quart jar filled with ants and he would ship them all over the world... To date, more than 20 million ant farms have been sold...

But the story doesn't end there. Frank took his fortune and worked to study the causes and possible solutions of world starvation, how to build airplane factories and air raid shelters within mountains. He designed military weapons, perfected electrical machinery and even invented a track hurdle used in the 1936 Olympics in Berlin...

... All because a young boy heard that single verse in church one Sunday morning and it stuck with him... All because he knew that God never abandons us in our time of need... All because he loved to work even when there was no work to do.

May Labor Day be a day when you are truly grateful for the work God gives you – for the creativity and energy and talent. Consider the ant – and be wise.

---

[1] *There is little recorded, actually, about Frank Austin's early life or even where he was born. All information before his graduation from Dartmouth is fictional. To read of his life, go to http://www.dartmouth.edu/library/Library_Bulletin/Apr1993/LB-A93-Cramer.html*
[2] *Frank's wife's real name (or that he even had a wife) could not be determined in my research.*
[3] *It is uncertain whether Frank Austin was a man of faith.*

THE SON
Romans 8:28-39.

An interesting thing happened to me as I began compiling and editing my "story sermons." I found this one. I had forgotten all about it or the fact that I had told the same story a couple of years earlier. If you have already read "Love Always Wins - Sometimes" you will see the similarities because it is the same true story told at a different time. I include it because it tells a bit more of the story and the whole in a bit different way.

Children being born into a family are, without doubt, the most momentous and wonderful of occasions. The day a child is born all of life changes. The young adult parents used to be, even if the most humble of persons, somewhat self-centered. They know there are other people in the world, but really, none quite so important as ol' no. 1. That's not a character flaw. It's just how life is. We look out for ourselves.

When we get married, things change a bit. Now No. 1 is the husband or wife - the spouse. But that doesn't last long. The honeymoon is over in a few months and, if the relationship is a good one, that new husband or wife hasn't actually become No. 2 but takes on the mantle of a second No. 1... "It's us against the world!" And it's a good thing. We were created to have a partner to share the struggles and the joys and the frustrations and the happiness with. Equality in the number 1 slot is a pretty good thing.

But when a baby is born something astounding happens. Everyone other than that tiny infant takes a demotion and this helpless little bundle of tears and poop becomes No. 1.

Back in 1980 a little boy was born to a young minister and his wife. They named him Allen. He was the joy of their lives and they watched him grow and learn to talk and walk and be a real person. He was a peculiar little fellow, though. As he grew, they sensed that something wasn't quite normal about him. He wasn't "abnormal" in any way that they could put a finger on. There was just something just a bit different about how he related to others and how he perceived the world, what gave him joy and what bothered him. He was, however, without doubt, the greatest joy that God had ever given them and they loved him without measure.

But parents seldom stop with the greatest joy of their lives. "If it was so great the first time, maybe we ought to do this again!" So a few years later, Andrew and Samantha had a second son. They named him Charles. And it happened again. Their joy was overwhelming. Their two sons were the greatest joys of their lives that any people on earth had ever experienced.... Andrew and Samantha and their sons Allen and Charles – any church would be glad to have such a lovely young family.

Andrew was a Methodist minister. Sam had studied theology, too, and had hoped to one day be ordained, but being a woman, that wasn't so easy in her conference and it never happened. She settled for being a school teacher - an amazingly good one, I might add. I've no doubt that THAT was her true calling.

Andrew's ministry was more typical than your minister's. He spent a few years in this church and that one and, by the end of his career he would pastor at least half a dozen parishes.

So that's who the family is – He a pastor. She a teacher (sounds familiar, doesn't it?). The two boys growing up in a good home, knowing lots of people, being loved (except for the fact that Andrew changed churches often and that they had boys instead of girls, Sue and my life runs pretty parallel).

In fact, it is even more so. Sam worked for the same campus Christian organization that I did before I went to seminary ...and we began, when our children began to be born, to attend the same Christian Family Camp in the Upper Peninsula on the same week every summer. We became friends – close friends – and we loved one another and knew we would for the rest of our lives.

Twenty years later......

The kids are all grown. They've all gone off to college. It turned out that Allen's problem could now be diagnosed. He had a mild form of Autism called Asperger's. He went to Minnesota to college and did well. Majored in Political Science and minored in art – a fine painter. Charles went to the same school – a freshman when Allen was a senior. But Charles' experience was rather different than his older brother. He found he didn't like to study and didn't have the discipline it takes to just DO what you have to do even if you don't like it... And that IS what college education is all about – perseverance....

He found some other like-minded students – not a hard thing to do in college or anywhere else. The wise person runs from them when he finds them. But Charles wasn't wise in that way. He spent his time playing cards and he discovered that he enjoyed drinking. He started doing a lot of it. He stopped going to class. He slept in and rather liked it.

But, of course, that sort of thing eventually catches up to you. He failed all of his classes. He was kicked out of school (even though he had a full ride scholarship – gone...). He went back home. But drinking (and now drugs) is a most difficult thing to stop once started, and Charles couldn't do it. If the truth be known, he didn't want to. He LIKED the buzz of drinking – the euphoria of the drugs. When high, he didn't have a worry in the world! What could be better than that?

Andrew and Sam were beside themselves. What do you do with a son who is acting like this? They loved him. They loved him dearly. They loved him far too much to let him ruin his life with drugs and booze. But what can you do?

"Charles," says Sam, "I know we can't stop you from this self-destructive life-style. Believe me, we would if we could. But you frighten me. We just can't have you doing these things in our house." (a little tough love, she thought, might do the trick).

The next day, when she came home from school, Charles was gone. He had taken the money from the cookie jar. He had taken a few of his clothes. He drove off in his father's car. He was gone.

Samantha blamed herself. Andrew blamed himself. Even brother Allen, still living at college, blamed himself. But, of course, no one was to blame. We all set our own course in life and live by the decisions we make.

They didn't know where Charles had gone. They had no idea. After a couple of days they called his college roommate to see if he had gone there. He hadn't. They contacted all of his friends they knew about. They hadn't heard from him, they said. They didn't know where he might have gone. They were worried sick.

A week passed. Then a month. Another week – another month. No word.

Even though they didn't know, let me tell you what happened....

Charles just started driving. He was so angry – not at his mother for telling him he couldn't do drugs and alcohol in her house. He was angry with himself for not being able to stop. He knew, beyond any doubt, that he was the most wretched of people. He was a drunk and a doper and he smelled and he felt dirty... and had no idea how to stop. So he drove until the car needed gas. Then he took the money he stole from his parents and filled the tank and drove some more. He didn't stop until he got to Minnesota and the home of one his college cronies who had also flunked out of school. His parents were cool. They turned their heads – pretended the "boys" weren't doing anything wrong. But it's expensive to keep two 21 year olds in liquor and drugs. After a month and a half, they made it pretty clear that Charles was no longer welcome in their home. But, of course, he had nowhere to go and no money to go there with. He emailed some of his friends, to see if they could help him out. (One of them – a family friend – contacted Andrew and Sam to let them know he was still alive). They were relieved – in a peculiar way. They had almost given up hope, now there was a glimmer again...

Charles made his way down to Iowa. He never did figure out how or why Iowa. He didn't know anyone who lived there... what a strange place to go. But, as it turned out, it was a good move. There was a job at the steel mill and he took it. But he was so lonely – so depressed. Thank God for the drugs and liquor. Their numbing effect was the only thing that kept him going.

But a drunk can't hold a job for very long and he was let go. It was winter by now and he couldn't pay his rent, so he was out on the streets in small-town Iowa. He had never been so alone – he had never been so desperate.

But God sent an angel to Charles one evening while he was shivering in the park, huddled near the frozen fountain. A man came along – a total stranger – and asked him if he needed help. He needed help more than he had ever needed help in his life. The man took him home – a little place where he and his wife lived in near poverty themselves. And they thawed him out. They let him shower. They washed his clothes. They got him clean. He stayed with them for a few weeks. They, like his parents, wouldn't allow the drugs or alcohol in the house, so he had no choice. He would either not drink – not get high – or freeze to death.

You've heard how hard it is to withdraw from drugs and alcohol. Charles experienced all of that. His angels stuck with him through it all... When spring came, they told him it was time to go home. They insisted he call his parents... "But they surely think I'm dead," he said. They did. "And even if they knew I was still alive they must hate me." They could never hate him.

And so Charles called home after having been gone for nearly a year. "Mom? It's me, Charles." And mom burst into tears of the deepest joy. "Charles – are you alright? Where are you? Are you coming home?"

"I'd like to come home – if you'd have me.... But I can't just now. I don't have any money."

"Dad will be on the next flight there! Tell me where you are!"

And Andrew was. He went to get his son and it was a reunion unlike you have ever seen. The tears and the hugging and the apologies and the promises and the words "I love you" punctuating every sentence.

And Charles knew he was still loved.

Page 2

It's now four years later. Charles went to AA and NA and everything else anonymous to get his life together. And he did. Andrew and Samantha went to the sister organizations for families of addicts. Charles was well! – something they never expected two years ago. He decided to join the Navy. The enforced discipline would do him good. No one argued with that decision. So off he went. Charles was a new young man. They had their son back – but more mature, more self-confident, more spiritual, more… everything good.

Last week Charles joined the family and a couple other families we love as we rented a cottage on a lake. It was a wonderful time of reunion and relationship and recreation and playing together and eating…

Late in the week I was taking a nap and Sue awakens me and says, "Sam's upset. You need to come and pray with her." I was still a bit dazed but, in the dining room I found Sam and Andrew were sitting there weeping. "What's going on?" I said. Andrew told me that he was looking for something in the cabin and bumped Charles' duffle and out fell a liquor bottle…

What to do? Confront him – humiliate him in front of life-long friends? Ignore it? Let him go back to his Naval base in California without acknowledging that you know? How do you "act" like you don't know when he comes in when you do and are worried sick? "Steve – pray for us and him."

The next day we all headed home. I can't say for certain exactly what happened next, but here is my suspicion: Andrew sits Charles down and tells him what happened. At first Charles is angry – then defensive – then belligerent – then contrite – then ashamed – then in tears of remorse and self-loathing.... Andrew tells him that he is deeply concerned and afraid. He isn't sure what it means and has no idea how he can help, especially since Charles is heading back to the west coast in two days. He says that he knows that Charles WANTS to stop. He knows that the pull is enormous. He knows that being all alone so far away from family and friends tempts fate… Andrew weeps with Charles – as any father would. About this time Sam comes into the room. Her eyes are red from crying and fear. She chokes out the words, "Oh Charles, we love you so much…"

And Charles tries to believe them. But it seems so impossible. How could they? To love him right now seems super-human. He has, once again, broken their hearts… He is a wretch…

Then Andrew says, "Charles, I don't know what is going to happen next. All we know is that we can't help you. But we do want you to know that no matter what happens you will still be loved. You will still be our son. You can't ever escape that. In our hearts is always your home."

Charles went back to California on Monday. As he went off, he had a renewed resolve to lick this demon. His parent's love, once again, amazed and humbled him. But he knew he was truly loved – by a love that seemed to transcend the human limitations of love. Knowing that he would once again climb back up on that wagon… knowing that he may fall off again – praying that always the love of his parents would be there to shore him up…

As you see, it's a story straight from the Bible. Like the Biblical story that Jesus told, it doesn't even mention God. But God is there in a most powerful way. It is God who allows us to sink to the bottom so that we can recover fully. It is God who sends angels into our lives. It is God who gives us the courage to call home. It is God who implants the seed of His own love into the hearts of parents and friends (What they can demonstrate is, indeed, only a splinter of what God has for us). It is God who calls us to account. It is God who gives courage to start again. It is God who, when no other is able, will be there for us and with us – at the lake shore or in California … or in Livonia.

If only we could comprehend what we have – how deep and full and all-encompassing and never ending God's love is for us we would be overwhelmed. We are all Charles in our own way. Andrew and Sam are inadequate actors playing God – yet even *their* love is unending…. How much deeper must be the real thing.

BILL IS BORED
Proverbs 22:6

As Bill and his son, Mac, tossed the baseball back and forth on this most beautiful Sunday afternoon, he couldn't help but to feel pretty good about life. He was truly blessed. He was 46 years old and he had been in the same job for 20 of those years. He loved being an engineer. His job was secure because he had been there so long. The company wasn't exactly doing great during the economic down-turn but it was more than solvent and there was no fear of disaster striking. He wasn't going to be unemployed.

A "charmed" life, he often thought. Nothing really bad had ever really happened to him. Some people, it seemed, had one disaster after the other. Tensions and stresses never stopped for them. But he was one of the lucky ones... "Thank you, God." Well – yes, his father had died suddenly a few years ago and that was devastating. 62 is too young... But dads die. And yes, his wife, Nora, had had breast cancer three years ago, but the treatments worked and she seems to be just fine now. Modern medicine is truly amazing... And, he supposed, you might call the motorcycle accident that his brother, Tom, had – the one that almost killed him – he was hospitalized for three months – he supposed that was something pretty bad. But that wasn't really "him" – it was his brother, even though he was quite worried throughout it all. And, of course there was the time he got sued because a neighbor tripped on his sidewalk and broke an ankle. That wasn't such a good time...

OK. So maybe his life was somewhat similar to everyone else's. But somehow Bill was able to keep it all in perspective and see God's hand – if not in the events while they unfolded, then certainly in the aftermath. Good things and bad things and, sometimes, horrible things happen. But for the person who trusts in God and believes what the Bible says, the perspective on personal history is quite different. And Bill DID believe the scriptures. He DID believe that all things work together, ultimately and in some mystical way, for the good. That's the amazing thing about God. He is somehow able to figure it all out and add all the components of life together and make it all come out OK. Pretty cool, really.

Bill grew up in church. It was a church very much like Mt. Hope. It had a choir; they sang hymns; they said the "Lord's Prayer" and sang the Gloria Patri and the Doxology. They had a kindly old minister that had been there since, probably, before God. He had really liked it although he would never admit such a thing. He told his parents that is was "SO BORING." That's what kids are supposed to say. And, really, it WAS a bit boring. But probably no more so than Social Studies in school or history... THOSE were boring.

Before "church" Bill went to Sunday School with his brother and sister. It wasn't much of a Sunday School. There were five kids in his class. Only 4 in each of his brother's and his sister's classes. In many ways it was rather pathetic, as he looked back. He couldn't remember even one thing he learned in that Sunday School. He couldn't remember one craft he made or one verse he learned or one song they sang. He really didn't like it all that much, but his parents made them go. So – when you're a kid, what are you going to do? You go. Back in those days, parents made the important decisions. Whether their kids liked those decisions or not was not really all that relevant. Parents know better than their children what is and what isn't good for them.

But he did remember one thing about that Sunday School so long ago. He remembered Mrs. Turner. She was his teacher in the first grade class. He could still remember her smile and the lavender soap smell whenever she gave him a hug. She gave great hugs. He loved her and he always knew that she loved him. She loved all the kids. And he remembered Mr. and Mrs. Sanders. They taught the second/third grade class together. He remembers them being rather old at the time but, so far as he knows, they are still living, now 40 years later. He saw them a couple of weeks ago. They must be in their 70's now... Which means they were only in their 30's when they taught that class... What a strange perspective children have about adult ages... He had thought they were OLD! He loved them too. They were like an older aunt and uncle.

The thing that Bill remembered most about Mrs. Turner and the Sanders' was the fact that, somehow, he knew, without any doubt whatsoever, that they loved Jesus. He didn't remember a thing they said in those early years. ...Didn't remember anything they tried to teach him. But he remembered that they somehow glowed when talked about Jesus. It was as though they actually knew him!

Good memories of church in those early years...

But something happened. He never knew exactly what it was, but for some reason, his family left that church. His parents never talked about it around the kids. They gave no explanation. They just, one Sunday morning, went to a different church. That was fine with Bill and his sister Judy and his brother Tim. At the Mt. Hope lookalike church the minister was old, the hymns put you to sleep, the choir sang ancient music. It was no place for a kid.

But this new place. Now THERE was a church. It didn't look like a church. It didn't smell like a church. It was so different from that Mt. Hope-like church that the two probably weren't even in the same category. There were dozens of kids in the Sunday School classes. The teachers were interesting. The songs they sang were upbeat and fun. The activities were great. They even had video games and TV's playing all kinds of cartoons non-stop (Christian ones, of course). THIS was great... And better yet, when it was over you went home. There was none of that grown-up palaver to put up with. When you arrived on a Sunday morning the kids went their way and the adults theirs. Everyone was happy!

But there seemed to be a fatal flaw in the system. When Bill was old enough to go to youth group (which met on Sunday evenings), there was no more Sunday School on Sunday mornings for him. Now what? Was he expected to go into the "auditorium" for "adult" worship? He didn't think so.... Not a chance. He went exactly once. He didn't know a soul. The minister, some young pup, was as boring as the old guy at the old church. He was confused as to when to stand up and when to sit down and when to wave his hands in the air and what to do with that bucket they passed down the rows. He didn't recognize the songs projected up on a large screen in front and the prayers seemed, somehow, disrespectful to God, and he absolutely hated it. He refused to go back. And if that was what was expected of him, he wouldn't go to that stupid youth group either. Who cares? There were two hundred kids there every week that no one knew by name. They'd never miss him... Sister Judy and brother Tim followed his example. They never even went once when he described how awkward it all felt.

Bill went away to college up in Mt. Pleasant. During his four years there he never darkened the doors of a church. Why should he? He didn't need it. He did some drinking, like most college students. He liked to party. He was pretty popular with the girls. He kept his grades up and finished in four years....

Along the way, though, he met a cute brunette with hazel eyes that you could get lost in. It didn't take him long to fall in love with her. She was amazing! He asked her to move into his apartment with him. She wouldn't. She, it seems, was a solidly Christian girl and believed that sex and living together ought best to be reserved for marriage. It was a rather old-fashioned idea, but what are you going to do? That high standard of morality and commitment to one's values was one of the most endearing things about her. So they'd get married. He could absolutely see spending a lifetime with Jenny...

She took him home to meet her parents. They were nice people. They welcomed him warmly. They chatted about all kinds of things and made him feel quite comfortable. On Saturday night, before they all headed for bed, Mr. Tracy said to Bill. "Bill, our family always goes to church on Sunday mornings. Jenny tells us that you aren't much of a church goer. And, although that concerns us as the two of you are getting serious, we accept it. If you want to go with us tomorrow, you are welcome. But if you don't, that's OK, too. You can just hang around here and we'll pick you up after church and we'll all go out to lunch together before the two of you head back to school."

Bill was no fool. If church is important to Jenny and her parents, he wasn't about to sleep in and have a black mark on his record. Church it was.

He hadn't been up so early on a Sunday morning for years... This was insane. A young man needed some sack time. Fortunately, they hadn't been up late on Saturday – no partying at Jenny's house. He would probably survive. ...What a guy does for love...

But as they pulled into the parking lot, Bill got the strangest feeling of déjà vu. This church looked strikingly like the church of his childhood. "Boring – here we come."

They went in and were greeted by several people. Jenny's parents were "pillars" of the church, as it turned out. They knew everyone and everyone knew them – lots of laughter and hand shaking and small talk... They found a seat and sat quietly listening to the prelude music (really quite lovely)... He was glad people were respectful of the organist. He clearly was very talented and had spent a lot of time practicing. Maybe he'd compliment the guy after service if he saw him.

But then the strangest thing in Bill's life began to happen. Jenny opened the hymnal to the page of the first song and everyone stood up and began to sing a song that Bill knew! How did he know it? He wasn't sure. But he knew every phrase before he read it. And, although he wasn't much of a singer, he sang along. It was kind of fun.

Throughout the service the same thing kept happening. That song they sang after the offering – he knew it! The little chorus they sang after the responsive reading – he knew it! When the minister read from the Bible, the words weren't new to him. He remembered, somewhere, having heard them before. The "Lord's Prayer" – he knew it (although they seemed to have changed a couple of the words – he remembered "trespasses" but they all said "debtors."). And it suddenly came to him. He had heard and learned all those things way back when he was 6 and 7 and 8 years old. The very word of God had been planted in his soul without him ever realizing it. He had soaked it up like a sponge and now it was flowing from him freely...

Tears ran down Bill's cheeks when he realized how much he missed all this. He missed the simplicity of people just loving Jesus. Not making a production of it – just loving Jesus. He remembered Mrs. Turner (he imagined he could smell lavender). He remembered the love she shared – and the Sanders – their "glow" in Jesus... And Bill wanted it all back. He wanted to glow. He wanted to sing those centuries old songs. He wanted to say the "Lord's Prayer" again. He wanted to listen to those boring sermons (although they seemed to make a lot of sense now and were, really, quite challenging and interesting). He wanted, like he had as a child, to know God like these people... And that day, in the silence of his own heart, Bill said "yes" to the love of Christ and "please" to the forgiveness of his sins.

Bill and Jenny got married in that church a couple of years later. It barely held all their family and friends... Plus he had made dozens of friends at the church who just had to be there... It was quite an event.

Bill and Jenny have been married for 18 years now. They have seldom missed a Sunday. It's just too important for their family. Mac, their son, used to find it boring, just like he did when he was little, but Bill knew that drawing pictures in church or reading a book or coloring or having to be shushed because he would get restless, was secondary to what was happening, by the power of God, in his little brain and in his heart. Bill knew that Mac would, one day, appreciate being dragged to church... would appreciate knowing the prayers and the hymns and the scriptures... and his own Mrs. Turner – still around after all these years (she exists in every "traditional" church) – giving hugs and smelling of lavender .

As Bill tosses the ball back to Mac, he knows one other thing – he wouldn't have given up that hour each Sunday morning with his son – bored as he might be – for anything in all the earth.

A LOT TO REMEMBER
Matthew 5:17-20

Lottie Haranson[1] arrived at the office before anyone else. The sun was up, but just barely. But if you are the mayor[2] and you hope to continue being mayor through the next election, you had better be on the job early and you'd better stay late and you'd better make sure you do things that get noticed and in the news. That's the name of the game. But civil service is hard work and Lottie wasn't sure how long he wanted to do this. SO much to do and the resources were always so tight... Failure was almost guaranteed. Success always a miracle... And even when there is success, at least half of the population – usually more – think you're a no-good bum.

Lottie's "to do" list this week was pretty long. He had to work on a new budget, he had to figure out how to curb the rash of violence that seemed to be plaguing the city, he had to convince some local businessmen to build a new hotel in town – visitors had a difficult time finding a place to spend the night (so much so that he sometimes, as mayor, invited people to stay with his family... Now, a mayor shouldn't have to do that - but it did play well in the newspapers). He had to schmooze city council to get them to give a license to yet another gay bar in town – these things were popping up everywhere. He had to, somehow, get a recreational facility planned and built for the young people – there seemed to be a lot or restlessness these days – not enough for them to do except get into trouble...

To top it all off, taped to his computer monitor was a note he had written to himself, lest he forget. He MUST contact the DJs and caterers for his daughters weddings. Believe it or not, he had TWO daughters getting married next fall. He didn't even want to think about the expense of that. He had suggested that they have a double service (thus increasing the guest list a bit but cutting most costs in half). They would have none of it. Neither would his wife. They must think money grows on trees!

He was about to get two sons-in-law that he didn't care for all that much for.[3] They were both pretty much alike. They were both good looking. They both had those plastic, toothy smiles – like a used car salesman – he wasn't sure he trusted them. They both dressed like they were rich. They both were so "sophisticated" it made you want to puke. They both seemed so phony... He didn't know what his daughters saw in either one of them.

And the worst part was that they weren't believers. UNBELIEVABLE! He and his wife had raised their daughters with the idea that any future mate MUST be a believer - a Godly man... Nothing but problems would come if they didn't. Even the Bible warned of it – "don't be unequally yoked with unbelievers…" But no. Dad and mom's wisdom – and the Bible's – apparently seemed like foolishness to them. THEY knew better. To them, it just didn't seem to matter. If you loved someone, that was enough. Love would see them through any religious differences they had. …Young people are so dumb.

And his wife – it all seemed OK with her now, even though she said she didn't like Jack and George any more than he did. What was she thinking? A wedding (**weddings**) are announced and suddenly she melts and thinks these two stud-muffins are just perfect. She even joins the girls in calling him an old fuddy-duddy. It all makes him so tired. It seems that nobody has any common sense any more.

Lottie has served on the board of his church for nearly 5 years now.[4] But even though church should be a place you go to find some peace, there hadn't been much there for a long time. The congregation was dwindling. Last Sunday morning there were less than a dozen people there – down from a year ago of 40 or 50. He wasn't sure they could stay open much longer. It was all so depressing.

Fortunately for Lottie, he was a wealthy man. He didn't really *need* to be mayor. He didn't really *need* to worry about the cost of the weddings. He didn't really *need* all the troubles that he faced every day. He could, if he wanted to, chuck it all and live quite a comfortable life. But he felt he was on a mission from God. He ought to serve others – in the community. He ought to use his talents, as best he could, to serve the church. He ought to be the kind of man God would be pleased with. He and Maggie[5] had always thought that. Being a "good" person was …. well, good.

The work day passed quickly. He had worked through his list pretty efficiently. He had gotten a lot done. He decided it was time to head home. Lottie was the last one out just like he was the first one in – a twelve hour day. The sun had been down for a while already. He was tired.

As he drove home, Lottie spotted a couple of young men walking down the sidewalk. The backpacks they were wearing told him they were from out of town. College students? Mormon missionaries? Who knows. But he did know one thing. If they were heading for the youth hostel they were in trouble. That place needed to go. Gangs owned it. It was a cesspool for violent people. Were they heading for campus – hoping to crash there? That was trouble, too. There didn't exist a place on earth as unwelcoming as the local campus. Why, last year, a carload of students from another school drove through the campus and riots practically started. The poor visitors were beaten senseless. He didn't know what it was, but somehow the campus was a hostile environment for any stranger. The college was only a couple blocks up the road. They, no doubt, were heading there. He needed to stop them before it was too late.

Lottie pulled his car over to the curb beside the two young guys. "Hey, fellas! Where you heading?"

"We're heading for the park. We're going to sack out there tonight."

"I'm afraid you can't do that. There is an ordinance against it."

"Well, can you tell us where a hotel is?"

"Sorry. There isn't one. Had one, but it was in such bad shape they had to condemn it."

"No problem. We'll find somewhere. Thanks."

Lottie saw trouble coming. Some drunken students were staggering down the street a block behind them. This could get ugly if something didn't happen soon.

"Fellas – hop in. I'll let you stay at my house tonight."

"That's very kind, but unnecessary. We'll be OK."

"I insist," Lottie said as he saw the students notice them. "Look – you can be inside. You can take showers – sleep in a good bed. You can even join us for dinner... Hop in."

After a bit more negotiating, the two young men got into the car and Lottie drove them to his house. He was relieved. No trouble tonight, thank you very much.

Lottie got them home, directed them to the shower and after they had cleaned up he invited them to join his wife and daughters and himself for dinner. They were the nicest young men. The girls shamelessly flirted with them. But, as they talked and he asked them what brought them to town, the conversation got very strange. They said they were there on a mission from God.

Lottie and his wife were skeptical. "What kind of mission exactly," Maggie asked.

They explained, "God has looked over your city and can find no redeeming value here. There is prostitution and gang violence. There is rape and drunkenness and corrupt politicians. There is homelessness and hunger with no charity. Murder and theft goes unchecked. Children are neglected and abused. Drug addiction is rampant. Sexual perversion is common. People gossip and slander one another with abandon. We know you are the mayor and a good man, but, and no offense intended, this is a terrible place. God searched the city for 50 good people, thinking that if there were even fifty he would be happy. Couldn't find them. He searched for forty-five. Couldn't find them. Forty? Nope. Thirty? Not even thirty. I think there were thirty in your church last year, weren't there? But not anymore. Even some of them have turned to evil. God searched and couldn't find so few as ten!

"Mr. Mayor. This is not good. Contact your future sons-in-law or any relatives you have in town or anyone you want. Tell them to get out of town because God is about to destroy it."

Lottie was stunned. Could this be possible? He didn't really think so. Yes, the town had problems, but was it really as bad as these young men said? He looked at Maggie and could see the fear in her eyes. He looked at the girls. They couldn't believe what they were hearing either. They couldn't even grasp that God knew about their town. Didn't He have better things to do?

"Fellas, exactly what are you carrying in those backpacks of yours? Explosives? Are you planning violence here?" He reached for his cell phone to call the police...

"No. No explosives... mostly underwear and toiletries. WE'RE not going to destroy the town. God is going to do it in His own way. But you all need to leave."

Then Maggie asked a question that only a woman can ask at a time like this. "There aren't ten righteous people in town? How many are there? Who are they?"

"Mrs. Haranson," one of the young men said, chuckling, "You and Lottie are two. Your daughters, Ruth and Leah are another two. God found no more."

Maggie smiled and cast her eyes down. They had done it. They had been found righteous in the midst of God-noticed evil. They had raised their daughters in such a way that they, too, were righteous in the sight of God. Praise be to Yahweh. Then she thought, "Could there possibly, EVER be a greater compliment than that – to be judged, on earth, by God, as righteous?" She doubted it. This revelation was humbling and most amazing.

Lottie's daughters immediately grabbed their cell phones and called their fiancés. They told them of the visitors and their warning and urged them to get out of the city as quickly as possible. They laughed at them. "God is going to destroy Sodom? Come on... you don't believe that stuff, do you? That's alarmism. Does your God do that sort of thing?" asked Jack. George was even more flip, "Don't you let your little God frighten you, Helen. Big George here will protect you. I'll see you tomorrow (you silly thing)."

Lottie and Maggie didn't really believe the strangers until a truly terrifying thing happened...

Someone knocked on the door. Maggie looked out the front window to see who it was. "Lottie – come here – quick. There is a crowd out on our front lawn!"

It looked like trouble, big time. Lottie gingerly opened the door to face a couple of large, rough looking men. "What do you want?" Lottie said.

"We want your visitors. We want those young punks who've trespassed on our turf. Send them out!"

"You've got to be kidding. What do you want them for? They haven't done anything to you. Get off my property."

One of the men stepped up on the porch and slapped Lottie on the face. "Give them to us or we'll walk all over you, old man. Then we'll get them anyway! Out of our way, fool!"

At this point, the young men opened the door, grabbed Lottie, and pulled him back inside, slamming the door shut. The men on the porch started hammering on the door, trying to knock it down. It was starting to splinter. Maggie and the girls were hysterical – screaming and crying... Lottie was reeling, not knowing what to do to save his family. One of the young men put his hands over Lottie's eyes and threw his hands towards the door and there was sudden silence. "What happened?" asked Lottie. He went to the window and saw the strangest thing he had ever witnessed. The thugs on his porch were groping around as though they were blind. The crowd behind them didn't know what was going on, but they knew something powerful was going on. They began to fade away... In a few minutes, friends of the guys on the porch came and lead them away – they were... clearly, they had been made blind...

Needless to say, Lottie nor Maggie nor his daughters slept much that night. They didn't know exactly who these young men under their roof were, but they knew that they possessed almost god-like power.

When the sun rose the next morning, things didn't seem quite so grim. The events of the evening before seemed almost like a dream – although they knew it wasn't a dream... Maggie served them all a hearty breakfast – kosher, of course – just in case... When they finished, one of the young men said, "Now it's time to go. Lottie, you've got to take your two daughters and Maggie and get out of here. Otherwise, you will be caught up in the coming destruction. It's happening today."

"Let me gather some things we'll need" Maggie said. "I'll get the silver," said Lottie. The girls were about to rush off to pack a few things into suitcases.

The young men said, "No. You don't understand. You must leave now – take nothing. Otherwise you will die in the conflagration that is coming. Come! Now! Hurry!"

Well, the Haranson family ran for their lives. And just in time. God did destroy that city with all the evil and corruption that had plagued it. It, and another city nearby and the plains around both were devoured in volcanic lava and ash and gas. Nobody except Lot and his family survived. Unfortunately, the woman who thought herself greatly complimented by God – Maggie – the woman found to be one of the only righteous people in the city, was a casualty. For some reason she lagged behind as the family fled and was caught in the ash and dust and gas of the volcanoes and died out on the plains…

I wonder what it takes to be considered "righteous" by God? Surely there were people in Sodom who would not be considered "evil." Yet they, apparently, were not considered "righteous" either. I'm pretty sure it is more than just doing the "right" (righteous) thing whenever possible. But Maggie was right – there is no greater compliment that God can bestow than that He considers you – or me – righteous.

Lot was the son of Haran, brother of Abraham.
[2] *There is no Biblical indication that Lot held any kind of public office.*
[3] *There is no Biblical indication that Lot did not care for them. In fact, he warned them to flee when it was clear the city would be destroyed. They DID laugh and not believe him. Nothing more is known of them.*
[4] *It is not known whether or not Lot and family attended worship anywhere.*
[5] *Very little is known about Lot's wife – not even her name. Even the meaning of her "turning to a pillar of salt" is unknown. It is often interpreted as being a longing after Sodom and the "good life."*

PROPHET NANCY GILL
Deuteronomy 13:1-5

Everyone has heard of the prophets in the Bible: Ezekiel, Elijah, Isaiah, Daniel, Jeremiah... Hosea, Amos, Obadiah, and Nahum, just to name a few. But most of us don't know what they were all about – what they had to say and why and how. And there is a very good reason for that. The prophets, for the most part, are real "downers." Oh, you may have heard of Ezekiel's "dry bones" (or at least the fun song that came from it...) and Isaiah's wonderful and amazingly specific prediction of the birth and death of Jesus 700 years before the events. We all, no doubt, know of Daniel's bout with the lion's den and, if we are a bit more Biblically literate, about Hosea marrying a prostitute or the Prophet Balaam having a verbal sparring match with his donkey. More obscure, of course, are the conversations Zechariah had with angels or Habakkuk's explanation as to why wicked people prosper and good people suffer (had his answer to that big question been more satisfying, he'd be a lot more famous)...

But the prophets, for the most part, are known for their incessant predictions of death and destruction and doom. Sometimes their predictions are moderated by "if you change, God will spare you," but generally not. Most of the time their words are just dire warnings so that, when disaster comes, you'll know from whence and why. ...There are not many sermons on prophetic predictions... because they are scary and depressing and because they were written to specific peoples concerning specific events going on in their specific society (except prophets like Daniel, whose prophecies are still to come).

Most of us wouldn't want to know a prophet. My guess is that being around one would be like being around a truly obnoxious person. "**I speak for God**" would be hard to take after a while. And, if we believed they really did speak for God, we would feel SO spiritually inferior. My guess is that they were more outspoken, more dogmatic, more uncompromising, more aggressive than most of us would be comfortable with. I don't think they used the term back in Biblical times, but you and I would call them... nuts – crazy – maybe even schizophrenic.

One of the truly amazing things about a prophet, however, is the fact that, when they are in their prophetic mode, they are NEVER wrong. I'm not sure exactly how that works. Somehow the Spirit of God communicates directly to them what they are to say and they become the conduit for God's message. Unless they mess it up, they hear it accurately and pass it on. "Don't blame me," might be their slogan, "I'm only the messenger." The penalty for being wrong in the heyday of the prophet, was death – because if you were wrong, you must certainly be a false prophet and we certainly don't want those in our midst, so they must go. The order was to stone them. Needless to say, the prophets were very careful to either KNOW they were speaking for God – knowing they wouldn't be wrong – or they would, wisely, make predictions for the distant future, for long after their natural life span (sorry – that's a bit cynical – they STILL were expected to be right and they would certainly be vindicated, even after they were dead, by the events happening). And, of course, all the predictions of all the prophets in the Bible came true. Otherwise they wouldn't have made it into the scriptures.

For the most part, everyone believes that the age of the prophets is past. Malachi was the last of the prophets and, in the final paragraph of his writings, he makes one last prophecy that one more prophet will appear on the scene – Elijah will return to prepare the way for Messiah. Then, for 400 years, not another peep from anyone believed to be a prophet of God.

By everyone's theological accounting, that predicted prophet was John the Baptist, who was the announcer of Jesus.

But there are still prophets in the world and I'd like to tell you about one that I met some forty years ago. My prophetical acquaintance (no one is really a "friend" of a prophet – acquaintance is as close as one dares to get) was a female. Her name: Nancy Gill.

Nancy was a short girl – probably under five feet tall. I usually think of prophets as tall people – but not Nancy. She was a bit on the heavy side. She had mousy brown hair and tended, always, to wear dark clothes. But wherever she went, you knew if she was in the room. She had a presence about her… almost like a dark cloud entering the room…

Nancy never considered herself a prophet. In fact, if you asked her, she would have told you outright that she wasn't smart enough or good enough or religious enough to be anything special in the Christian world. But I noticed something about Nancy that made me suspicious…

Nancy was a senior at Eastern Michigan University when I met her. "Good morning, Nancy."

"What's good about it? I've got a test at 10:00 and I'm going to fail it."

"Wow. Sorry. Tough course? No time to study?"

"I studied for 10 minutes and gave up. What's the use. I don't get this stuff."

I heard later that she failed the test. ...My first clue of her "Prophetess" status...

[Whoever has will be given more, and he will have an abundance. Whoever does not have, even what he has will be taken from him. Matthew 13:12]

As time went on, I had numerous opportunities to observe Nancy and found her life fascinating. I didn't really like being around her all that much, but she was part of the campus Christian group I was training with, so I had little choice. We were thrown together time and time again...

Our Inter Varsity Christian Fellowship group joined with other groups twice a year for a weekend retreat over at Mill Lake State Park near Chelsea. Just about everyone went. They were great times of fun and fellowship and learning and meeting girls and guys from other campuses (Let's see... I met Karen from Adrian and Joann from U of M and Marsha from Toledo... I must have met some guys too, but I'm afraid I don't remember any of them...). Nancy, of course, went along. She predicted that the weather would be terrible. And, as it turned out, her prophet sense was right on. On this particular weekend the weather didn't cooperate. It rained. It wasn't a hard rain but it was pretty steady. I heard Nancy say to someone, "I knew it was going to be miserable here. I don't know why God can't give us good weather when we come out here to this musty old campground. We're probably all going to get sick. This is going to really be fun..."

[The LORD opens the heavens, the storehouse of his bounty, to send rain on your land in season and to bless all the work of your hands. Deut. 28:12... He sends rain on the righteous and the unrighteous alike. Matt. 5:28]

And several of us did catch colds by Tuesday. And, she was right, we did have fun. I think it was at that retreat that someone talked to Sue (my wife now) and the Holy Spirit moved and she first welcomed Jesus into her life. I don't remember if she caught a cold or not. I do know she caught something, though, that has infected her to this very day and it's been wonderful.

[... whoever believes in him [Jesus] shall not perish but have eternal life. John 3:16]

Nancy was never a happy person. But what prophet is? When you see things the way they really are, there is often not much to recommend them. But she WAS a passionate young woman. If she liked you, you were a rarity. But if she didn't, you'd better watch out.

She had a pretty quick tongue and could criticize and castigate with the best of them, even at the tender age of 20. If the truth be known, she didn't really like people very much. She believed that everyone had some kind of major flaw that made them unappealing.

[... all have sinned and fall short of the glory of God. Romans 3:23]

I suppose that everyone has a philosophy of life. Some of it comes from our parents. Some of it from friends and others we meet along the way. Some of it from our studies and books and listening to teachers and preachers and lecturers… from TV shows and music and magazines and newspapers. And probably Nancy's philosophy of life came from all of those. But I always suspected that some of who she was was just … who she was. She was born with a perspective of always seeing the dark side – always knowing she was right – always ready to proclaim that the sky was falling – that disaster was just around the corner – that God would "get" us in the end. She was uniquely able to see truth and allow it to bind her mind and spirit in the most secure of ways.

["If you hold to my teaching, you are really my disciples. …you will know the truth, and the truth will set you free." John 8:32]

I remember on one occasion her prescience was especially keen. It was a beautiful spring day and a fairly large group of us decided to go to a nearby stable and go horseback riding. She thought it a terrible idea. "First of all," she said, "many of the people who say they will go will decide not to and leave us holding the bag." As it turned out, she was right. On second thought, about a third of the other students decided that horseback riding was too expensive or simply not for them. They had never done any of it and always thought they'd like to, but when the real possibility presented itself, they decided they weren't all that crazy about horses…

"And you know those horses are going to stink and we will, too, after riding them," she said. Again, Nancy was right. We should have asked for non-smelly beasts…

"Besides, I've ridden before and I know how stiff and sore you are after a couple of hours of riding. None of us will be able to move." And I don't think any of us, in our young lives had ever been in so much pain as we were that evening… I tell you, this young prophetess was a genius. But we were all glad we went (except Nancy, of course). Our enjoyment was full and the suffering bonded our group like nothing else and gave us a story to share for years to come whenever we saw one another.

[Enjoy life! ... Enjoy all the days of this...life that God has given you ...Whatever your hand finds to do, do it with all your might, for in the grave, where you are going, there is neither working nor planning nor knowledge nor wisdom. Ecc. 9:9, 10]

Nancy was a senior the year I knew her. And in that short nine months she affected my life like no one ever has. Her certainty that whatever could possibly go wrong, would, astounded me. I saw in her a different perspective on God and how the Divine interacts with people than I had known existed. I had no doubt that she was a believer in Christ. I had no doubt that she worshiped and served the same God as I did. But the God I knew was generous and loving and forgiving and helpful. The God I knew wanted us to be holy but is not surprised when we aren't. The God I followed was a God of compassion and tenderness... I learned that my understanding of God and how others perceive Him was quite narrow. I learned that, often, the prophecies we make about the future do, actually, come true. Someone once said, "Whether you think the future will be good or whether you think the future will be bad, you are probably right."

Our acquaintance ended when I was sent off on an assignment at another school and I never knew whether or not Nancy Gill graduated. I rather think she must have - she was very close - but I have every confidence that graduation day must have surprised her. Or, more aptly, that she looked at her sheepskin and knew it wasn't going to get her a job and that she had surely just wasted four years of her life. And I've no doubt that she was right again.

I knew Nancy for only a year, although it seemed a lot longer. I went off to work with students in North Dakota and I never heard about nor saw her again (I didn't mind). But I've thought of her often. I've wondered what she ended up doing or being. So last week I Googled her – and found 1,310,000 references to Nancy Gill. And I couldn't help but wonder whether they are all her. And I still can't help wondering if there isn't a bit of her in each of us – and what we can do about it.

Seek first the Kingdom of God and His righteousness, and all these things will be given to you. Do not worry about tomorrow, for tomorrow will worry about itself. Each day has enough trouble of its own.
--Matt. 6:33-34

JEFFREY GOES TO HEAVEN
Mark 10:13-16

They say she died in her sleep, but everyone who knew her knew that couldn't be true. Florence was an insomniac and, try as she would, she seldom got more than a cat nap now and then. What actually happened was that she was reading in bed – a novel she had been wanting to read for a long time (she had been on the waiting list at the library and it was finally hers – she was about 2/3 through). She sensed that someone was in the room with her and, as she looked up, she saw an angel... She knew instinctively what was going on. She said, "I'm not ready to go yet! I've got things to do... I've got to finish this book. I've waited weeks to get it..."

The angel shook her head and smiled – the highlights of her long, golden locks shimmered in the dim light. Everyone always said the same thing. "Sorry, Florence. It's time to go." She let her book slip from her hands onto the floor and they were off.

Dying is an amazing sensation. Florence was 87 years old when she died. She had moderate arthritis, dimming eyesight, failing memory – but, ironically, when she died, she had never felt quite so alive. She stretched her hands and wiggled her fingers and bent her knees – no pain. How cool was that? She looked out, across the city, as she and the angel ascended into the heavens and she could see forever. It was like watching Jason's High Definition TV. The colors were more vibrant than ever. She could see details she had forgotten existed – and she could see for miles and miles in every direction. This was awesome! "Angel – I had no idea it would be like this. This is... this is wonderful!" The angel just smiled and said, "You haven't seen anything yet."

Florence wasn't sure if it was because they were getting so high and it just seemed like it or if they were actually slowing down, but the earth she loved didn't seem to be receding so quickly now. And Florence had time to think about what was going on. She knew, without any doubt, that she was dead. What else could this be? She pinched herself to make sure she wasn't just sleeping. Although the pinch didn't hurt, neither did she awaken. She was quite dead all right. There could be no doubt.

Florence was a woman of faith, so she wasn't worried about dying or where the angel was taking her. She knew that she was headed for heaven. She had had a rather raucous youth – people called her a "hellion," but she met Jesus in college and had been walking with Him ever since – 66 years now. How clearly she remembered those days – *this renewed memory thing was great!*... She went to college an agnostic. An agnostic is someone who doesn't have the courage to say they don't believe in God (if God exists He might zap you) but knows that saying you DO believe in God has some baggage attached to it – certain expectations of how one lives and what one believes and what values one holds. Agnosticism is a good place to be. You don't chance offending God ("God – I'm just not sure you're there – but I'm open to the possibility – be patient with me...") and you don't have to DO or BE anything you don't want to do or be because you haven't committed yourself. She rather liked being an agnostic. Over the years she had concluded that most Christians actually were - in practice if not in fact.

Florence loved to read. But in college there was no time for the kind of reading she most enjoyed – novels of adventure and love. The textbook reading load was as much reading as anyone would want to do. But one day she happened upon a book that her roommate had for a comparative religions class. She wasn't in the mood to study her own textbooks just then but there is a strange appeal to a textbook that belongs to someone else that isn't assigned to you... somehow the knowledge inside seems more interesting and intriguing... It was a weekend and her roommate had gone home – it was a Saturday night and she didn't have a date and nothing else to do, so she began reading. It was fascinating, especially the numbers of adherents claimed. Some of these religions had hundreds of millions of adherents – Buddhism 360 million (more than the entire population of the United States); Hinduism has twice that many. Islam has over a billion. And Christianity has over 2 billion! [1]How many people are there in the world anyway?... Does EVERYONE believe in God? And this book seemed to be written quite objectively (maybe she should take the course) and, clearly, by a man who knew his subject – he was obviously no dummy.

Florence read that book all day and far into the night. This was fascinating stuff! She read about Hinduism and their strange adherence to reincarnation. She wasn't sure she wanted to come back as a cow – but it was nice that they didn't eat you if you did. She read of Buddhism and their attempt to reach Nirvana by having no desires nor expectations in life. She wasn't sure she could handle that. She was way too much an American – too much ambition and hopes for the future. She WANTED to want things. She read about Judaism and admired the "system" of rules and rituals they teach – how could you remember them all? Islam, she found had a strong emphasis of doing good in order to reach heaven, but the not knowing until you get wherever it is you're going made her rather nervous... Christianity?

They believe some pretty strange things – Jesus raising from the dead? Salvation through simply believing (You don't have to DO anything?). The miracles? Pretty far-out...

But in a few hours it would be Sunday morning, so she decided she would go to church (there were no mosques or synagogues or Buddhist temples in town – plenty of churches, though).

The minister, as it turned out, wasn't very good. His sermon was rather boring. The choir was just a bit off-key. The kids in the pews were distracting. But there was something about the people. Before the service and after the service and during the service (they had one of those awkward 'greet your neighbor' times some churches have mid-service – she didn't like it much)... before and after and during the service it was SO OBVIOUS that these people really did like one another – that they really did care about one another – that they actually loved HER even though they had never met her... She was so blown away by their love that she pulled one of the young men aside who was chatting with her after the service and asked him if this was real and how and why. He told her it was because they were all part of the family of God – brothers and sisters to Jesus and to one another... that they had sought Jesus' forgiveness, gotten it, were striving to live righteous lives and live without guilt. That very morning she asked how and she became a believer.

Florence's life hadn't been an easy one. She got married (married that young man she had talked to in church). She and Josh had two children. The girl, Grace, died as an infant – broke their hearts... Jeffrey grew into a good enough man. He had followed Jesus as a child but had left the church – calling us all fools who needed a crutch. He didn't. He had died five years ago, unrepentant. She hoped (but doubted) that he had turned back to God before he lapsed into that final coma as cancer took its toll...

Florence remembered it all now, with crystal clarity. She remembered the good times and the bad times and the times she wished she could forget forever... She remembered her pets and her garden and vacations and laughter and sunshine on her face... She suddenly realized that somehow even the bad things that happened along the way served a greater purpose – dots she had never connected before. The whole universe was operating as a finely tuned instrument – as an orchestra where the piccolo and the bass have parts to play – where notes played in minor keys and major chords work together to make beautiful music. All is good as God conducts... She found herself laughing out loud, she felt so good – so alive – so filled with joy – she felt like she could almost not contain it...

Now she looked back toward the earth. It was, indeed, receding. They were making headway into the great, vast unknown. She wondered what was ahead. She didn't fear it. She knew it would be good. But she still couldn't comprehend what heaven would be like...

Then, as she watched, the earth began to fade away. It wasn't moving further off, it was just vanishing and, in its place, beginning to materialize, was something quite different, yet strikingly familiar and they were descending/ascending (she couldn't tell which, if either one) toward it. Florence knew it must be heaven, but it looked exactly – yet not at all – like where she had just come from. There was her house. But the white siding was whiter. The grass was greener. The flowers more vibrant in color. The air fresher. The birds singing more beautiful, the neighbors more cheerful... everything exactly like it was when she left but infinitely better in every inconceivable way. She looked at the angel and the angel just smiled and said, "Welcome home. Your heavenly father looks forward to meeting you whenever you are ready. If you want, you can finish your book now."

But Florence didn't want to finish the book. It seemed so trite and unimportant now...

She went into her house and the first thing she heard was the sharp bark of her little dog that had died years ago. It came running across the kitchen floor, skidding it's little paws and literally leaped into her arms. She was so happy tears came to her eyes. Then she heard someone singing. She recognized the voice. It was Josh, of course. She wasn't surprised to see him. She knew he would be there. But her joy at seeing him again was overwhelming... They hugged and kissed and held each other for a very long time. He felt SO good. "Where's Grace?" said Florence in a faltering, laughing voice. "I need to see my baby." Josh pointed to the first bedroom... and inside was a little girl Florence didn't recognize except that she had Josh's eyes and her own nose and chin... Grace had died an infant but seemed now to be a beautiful seven year old – the joy of any mother's heart...

"Flo – it is so good to have you here," said Joshua. And he hugged her again and his face just beamed with delight. It was like being young lovers again. "I've got a surprise for you. Look in the den."

Florence walked to the den and peeked around the corner. There, to her utter astonishment, was their son, Jeffrey. "Jeffrey, what are you doing here? I thought heaven was only for believers?"

"I know, mom. I am still in shock, myself. I didn't believe any of that stuff and here I am. Believe me, I believe it now! I haven't gone to see the big guy yet. I'm afraid he'll tell me it was a mistake and I'll be sent away. This really is an amazing place... The flowers never wilt. The sun never burns. The food is always delicious. The neighbors are always thoughtful. No one is ever sick. The movies are always good – and holographic and interactive. Nobody is ever depressed or sad. The whole place is at peace. There is no poverty or hunger or homelessness or want. Our jobs aren't tedious or boring or dead-end. We never get tired but are able to sleep soundly. There is so much joy around that it makes you just happy to be alive (back on earth they call it dead but I've never been more alive). Wait until you've been here a while and see more of it... You'll be astounded."

Florence reveled in her new/old home for a long time – or perhaps it was only a moment – time there is meaningless... But being with her family again – talking with them and doing things and reminiscing and speculating about what is yet to be... She couldn't have been happier. The more she saw of it the better she liked it. But finally she decided she had to see Jesus. She had followed him so long that seeing him face to face was almost more than she could imagine. He lived just next door (how did he manage to live next door to everyone? She didn't know but thought it wonderful)...

She knocked on his door (she thought she would never have the courage, but her newfound boldness to approach the Lord of Life astounded her). Jesus opened the door himself and welcomed her in by name and told her how much he loved her and she felt, in the deepest sense, that he was telling the absolute truth. His love for her was deep and rich and full and pure and complete.

"Florence, I know that yesterday you had a zillion questions. And I know that most all of them have already been answered or have become irrelevant – except for the one you feel you can't express. And I won't ask you to. You want to know why Jeffrey is here. He left the faith. He broke your heart. You feared for his soul. I hurt too. His rejection of me gave me pain for ten thousand years. But you took him to church when he was little. You insisted that he go to Sunday School. You took him to Vacation Bible School at that little Mt. Hope Church on Livernois in Detroit. You read him Bible stories and prayed with him. You exposed him to me in every way you could think of and you were thrilled when he, in his child-like way, said yes to me. That day he became my brother - God's son and God his Father. Tell me, Florence, when he left the faith, did he cease being your son? Of course not. Did you love him any less? No. ...Same with me. When he became my son and I his brother and our Father his Father, the relationship was sealed. I was bound to love him forever even if he stopped loving me – even if he stopped believing in me – even if he ridiculed me or those who believe in me. When he said 'yes,' even as a child, he was mine forever, just like he was yours forever on the day he was born. Nothing can change that fact – not even if he wanted to…"

And Florence went back to her heavenly home that day with an understanding of the love of God unlike any she had ever conceived – a love so all- encompassing, so all-pervasive, so… so deep… and she knew why, for the first time, the angels were said to sing of God's love and greatness and holiness continually throughout all of heaven. …Oh, the awesomely deep, deep love of Jesus.

O the deep, deep love of Jesus, vast, unmeasured, boundless, free! Rolling as a mighty ocean in its fullness over me! Underneath me, all around me, is the current of Thy love Leading onward, leading homeward to Thy glorious rest above!

O the deep, deep love of Jesus, spread His praise from shore to shore! How He loveth, ever loveth, changeth never, nevermore! How He watches o'er His loved ones, died to call them all His own; How for them He intercedeth, watcheth o'er them from the throne!

O the deep, deep love of Jesus, love of every love the best! 'Tis an ocean vast of blessing, 'tis a haven sweet of rest! O the deep, deep love of Jesus, 'tis a heaven of heavens to me; And it lifts me up to glory, for it lifts me up to Thee!

- Samuel Trevor Francis

---

[1] *These statistics are current and not actually what Florence would have seen 66 years ago.*

THE STORY OF JERUBAL AND THE WAR
Judges 7:2-8

A True Story.

I've never been to war. Someone who once said that "War is hell." And, from the descriptions I've heard from people who actually have been to war, I think that is probably an apt analogy. I've never been to hell either, but hell must be just about as bad as existence can get. War is like that. There is the smell of cordite and gunpowder. There is the flash of explosions and the debris and dirt flying through the air to seek out unwilling victims. There is the noise. ...If you are too close your eardrums may burst and you are deaf for a while – seeing explosions and the pained screams of the wounded but as though watching a silent movie. There is the distinct odor of sweat and fear... the visible aging of young men and women almost before one's eyes... He who was 19 yesterday is 43 today – older – wiser – not the same person as yesterday at all. Yesterday he was a student – at the university or just finishing high school – today he is a leader of men. He has little metal pins on his uniform to prove it. He acts as though he knows just what he is doing – just what to do – he doesn't. His biggest fear is that his men can hear the pounding of his heart and sense the uncertainty inside...

God started on earth in the Middle East. There has always been a most uncanny connection between God and the people of those lands. They know that they don't have a corner on relationship with God, but they also know that the connection they have is closer and more personal. There is even an unspoken tendency to believe that any thought that comes into one's mind is God speaking. You saw "Fiddler on the Roof." You know what I mean. Old Tevye walks around talking to himself, it seems, but is actually talking to God – and it is clear that he thinks God is speaking to him – a dialog that makes most of us wish we had that kind of relationship with the divine.

There was once a man named Jerub-baal Joashson[1] who lived in the tiny village of Abierez.[2] It was a sleepy little town – not much ever went on there. The main industry was the growing of grapes for winemaking and the making and selling of the wine. Most of the people were poor. Jerbu-baal wanted desperately to get out of the tiny village and find some adventure in life but, if the typical pattern for young people continued with him, he never would. He would live in Abierez – get married in Abierez – raise his family in Abierez – and eventually die in Abierez. Jerub-baal did have one possibility of getting out though. He joined the National Guard. Once a month he would go to the regional armory for a weekend of training and mock battles. He learned tactics and war strategies. They taught him about the nation's enemies and warned the recruits of their ruthlessness and the dangers of associating with them.

Jerub-baal discovered that he was pretty good at the soldiering thing and he rose in the ranks of the "Guard" to the position of "General." He liked the sound of it: General Joashson… General Jerub-baal Joashson – it had a nice sound – official – dignified – authoritative.

There was one thing that set Jerub-baal apart from others in the village of Abierez. He didn't buy into that Middle Eastern foolishness that when an idea comes into your head it is God speaking. He was pretty sure that ideas were just ideas and God speaking is much more profound than just ideas floating around inside your brain. But the concept was so pervasive in his culture that he wasn't always sure. MAYBE God speaks in such a simple manner. MAYBE that "still small voice" of Elijah's experience IS how God speaks… but he didn't think so. Wouldn't you think that when the creator of the universe speaks – the one who said **"Let there be light"** and there was light – it would be more than a flitting thought?

Did I mention that Abierez is in Israel? Jerub-baal was a Jew. And like most Jews today, Jerub-baal was not a believer. He was a skeptic. What has God ever done for me? Why should we be so honored to be "chosen" by God when all that ever happens to our people – throughout history – is to get dumped on? Those stories in the Bible of God's watching out for us--- doesn't really look like it, does it? Look around. Poverty. Danger. Struggle to stay alive… Jerub-baal was what I'd call "God angry." He knew God existed. What thinking person can deny that? But God is not good – at least to him and his people.

Well, maybe that is the way it is with young people of every generation. They hear the old stories and see no relevance. They want something to happen NOW! Jerub-baal didn't know it but that is exactly what was about to happen.

In Jerub-baal's day, Israel was the what we know of as Israel today, but only that part that is west of the Jordan River – we call it the "west bank." Wars are fought there on a regular basis. But not so much in Jerub-baal's day.

The people over on the east bank, the Mitanni, were a ruthless, aggressive people and they had crossed the river and occupied Israel. They were thugs. They would steal and pillage. There was no peace when a band of them came through. No one was happy. Being ruled by an enemy is always a very grievous thing. No one quite knew what to do. So no one did anything.

Now, you may think it strange that God would speak to such a skeptic as Jerub-baal, but he did. One day he was out sitting under a big oak tree – taking a break – and a stranger came along and asked him if he might join him. "It's a free country," says Jerub-baal. *Why can't this guy find his own shade tree? Now he's going to want to prattle on about something or other.*

"So, how's it going with you?" *Great! This guy doesn't just want to pontificate, he wants conversation.*

"Fine, I guess – as good as for anyone else. Those blasted invaders from Mitanni aren't any fun to have around, I can tell you that."

"Aren't you guys Jews? I thought God's always got your back. You're a general. Why don't you do something about these devils?"

"God – phfff – what's God ever done for us? Those stories about rescuing us from Egypt and the Red Sea parting and the 40 years in the wilderness… Maybe God used to do great things, but not lately. You'd think he could get rid of these gnats in our hair easier than opening up the sea for a million people to cross. It's not happening."

"How about this: YOU do something. Rid Israel of the Mitanni. I'll help."

"Are you kidding me? Abierez is an anemic little village. If we got every man, woman and child to kill 20 Mitanni each, we'd still be outnumbered and overrun."

"But aren't you a general?"

"In the National Guard!! I'm a general in the NATIONAL GUARD! We PLAY at it. We aren't real soldiers! And what do you mean, 'I'll help.' Who do you think you are?"

"Trust me. I'll stand beside you and together we will drive them out."

Now, like I said, Middle Easterners often think God speaks directly to them – a new idea – a revelation – an insight – an epiphany – it must be from God! In fact, for most people Jerub-baal knew, that little conversation would have been God speaking – calling him to action. But Jerub-baal was not a fool nor was he about to be made a fool. There was something about this stranger that he liked – but a lot that he didn't like too... Such bold talk. Such vision. Such confidence. Such disaster waiting to happen.

Jerub-baal says, "Let's have some lunch. I'll go into the house and fix something. You'll wait for me, won't you? I'll be right back."

Jerub-baal was hoping beyond hope that the stranger would be gone when he came back. In fact, he took an extra long time making lunch so that he would get bored and go away. He didn't actually have anything in the house for a decent lunch – just some stale bread and some dried up peanut butter. His mother taught him better than that. "You can't serve that to anyone" she'd say. So he went out to the pasture and caught a lamb. He killed it, skinned it, cut it up, put it in the oven. About three hours later, lunch was ready. "Just about right," he thought. "The stranger should be gone by now."

So he piled the lamb chops on a platter with some mashed potatoes and some green beans and the dry bread slathered with butter and takes them to the oak tree. Unbelievable! "Unbelievable!" he thinks. "The guy is still there. Fine... Whatever..."

The stranger greets him with a smile and a not, as though he had been gone for ten minutes. Jarub-baal sits down and offers him a chop. But instead of putting it on the plate he offered him, the man put it on a rock there under the tree and then he takes the bread and puts it on top of the lamb chop. "Watch this," he says. And he gently touches the bread and P-O-O-F – the whole thing bursts into flame and is incinerated. But even more incredible, when Jarub-baal opens his eyes again after the flash, the stranger is gone.

"My God," he says, "I've seen an angel of God face to face. That can't be good..."

As powerful of an experience as all that had been, Jerub-baal hadn't seen anything yet. He heard a voice that he was quite sure wasn't coming through his ears. "Jerub-baal, do you believe in me now? Tear down the idol in the town square. Use the scraps to build me an altar."

"OK," he thinks. "But destruction of public property can get me into a lot of trouble." So he waited until dark and does as he believed the Lord had told him.

The next morning the whole town is in an uproar. The men of the village are beside themselves. It would be like some unknown vandal breaking in here some evening and ripping the cross off our front wall. What an outrage! What a sacrilege! What a truly awful thing to do!

It didn't take too much investigation to discover that Jerub-baal had done it. He didn't have much of a poker face. And standing beside his newly constructed altar to God, clearly made of the idol's wood didn't help his case much. The men of the town wanted blood. But Jerub-baal's father interceded (as good father's always do) and suggested that if the god of the idol had any ability at all, **HE** could punish Jerub-baal. Was **that** idea a word from God? Maybe so. "We'll go with that – interesting idea – god defending himself" the men said. So Jerub-baal didn't die that day.

Now, we're a long way into the story titled "Jerub-baal and the War" and so far no war – but it's coming…

The Mitanni-ites[3] were getting restless. They talked to other like minded nations about getting rid of the Israelites once and for all – to wage a war of purification against them and to take their land and wipe them off the face of the earth (a fairly common theme when it comes to Israel throughout human history – no wonder why they wondered why it is such an honor to be "chosen" by God – nothing but trouble)… They united and began gathering their troops in the valley of Jezreel – in the Bible that valley is sometimes called Armageddon – the place predicted as the location of the last great battle on earth.

Jerub-baal knew the score. He knew that Israel was in the deepest kind of trouble. It simply could not resist the amassed strength of the surrounding enemy nations. It was about to become extinct. Unless…

"But I won't be anybody's fool. God – WAS that your angel I met with? WAS that your voice I heard?"

So Jerub-baal, earlier in his life going by the name of Gideon, put God to the test – the famous test you have all heard of. "God, here's the deal. So that I know that it is really you that I heard speaking and not just some figment of my imagination or simple foolishness, I'm going to place this lamb's wool here on the ground. When I get up tomorrow, if it is wet with dew but the ground all around it is dry, I'll know it was you." …next morning – it was. "I wonder if that could have been a coincidence or just a fluke of nature. Maybe fleece gathers moisture much faster than grass…. So God, let's go the other direction. Tomorrow wet ground and dry fleece…" And the next morning it was.

So Gideon began gathering the troops. He sent an urgent message to all the neighboring communities to send their men – young and old – to fight the Mitanni and all their friends. When Gideon's troops were gathered, he looked at them and realized that these untrained men really didn't have much of a chance against trained soldiers. But maybe, if God wants, they can be victorious.

God speaks inside Jerub-baal's head again. "Gideon – too many men. If you should happen to win, it is possible that everyone will think it was because of your leadership and their courage – they ARE brave, aren't they? Everyone must know that *I* gave the victory. Cull them out." So Jerub-baal reduced the men. He asked if anyone was afraid. If so, he sent them home. (Now, I've got to say, I have to question the twenty-two thousand who stayed, saying they weren't afraid. How is it possible to face war with barbaric people outnumbering you, with better weapons, trained soldiers, and to honestly say, "no problem – I'm not afraid."). But it didn't matter. God told Jerub-baal that even those twenty two thousand were way too many. So they pared the numbers down two more times to an army of three hundred! Think about that: three hundred untrained soldiers – about as many as might be in Target on a weekend or a Wallmart - to go into battle against at least three other armies… As Gideon and his captains looked over the valley of Armageddon they described what they saw as swarms of locusts – so many warriors that they looked like the sands of the seashore. It is simply not possible to even think of winning a war against those odds… three hundred vs. swarms of soldiers. What can God be thinking?! But somehow Gideon knew, at that point, that the war was as good as over and that his army would, in fact, win – God had said so.

But, of course, no rational person would believe victory possible even with God. But God doesn't ask for rational. He asks for faithful. God tells Gideon to think outside the box. "You know, Gideon, if you march in there and try to kill that hoard you will be die. There is no doubt about that. You need to think creatively. You need to capitalize on their fears. They know the stories of my power and my preservation of this nation in overwhelming odds against it. Believe it or not, they are afraid of you. They don't believe you can possibly beat them, but they are afraid that I can. Use that."

Gideon waits until midnight. He tells his men to put down their weapons and gives each a torch and a pot and a trumpet. He tells them to spread out and surround the valley of Jezreel – to make a circle around the entire enemy army. "Then watch for the signal. When it comes, break your pots with the lit torches inside and blow your trumpets and cry out as loud as you can, 'A sword for the Lord and for Gideon!'" When the signal came and his men did as they were told, the Mitannionites awoke with a start from their sleep and saw the torches and thought each one was a battalion of Israelites – three hundred battalions. They heard the word 'sword' being shouted so they grabbed their own swords and started slashing away in the darkness, literally killing one another as they ran, in panic, for safety.

That night, without killing a single enemy, the Israelites won the war. What was left of their enemy armies slunk off in humiliation and disgrace back across the Jordan with the handful of Israelites chasing after.

It wasn't the end of Israel's enemies, of course. Enemies are a part of life for us all. Oftentimes we can't beat them – but neither should we join them. We should be creative and seek God's assistance. He's done some pretty amazing things in the past. Maybe He's still got a few tricks up his sleeve for you and me.

---

[1] *Jerub-baal is the name Gideon (meaning warrier) was given after he destroyed the idol pole dedicated to the god Baal. Joash was the name of Gideon's father. His name would have been, in our parlance, "Joashson."*

[2] *Abierez may or may not be the name of the town of birth. Joash and Gideon were Abierezites, so I've assumed that the town's name was something like that.*

[3] *"Mitanni" was the region from which came Israel's most feared enemies at the time. The word comes to us as "Midianites."*

THE HOME RUN
Romans 8:26-31

ALL THINGS

Eric was a pretty typical teenager – all the same self-doubts and insecurities and immaturities and surliness as any American teenager. But typical was the word. He was a good looking boy – or at least as handsome as any young man – with a few zits, somewhat unmanageable hair (so he wore it cut short most of the time – made him look a little like he was in the military), growing faster than his mother could buy him clothes... He thought his ears were a too large and his face too long – but no one would ever think that... just him. But he had a nice smile and a good sense of humor most of the time. Eric was born in Wichita, Kansas but he never really thought of that city as his home nor Kansas as his home state.

Eric was what is referred to as a "military brat." His father was in the Air Force so the family moved a lot. Kansas, when Eric was born, then to New York, then to another assignment... It seemed that Eric and his older brother, Kevin, were always the "new kids" in school. That isn't easy for anyone and Eric and Kevin fell into the "military brat" pattern of not making friends because going to all the effort to make friend and then saying good-bye just when you were getting close was just too painful. Eric became a loner, as so many teens do whose parents have no roots. All through grade school there was not one other boy – certainly not a group of boys – who could be named as Eric's friends. Kevin, being more outgoing, gathered a few friends – he was willing to take the chance of being hurt at the next move – knowing that friends (even if temporary) were worth it. But when Eric was in junior high school – Kevin in high school – something wonderful happened. His father's commitment to the military was over and he decided to retire. Mom and dad had always loved the mountains so they decided to rent an apartment in the shadow of the great Rocky Mountains of Colorado until they could find a house. Eric and Kevin were suspicious that, because they were only renting that this, too, was a temporary stay. But it wasn't. They lived in that cramped apartment for three years, but finally found a very nice house in a small town near the mountains. It looked like this was going to finally be permanent. Eric's mother was delighted. She was tired of moving every few years. Eric's father decided he needed to get out of the house daily, so he took on a part time job in town. Eric and Kevin worked hard to adjust to permanence.

It was that year that Eric made his first real friend at school – Dylan. Dylan had lived in their small town all his life. His family attended the Lutheran church. He went to Sunday School and had just suffered through his church's really long confirmation series of classes (Lutherans go weekly for two years!) and believed most of it, he supposed. He joined the church when he finished the classes.

Dylan's mother was Jewish, so at home they observed some of those traditions although Christianity was his religion of choice. After all, you've got to love a religion that sponsors something like Christmas… Like Eric, Dylan was a bit of a nerd. He was in the academically gifted classes in school – quite a smart young man. He didn't have to spend much time studying because it all came pretty naturally to him. By and large, he was bored with school and, even though he did well, he really hated getting up every day and trudging off. And he seemed to constantly be the butt of jokes. Kids who are clearly smarter than their peers often are…

When Eric met and became friends with Dylan, Dylan already had a best friend; his name was Brooks Brown. They had known one another since elementary school. The grew up together and were pretty much inseparable. Brooks, too, was in that "gifted" category – very smart – a bit socially awkward – but a good kid. It looked as though the three boys would be best friends – they went to the same school, they liked the same things, they were all three smart, they all three were somewhat nerds…

Eric had friends! His parents were delighted. They had started to think he'd ever have any. Dylan was his first, really. Eric was pretty happy about it himself, although he'd never admit it. It seemed that Dylan really did like him! Life was good. Except for one thing – Brooks. Eric couldn't quite get the fact that Dylan could have two best friends. How can you do that? Either HE is your best friend or I am. It's not possible to have more than one "best" – that's what "best" means. He resented Dylan's relationship with Brooks and, although Brooks was a perfectly fine guy, Eric set out to do whatever he could to undermine his relationship with Dylan. Eric began to taunt Brooks – to make fun of him – to criticize everything he did – to, essentially, make his life miserable. And Eric was pretty good at it. Every school where he had ever been the "new kid" he was the butt of jokes and teasing and ridicule. Other students mocked his accent. His clothes weren't what everyone else was wearing. His way of thinking was so much different than the thinking of the other kids in the new school.

Eric understood persecution so he thought he'd try some. He did everything he could to drive a wedge between Dylan and Brooks. Dylan rather liked it. Two guys he liked fighting over being his best friend. Pretty cool!

ALL THINGS WORK TOGETHER FOR GOOD

Before long Brooks withdrew from the threesome and found other friends. Who needed all that drama? Who needed Dylan if he wouldn't stand up for him when Eric was putting him down? What kind of a friend was he, anyway – what a wimp! And Brooks moved on. Junior high can be a pretty brutal place, can't it?

Eric and Dylan were inseparable after Brooks was gone. As they entered high school they spent countless hours together. They studied together. They hung out at malls together. They went to school activities together. They both loved computer games so they played a zillion hours of those against one another. They linked their computers over the internet and challenged one another and the faceless strangers out in cyberspace to do battle. Most of all they loved war games. They loved the blood and gore and the shooting and killing one another and all their enemies. But all that was just in electronic bits and bytes. In reality they were still nerds and they took a lot of guff from the other students. Their relationship was called "gay" (neither of them seemed interested in girls) and they were teased mercilessly by some of their fellow students. They were put down and made fun of and basically "bullied" in the devastating way high schoolers can to one another. But, for both of them, this sort of thing had been going on for years. It was really getting old...

By the time they were juniors and seniors in high school, Eric and Dylan knew all the best bullying tactics so they started bullying the younger students. "Hey – they give it to us – we give it to them – the natural pecking order..." I think they found out why others picked on them so much. It was fun to watch others squirm and feel inferior and cower. It was a rush having authority over others weaker than yourself. You felt powerful and in control and almighty... It was almost like being a god.

Eric was pretty good at computers and he put together a couple of websites that were really pretty scary. On them he talked about how much he hated the people in his neighborhood, how he hated the students in his school who had persecuted him and how he just hated people in general. And then one day Eric and Dylan did the unthinkable. They made their war games reality. They took real guns to their high school in Columbine, Colorado with the intent of killing their enemies...

As they were about to enter the building, Dylan saw his old friend Brooks, "Brooks, I like you. Go home NOW!" And Eric and Dylan entered the school and killed 13 and wounded an additional 21 before ending their own lives.

And the nation mourned. HOW could such a thing have happened? WHY? Didn't anyone know what was going on in these young men's minds? Where did society fail? And no one had any answers.

ALL THINGS WORK TOGETHER OR GOOD TO THOSE WHO LOVE GOD

A small church in Livonia, Michigan didn't have to worry much about that sort of thing – at least they assumed that to be true. There was no one even remotely like Eric or Dylan involved in their youth programs. But they wondered if maybe there should be. If young men and women had a place to go where they were always accepted and loved that would be a good thing. If teens could be convinced that we are sons and daughters of God and that we're in it together – if teens could KNOW they have a place of safety and security where they can be themselves and loved – if young people could learn to deal with the guilt of their sins through the forgiveness of Jesus – maybe Columbine would never come to their community. Maybe if churches all around the country provided a place for the youth of their communities, lives might be healed and lives might be saved.

Timing is everything, of course. And God's timing is sometimes astounding. Columbine happened at the same time that that little church was growing concerned about an ever more obvious fact: Families were leaving the church as their children approached the teen years because there was nothing for them – or at least not very much. They had a few great volunteers but a very limited amount of time to give and no education or training at all in youth ministry. They worked hard, but there were only three or four at their "meetings" – not really too much fun for anyone... Could it be they needed a "Youth" minister? They had been toying with the idea, but it seemed absurd. There was no money for another person on staff... The budget was perpetually in the pink if not fully red. The best advice: Just stop thinking and talking about it – right now!

But there, in that small town in Colorado, were 13 bodies – teenage bodies. Could they ignore that? What would God say if they did? How would they live with themselves if such a thing happened here and they hadn't been willing to make the sacrifice it would take to provide a loving place for any teen who wanted love and friendship – who needed to find God? What if they didn't at least try?

Back in the year 2000 all you had to do was put your line in the youth minister pond and whole schools of potential youth ministers would start biting. Dozens of resumes came in wanting to serve as youth minister at Mt. Hope Congregational Church (what IS "congregational" by the way?). Most were rejected at first glance. You really ought to be able to spell and use proper grammar and have SOME idea what youth ministry is all about before you apply… Astoundingly, many didn't. But there were four, as I recall, who stood out. Our first interview was with a young man who we would have rejected just from his resume except that he took some impressive initiative. A week after we received his resume, he called the search committee chairperson. He wanted to know a bit about the church ("I've never heard of "Congregational." Is this a Christian church?). "Do you have a positive, upbeat service?"
" Yes, we do."
"Do people love coming to worship? Is it 'fun.'"
"Well, 'fun' is a strange word to use in referring to worship, but, sure. I guess you could say that."
"Are you Bible based?"
"Yes, of course." (What church would say 'no' to that question?)
"It just so happens that I'm going to be in your area in two weeks for a wedding. I'd like to take that opportunity to worship with you and meet with your committee."
Wow! A real go-getter! I don't really think anyone believed he had a wedding here – way too convenient – but the committee liked his initiative.

After worship two weeks later we had him over to our house, with the committee, for lunch. No one on the committee really remembers anything about the interview after his first comment. "So, what did you think of our worship service?"
"I thought you said you had an enjoyable service. I've never been to a church that uses hymnals and an organ. How can anyone enjoy that?" The committee didn't think he was a very good fit.
One young man came up to interview from Missouri or somewhere. We liked him a lot but he wasn't sure his wife was willing to leave her family. We weren't sure we could easily move

our congregation to Missouri, so that didn't look like it would work out.

Then we hit the jackpot. There was a young man doing youth ministry at a large church in Plymouth or Northville at an Assemblies of God church who had a remarkable track record. He grew the teen program there from nothing to 150 in the 3 years he had been there. He was no longer enamored with the Assemblies of God theology, he said, and burned out with such a large church. He wanted to start over with a smaller church. We were exactly what he was hoping for.

At the same time the committee got a resume from a young man from Colorado – or at least he had been doing an internship in Colorado – not so very far from Columbine – a bit of experience as an intern, but not much – none working on his own – but his theology was far more in the ballpark than the other fellow and he had at least HEARD of Congregational ("tell me exactly what it is? I know it has something to do with the Pilgrims, but it's all a bit hazy…).

…but growing a group to 150 – that's mighty appealing… This upstart just coming off of an internship may not be what we need – no real track record… And look at this picture of himself he sent – is that a urinal in the background? Pretty goofy… "But maybe goofy is what we need," the minister said. The committee bit the bullet and paid to have him come to Livonia for an interview. Interviewing the other guy was free, he was from Northville.

No one seemed to be able to keep this candidate's name straight. At one time or another, every member of the committee called him Jason - maybe just to see if he could laugh it off. He seemed to be able to find humor in just about anything. He seemed like a pretty decent guy. But 150 teens in three years with the other fellow…

I suppose I don't need to tell you which of the final two we chose. We chose the local guy who had the potential to grow our group to 150 in three years, of course. He said he'd let us know his decision in two weeks. We were very excited…

ALL THINGS WORK TOGETHER FOR GOOD TO THOSE WHO LOVE GOD AND ARE CALLED ACCORDING TO HIS PURPOSE.

Curt MacRae was assigned to keeping Jason (or was it Justin? – somebody get out his resume and see) at bay until we had a final decision – just in case the super star turned us down. And Curt can tell you of that phone call that changed all our lives. He called Justin to tell him we were putting him on hold for a couple of weeks and

Justin said to him, "If you decide to call me, I will say 'yes' immediately. I think God wants me at Mt. Hope." And suddenly it simply didn't matter what the other guy could or couldn't do. Perspective was gained that day. We want the young man God has chosen and who knows it. We want the man who believes this to be a calling and not just a job or a stepping stone. We want someone who wants to love us and believes he will be loved by us... A man who told the minister he hopes to be, like him, a "long termer." ...Ten years so far...

Not long after Pastor Justin began his youth ministry, calling it "Firm Faith Ministries," a church in town began having some extremely serious problems and families began looking for a different place to worship and serve. Some were families with teens – some were families who simply loved teens. They wouldn't, of course, even consider a church without something for their youth... or some service they could perform that involved youth... and God had already prepared the way... God had taken the tragedy of two angry young men – neither they nor their families nor their victims nor their families having ever heard of a place called Livonia, Michigan and turned it, right here, into something very good. And this is just one strand of the tapestry God is perpetually weaving – making something good out of whatever happens in our world. ... All things work together for good to those who love God and who are called according to His purpose. Praise be to God.

THE MONARCH AND THE EAGLE
Isaiah 40: 25-31

Every summer for virtually forever, our family has had the opportunity to spend a week in the Upper Peninsula of Michigan doing virtually nothing. For 25 years we attended a family camp that sits on beautiful Lake Huron – in my opinion the greatest of the Great Lakes. Have you ever crossed the Mackinac Bridge? We always drive across at the slowest allowable speed just to enjoy the magnificence and splendor and the azure blue of the water 200 feet below. We look out and see the spouts of the Mackinac ferry, knowing it is carrying tourists for a day of fun on the island. The water is dotted with the billowing sails of boats – but never crowded because the lake is so huge. There is plenty of open water for everyone. At camp we always did a little sailing in colorful little two person sailboats - Sunfish, a little kayaking, a little hiking and picnicking and reading in the shade of a beautiful porch, from time to time looking up from our books to gaze at the horizon or to see what delight caused that little one to squeal out on the beach. At camp we attended Bible lectures and Bible Studies and talked informally about spiritual things and shared our lives with other families who attended for as long or longer than we had. We've told our girls that some day they should spread our ashes on the shore there at the camp. I've even shown them the exact spot on an isolated little spit of land. We don't have permission, but what are they going to do, scoop us up and move us to a more acceptable spot. I don't think so.

We haven't actually attended the camp for the past three years. It's a "family" camp and, once our family ran out of children and then out of teens and then out of college students and everyone got jobs and lived away, we decided we ought to stop going, making room for other families with children and teens and young adults so that they might begin the family tradition we have so cherished.

Now we, along with three other families from the camp, rent a log house about four miles from the camp and pretend we are there. We talk and we eat and we hike and we read and we watch the water and the gulls and do nothing unless we want to.

This summer was one of observing nature for me. I watched deer and hares (different from rabbits I've discovered), and little furry woodland creatures scurrying through the underbrush. I watched insects – spiders building incredible webs, little unidentifiable bugs of all sorts on the ground, lots of mosquitoes and even a little mouse in the house. And I did a lot of thinking about nature and all that God has wrought.

Migration is one of those strange and wonderful things built into the souls of many animals. Salmon, hatched from eggs laid in some shallow mountain stream, hundreds of miles from the ocean, find their way downstream to the sea where they will live out their lives, only to return years later, fighting their way upstream to find the exact spot where they were born, to spawn and then die. How does a fish who is said to have a memory of three seconds (scientists have actually found that a fish's memory is about five months). How does that fish know where to go and how to get there? A great mystery – amazing… Whales, geese, hummingbirds – all sorts of creatures pull off harrowing migrations – and it's all built in. Except the Monarch butterfly.

What really got me thinking about nature this summer was the Monarch butterfly. Like so many creatures in the animal world, the Monarch migrates. But, as I watched one a few weeks ago I was struck by how fragile a butterfly really is. This one would sit on a tall weed and gently move its beautiful wings as though it were trying to rest before taking off again. After a few minutes of catching its breath, it fluttered its wings and, in a somewhat unsteady path, it seemed to me, flew away.

Monarch butterflies migrate. They come from southern Canada and throughout the Midwest and the east coast. At just the right time, clouds of them arise from the forests and begin their flight south and they make their way down the mountain chains of the eastern states into and through Mexico and on into Central America, where they gather by the millions – maybe billions – in small enclaves of a few square miles. In hushed forest cathedrals of unimaginable quiet and color, the Monarchs come to rest, covering every twig, every leaf, every tree trunk, every blade of grass, every square inch of ground for as far as the eye can see… Someday I must go there to worship, for surely God is in that place in a profound way.

But here is the thing. Butterflies don't fly south at the same rate as the geese you see every fall forming their V in the sky, flying at 30 or 40 miles per hour. The Monarch flies at a couple miles per hour, never in the rain or into the wind. It takes the Monarch two months to make the journey from Michigan to it's winter home in Central America. But here is a fascinating fact about the Monarch that makes their migration truly astounding: The life span of a Monarch is four to six weeks – six weeks! Do the math. The journey takes at least eight weeks if the weather cooperates. More typical is twelve weeks.

The butterflies that begin their migration are not the same butterflies that arrive in Central America! And the ones that return to the north to beautify our summers are not the same ones who LEFT Central America. The Salmon and the goose and the hummingbird have migratory powers built into their psyche. Something inside them transcends their limited memories. But the Monarch's migratory abilities are generational! One Monarch begins the journey to Central America, stops along the way to have offspring and to die. That next generation continues the journey, not knowing where they are going nor where they came from and arrives in the tropical forest. Then THEY die there and then the NEXT generation heads back home (but has no idea where "home" is) – to die on the way for yet another generation to finally arrive in Michigan where it all started... Think about that! It's mind boggling...

So, in the quiet hours, sitting on a boulder at the edge of the lake, soaking in the sunshine, comes the question: Where do we come from? Where are we going? What are we doing here in the meantime, in the middle? Why are we here?...

There comes at time, when you've lived long enough, that where you came from means little or nothing – where you began – where you started – is unimportant. The event of your birth is so far in the past and "so much water under the bridge" and you've changed from your beginnings so much that your first appearance on this planet needs to be marked only with a few official papers – a birth certificate and driver's license.

And the end of the journey – it is almost as remote as the beginning. You can't imagine it. It will surely come, as it does to all people, but there is no use thinking much about it. You have good reason to believe that it won't be here for years and years.

But in these middle years – the central part of our journey – why are we here? To survive? To get through the day, the week, another year? Another Christmas – birthday – new year... to jump through hoops, pay bills, eat, drink, watch TV? Are we like those Monarchs in the central part of their journey? Not really needing to know anything about our past or our future? Isn't there SOMETHING we ought to know that we don't? ...And somewhere, sitting on a bare twig on a bush, in an unseen corner of the north woods, a butterfly sits. It slowly lifts it's wings and they fall and lift again... and the change begins.

In the fall of every year, the weather systems change their energy and their patterns. The cold fronts of autumn penetrate deeper and further into the south, temperatures fall and winds begin to whistle. Somehow the eagles and the hawks and the buzzards and the butterflies know that it is time to go. And they know the best routes to take. They invariably head east – their goal: to reach the long chain of mountains that goes through New England and New York, through the Mid-Atlantic states, into West Virginia and Tennessee and across the corner of northern Georgia, into Alabama and on into Mississippi and south. They travel the extra distance to reach the mountains because of the updrafts. If they can catch the drafts coming up from the valleys, winging their way is infinitely easier. The winds travel over the land, hugging it closely and then, as the land rises in hills, some of the wind continues to rise, like going over a speed bump, but continuing upward...

The master of the updraft is the eagle. The eagle isn't really engineered very well. It's a bird, but isn't designed to be able to flap its wings for long periods of time. It doesn't have the strength or the right weight distribution. Hawks, buzzards, seagulls, eagles – all the same. Their muscle proportions are OK for short trips and for diving down and snatching a fish from the lake, but to cover any kind of distance, they have to find lift and then simply soar on the currents with their wings held outstretched in place.

Can that be? Our national emblem is weak? Our powerful national bird can't go the distance? What does that symbolize?

My very favorite passage of scripture is found in the Old Testament. It's about giving us encouragement when we feel weak and have lost our way. ...Like maybe there, in the middle years looking for meaning and motivation and purpose in life...when we need to see a little hope. It says, "They that wait upon the Lord shall renew their strength. They will mount up with wings as eagles." As eagles? If an eagle can't go the distance, I'm not sure that is so encouraging. I want to be able to get to the end of the journey and succeed in life. I want to win! I was taught early and often that the definition of strength is muscle and might.

But the 'strength of eagles' is that they have a unique gift. They are wholly dependent beings. They are designed to work in relationship to their surroundings. Their strength is not IN them. It is OUT THERE. The 'strength of eagles' is a recognition of the purpose of our design and the potential that is all around us, above and below...

You and I are created *weak* in a way, designed for dependence and fueled by faith. The energies of youth are an illusion – or at least temporary. That energy fades away all too quickly. And the strength for the rest of the journey is not built into us. We do not have the energy to make it to the end. We were designed to soar – to find the updrafts and to use them – to know who we are and the limits of our abilities. We were designed with just the right weaknesses that we NEED some help on our journey through life – wherever it is we have come from and wherever it may be that we are going, we need the wind to hold us up... And I think it is no accident that, in the Greek language, the word for wind and the word for Holy Spirit are the same – "pneuma" – and as the spirit – or the wind – gathers around us and moves across the land, we are lifted up and carried... not in our own strength, but in God's. And those who sense it – those who have been waiting, will rise to make their way down through the years in majestic flight, far from where they were first launched, not always aware of where they are heading, it not mattering where they have come from... being only dependent on lift. Lean on the wind – the spirit – learn faith. Don't look down. Don't look back. Press onward for what God yet has in store for you... knowing it will be good.

"They that wait upon the Lord, will renew their strength. They will mount up on wings, like eagles..." Like eagles... *"they will run and not grow weary. They will walk and not grow faint."*

THE SISYPHUS SOLUTION
Ecclesiastes 1:1-8

Since the earliest days of man on earth, human beings have been aware that we are not alone. SOMEHOW the sun runs its course, the seasons change, the rains come, the crops grow or fail, women give birth, animals migrate... SOMEHOW creation works. How can the complexity be explained if not the existence of the unseen gods of the universe? To think that it all just happens has always seemed the most naïve thought to have ever existed – an idea held only by people who are blind or have never thought a thought or are, simply, fools. We are not alone.

There once lived a man named Abraham. From this one man the three great religions of the world have come. The Jews claim he began their religion as he obeyed God and was promised that his descendants would be as numerous as the grains of sand on the seashore or as the stars of the sky. The Muslims, tracing their ancestry back to Abraham through his first son, born to his servant, claim the same thing. Christians, tracing their heritage to the Jews, naturally can continue tracing that heritage back to Abraham. Abraham is, perhaps, the man who has influenced more lives than any other who has ever lived.

What was it about Abraham that was so unique and special that hundreds of billions of people, over the course of four thousand years revere him and call him the father of their faith?

It is that Abraham was, what we would call, a Renaissance Man. He had ideas that were ahead of his time. In fact, his ideas were ahead of the next generation's time and the next and the next and the next. He had an idea that wouldn't really become all that popular for another couple thousand years. The idea? That there is only one God.

One God – a new idea? It's not new today, but it used to be. To us it is a given. But to people of ages past it was quite an outlandish concept.

It was not only a new idea, it was an absurd idea. It was the epitome of foolishness. It was, perhaps, the most dangerous idea to come along in - - well - to ever come along. To even say it out loud was an affront to the gods. It was an insult. It was blasphemy. It was putting oneself and the whole of society in jeopardy of godly retribution. Babies would die. Lightening would flash. Plagues would be unleashed. Horrors unspeakable would, no doubt, be visited upon the earth. Hush. You must not suggest such nonsense.

Twelve hundred years after Abraham first came to his astounding conclusion, the popular view was still that there most certainly were a pantheon of gods controlling and overseeing every aspect of human life and every aspect of the created world. Logically, creation and life are so complex, to think that a single god would be capable of keeping it all together was like us trying to understand how a super computer works. It is simply beyond our ability to understand.

I'd like to tell you a story about some of THOSE gods – with a small "g" - that were believed in even twelve hundred years after Father Abraham made his discovery that God is a singular word.

There was once a young man with the quite peculiar name of Sisyphus. He wasn't just any ordinary young man. He was the son of a king. And when you are the son of a king you have all kinds of opportunities that other young men never even dream of. He wanted to be king himself, but he was not a patient young man and he couldn't wait. Unseating his father was out of the question. His father was a good and powerful and benevolent ruler. Everyone loved him. And worst of all, he was in excellent health. He wouldn't die for years, maybe decades… So Sisyphus, instead of waiting to inherit the throne when his father died and he was, perhaps, an old man himself, decided that he would found his own city and become it's king. It had never been done before – having a king over just a single city. But he felt it was better to be the king of only a city than not a king at all.

Sisyphus was a bit of a schemer. He took shortcuts, he plotted out intrigues, he was always looking out for ol' number 1. Like all kings, Sisyphus worried constantly about someone overthrowing him and taking his thrown – no doubt killing him in the process (that's usually the best way of dethroning a king – leave no possibility of a counter-revolution). So Sisyphus took a few extreme measures to ensure his throne and his safety. He wasn't worried about the residents of his city. They were loyal and trustworthy. It was strangers he didn't trust. If he could prevent strangers from entering his city, he would feel much more secure. So he issued a dictate saying that any stranger entering the city limits would be summarily executed.

Now, obviously, here was a man not dependant on tourism for revenue – and not a man who was willing to offer the common grace of hospitality that his culture was known for. Killing strangers inside your gates – pretty crude and pretty rude.

Killing total strangers really didn't go over very well with the city's population. In fact, Sisyphus' outlandish policy even got the attention of the big god in the Greek pantheon of gods, Zeus. And, whether you believe in one God or dozens, you don't want to do things that really tick them off. To make matters worse, Sisyphus had something on Zeus. Now, I don't know how you know secrets about a god and I don't know exactly what you do with that knowledge, but Sisyphus did. He told Zeus' secrets and Zeus was really angry about it. Zeus (the father of all the other gods), sent the death god, Thanatos, to go to Sisyphus, arrest him and take him to hell.

But underestimating Sisyphus was a mistake, even for death. Sisyphus was, really, a pretty clever guy. When Thanatos arrived, he engaged him in conversation, paying special attention to the new-fangled handcuffs Thanatos had on his belt. Thanatos had designed them himself and was pretty proud of his handiwork. "Hey, those bracelets are pretty cool. Put those shiny babies on. Let me see how they work," said Sisyphus. And soaking up the flattery, Thanatos was more than happy to demonstrate. He put one on his wrist and snapped is shut.

"Wow! What a great invention. But there are two bracelets. What do you do with the other one?"

"Oh. You put that one on the other wrist so the prisoner can't escape."

"No kidding! Does it really work? Let's see."

So Thanatos put the other handcuff on his other wrist and Sisyphus reached out and snapped it shut. And, once shackled, Sisyphus threw the god of death into prison where he felt he belonged. He had out-foxed death and now he would never die.

The big problem with putting Death in chains and taking him out of commission is that **no one** dies. A guy could have all his arms and legs cut off; he could have swords piercing his body; his flesh could be in a state of total decay but he wouldn't die. The Generals were going crazy because no matter how well their battles went, they just couldn't finish the enemy off. So one of the Generals went and rescued Death, allowing Thanatos to go on doing his business, and Sisyphus was arrested and delivered to the Underworld.

As one might expect, life in hell is not a bed of roses. You are given an assignment and there is nothing you can do to resist it. Sisyphus' punishment was to push a boulder up a steep hill, so steep that no one could succeed in pushing it over the top. The boulder would, at some point, roll back down the hill, all the way to the bottom. Sisyphus would then have to trudge back down the hill and try to push it up again. Over and over, for eternity, Sisyphus was to try to push that boulder over the top and he never could do it. Sisyphus was condemned to perform a task that he could never hope to complete, yet he was never allowed to stop trying - truly hell.

And I wonder if many people feel a bit like Sisyphus in their earthly lives... Every day they go to work, do their job, go home at the end of the day and go again tomorrow and push that same rock up that same hill, knowing, with certainty, that the next day will be pretty much the same as this one.

It's Labor Day and, for way too many workers in the world today, work is Sisyphus' rock.

There was, at about this same time, another king – a real king – not one from Greek mythology. He, like Sisyphus, was the son of a great king and had become king, himself, without the proper perspective on the job nor on life itself. His name was Solomon. He was the son of David – the unexpected heir to the throne. Like Sisyphus he was a believer in God – but unlike Sisyphus, he was a believer in the God of Abraham and Isaac and Jacob. He believed in one God – the Lord, Jehovah. But his work overwhelmed him and he forgot God. He had more smarts than any king ever born and began to think he could do it on his own. But before long he found himself in hell, pushing that rock up the hill. He said, "Meaningless! Meaningless!... Utterly meaningless! Everything is meaningless. What does man gain from all his labor at which he toils under the sun? Generations come and generations go, but the earth remains forever. The sun rises and the sun sets, and hurries back to where it rises. The wind blows to the south and turns to the north; round and round it goes, ever returning on its course. All streams flow into the sea, yet the sea is never full.
To the place the streams come from, there they return again.
All things are wearisome, more than one can say."[1]

I myself have seen people...people who made choices that landed them in horrible circumstances; and people who, through no fault of their own, found themselves in circumstances that are awful...but some of those people who, through their own faithfulness and trust *in God's grace and power*, found a way to "make a heaven of hell," to quote Milton's great poem.

God calls us to trust that, through the power of grace, good can come even from the cursed rock that we're given...

---

[1] Ecclesiastes 1: 1-8.

A PLAIN STORY: ARTHUR
Matthew 25: 34-40

If you head down I-275 until it merges into I-75 and stay on the freeway for about an hour you will come to a city with a most peculiar name. You and I don't think it so peculiar, but apparently it is. I once heard a visitor to the area, who had apparently never seen the word in print, laugh at the strange name of a city he passed on the freeway. He pronounced it: To-le-do.

If you continue on down the freeway a bit further, you will pass the exit to the small town of Perrysburg. At that exit you can look to your left and see, in the middle of a corn field, a huge and beautiful Mosque – a strange place for a Mosque, I've always thought. How many Moslems can there be in Perrysburg, Ohio? They built it in 1970. I know because I was a student in the 70's and travelled that road from time to time and watched it being built.

A little further and you come to the exit for Bowling Green, Ohio. My guess is that most of you have never taken that exit. You've never explored the city of Bowling Green. Where's your adventurous spirit? Surely a city that carries the name of an old fashioned English sport ought to be an interesting place to visit... But it's not. You've done well to keep going. Bowling Green is a sleepy city with nothing much to recommend it except for one of the finest universities on the face of the earth (or at least that's what the alumni association wants us BGSU graduates to tell everyone - so I have).

I spent four of the best years of my life in Bowling Green. I can honestly say that I learned more about life and ministry and people and hard work during that four years than I have in any four years of my life before or since. I also learned that I am not a great student – graduated somewhere near the middle of my class, but staying in and eventual graduation was the thing I was aiming for and I did that. While in college I discovered that I am politically wishy-washy even thought I majored in Political Science (I was there in the midst of Vietnam and scratched my head about it all for the entire four years). Never could decide what it was all about nor whether I was in favor or opposed. I like to think it was because I was young and naive. I think I could decide now. But that's hindsight.

I got involved in a campus Christian organization called Inter Varsity Christian Fellowship. I'd love to tell you about my experiences with Inter Varsity or my exploits as a student, but that's a different story and has nothing to do with Arthur, the one this story is about.

The churches in Bowling Green have tried to avoid campus ministry like the plague (at least in those days when I lived there) so every one of them built their churches far enough from campus that no student could easily walk to any of them on a Sunday morning. Except the Baptists. There is a Baptist church near enough to walk, but that was an accident I think. I attended that Baptist church throughout my freshman year – all by myself. I seldom went home on weekends so I always got up early and trudged over to First Baptist on Sunday mornings. And no one in that church showed the slightest interest in me or seemed to care if I was there or not. Nine months I attended and I didn't know a soul nor did any of them so much as know my name. I'm not too bright and it took me an entire school year to figure out that sleeping in might have been a better option.

But that next summer I got a car. I was the only one in our little Inter-Varsity group that had a car and so I became the designated driver to get half a dozen of us to church. We didn't know much about churches so we went to a church of the denomination that my roommate attended back home. It was pretty awful, but church shopping was harder work than just going to this one by default… So we did – for a year and a semester.

In the winter of my third year I was at home for the holidays (rural Ohio) and slid off an icy road into a shallow ditch and rolled the car. No injuries, but the car was out of commission for a while… I wasn't going back to that Baptist church – they had had their year with me. No more of them. Trying to find a way to get to the church we had been attending but hated didn't seem worth the bother. But going to church was our "thing" and other students in the dorm would have been disappointed if we didn't… We were a religious curiosity, but they enjoyed seeing our discipline, I think. Christians are supposed to be a bit peculiar so going to church was our way of proving it and how devoted we were to God.

A girl in the group spotted a little note on her dormitory bulletin board. Someone was offering rides to church.

"What kind of church is it?" we asked.

"Congressional – no – Congregational. Anyone know what that is?"

"Not a clue. Do you think it's some kind of cult?"

"I think I've heard of it," said one fellow. "I think it's one of those very liberal churches. They don't believe in anything."

"Might be fun. We've no way of going anywhere else. Give the lady a call. See if she can take six of us."

I'm pretty sure the woman was a bit overwhelmed and somewhat confused. SIX college students needing a ride to church? But she said she could squeeze us all in. Unfortunately the mini-van hadn't been invented yet and we did, indeed, have to squeeze in.

She took the campus streets to the north side of campus, to Poe Road, near the airport. She headed west on Poe, crossed Main Street, crossed Fairview Ave. Crossed Haskins Road – now we are out of Bowling Green in the midst of wheat fields... and she kept going. Where was she taking us?

This was the era of cults and cult kidnappings. Were we in some kind of trouble? We were getting a bit concerned... But there were six of us and one woman – we could probably take her... We crossed Mitchell Road and she kept driving – another mile and we saw it. A tiny brick church – probably wouldn't hold more than 120 people – kind of cute. The name on the sign said, "Plain Congregational Church." What a strange name for a church.

We pulled into the parking lot, not expecting much. "This is bumpkinsville," we thought – tiny church in a tiny town in the middle of nowhere. We'd probably not be coming back here any time soon...

...But we did. The minister was fascinating to listen to. The people were as friendly as could be. The message spoke to our hearts and applied to our lives. He talked about commitment to God and freedom in Christ. He talked about how we don't need to believe whatever comes from a pulpit – how we ought to read the Bible for ourselves and decide what God is saying to us as individual believers and as Christians and as Jesus' friends...

That day I became a Congregationalist. The six of us told all our friends about the church and before long there were about twenty of us attending. Over the course of the next six or seven years fourteen college students (after they graduated) decided to go into some kind of full time Christian work because of that church and that minister – ministers and missionaries and Christian counselors and youth workers... FOURTEEN! Over the years we became known as "Tom's Boys" (the minister's name was Tom) – even thought there were girls too...

But this story isn't about me nor is it about that church and it's not about all that happened there forty years ago (although those would be good stories).

This story is about the little town in which the church is located... The town of Plain, nestled in the center of Plain Township, Ohio – and takes place today.

Northwestern Ohio is so flat that they would think of us here in Michigan as mountain people. The soil is rich, so all the trees have been cut to open up the land for farming. You can see, literally, for miles in every direction. Really, a great plain. Thus the name, "Plain" for the township and "Plain" for the church.

All of that is a prelude to what happened last year.

A man died. His name was Arthur. He was poor, unkempt, somewhat obscene, lonely, and bitter. He had been a member of the Congregational Church for decades but, in his old age, most of the congregation was rather relieved that he wasn't able to attend. It was always awkward having him around. He was an embarrassment. He was crude and rude and spoke loudly of his strong opinions about everything. No one mourned his passing… Almost no one attended his funeral.

Except one deacon. Bill Robinson had Arthur on his "list" of people he was to watch over. Bill had never met Arthur until shortly before his death but he had heard stories about him. He probably wasn't as bad as some of the things he had heard. He was practically a legend around the church. Stories of Arthur were always sad and often unbelievable. But Bill was a good deacon and took his charge seriously – especially now – Plain Congregational was without a minister right then, so the deacons were stepping up to make sure ministry got done – the sick and home-bound visited, the needy tended to, the weekly worship running smoothly, the guest ministers lined up, weddings officiated at, and the church keeping its doors open…

Bill decided to visit Arthur.

Arthur lived in what is called a "shotgun" house. Shotgun houses are deep, narrow fronted houses. Called "shotgun" because you could open the front door and the back door and shoot a shotgun all the way through. Arthur lived, essentially, in one room of the house and, within that one room, spent most of his day in a rotting stuffed chair in front of a television set.

Bill knocks on the door.

"Whose there!? What do you want? Go away!" a voice bellows from inside.

"It's Bill Robinson. I'm your deacon from the church. I've come to visit."

"Aww, crap. Come on in if you've got to" Arthur called out.

Jim should have known, from the greeting, a bit of what to expect, but he totally missed the mark in guessing the kinds of conditions a person can live in…

Months of sitting in that chair watching TV hadn't done Arthur nor his surroundings any good. The place was filthy – Arthur was filthy. Bill could see cockroaches skittering in the corners, chasing after food crumbs that had been dropped, unceremoniously, on the floor. There were newspapers scattered everywhere. A moldy/mildewy wet odor was strong in the air, covered a bit by the cloud of smoke that hung around Arthur. Arthur was a chain smoker – a rather dangerous one... When a cigarette had burned to about three quarters of an inch, he'd toss it toward the TV still lit, trusting the dampness of the newspapers to keep them from bursting into flame and torching the place. Fortunately, his system seemed to work...

"Sit down!!" he rasped. "What took you so long to getting around to visiting Plain Church's oldest member? – I was starting to think no one cared." And Arthur chuckled and coughed...

Sitting didn't really appeal to Bill in the slightest. He wasn't exactly roach-phobic, but still... The thought of sitting on that filthy cushion was about as unappealing as anything he could imagine. He sat on the edge, trying not to touch anything any more than absolutely necessary.

It became clear right away that Arthur wasn't interested in a quick Psalm reading and prayer from his deacon. He wasn't interested in discussing his health or the weather or the church. He had a captive audience and he wanted to talk about God. He wasn't happy with Him.

"Look around you, son. What do you see?"
Jim looked around. "I see a man who could use a little help cleaning up this place. I see a man who is, maybe, mad at the world and can use a friend."

"Don't give me your counseling class B.S. You see a man who has been abandoned by God and by all those hypocrites down at the church. I used to believe in the Almighty. I used to be a Trustee over at your church. I lost my job and my family. I lost my health and ran out of savings. Did God watch over me then? Not on your life. 'Sorry, Charlie – you're on your own now.' When I was at the lowest point of my life, God stomped on me and ground me into the pavement with his heel. Look around. This is how I have to live now. This is as good as it's going to get. Who can believe in a God that allows a man to live like this? And if God exists, he's got to be a sadistic s-o-b."

Arthur made good points. It DID seem that OK times had turned to bad and bad times to really bad times. It did seem that God had abandoned Arthur. It did seem that there wasn't much in Arthur's life that was good. Where was God?

Bill started to give Arthur the arguments he had learned from past ministers. He was about to say that God had not abandoned him. That God allows free will and things happen because of choices we make or others make that impact us and the consequences come naturally in a cause and effect kind of way. He was about to say that storms come to the just and the unjust alike… and he believed all that to be true. But he knew those things wouldn't be well received. So he said, "I'm sorry, Arthur. I'm so sorry you feel abandoned by God and God's people. I'm sorry I haven't been here before now…" And he meant it. "But I'm here now and I'll come back every day if you want."

Did he just say 'every day?' How could he have said that? He had a job... He had responsibilities. He surely wouldn't be able to come on his day off… Did I just say *every day*!? What kind of diseases would a person get coming into this disgusting place every day?! I can't come every day… but that's what I just said! God help me!

Arthur was silent. As the TV screen flickered, Bill could see the glint of a tear in the old man's eye… He knew he had committed himself to something he really *really* didn't want to do. It may have been the most foolish thing he had ever done… but Arthur had a tear… That rash promise meant something to the old guy.

"Don't be a fool. Nobody visits nobody every day. You think I need a nurse?… I don't need no hand holding. Just leave me alone."

"I'll be here every day. I promise." There it was again! What was he doing? He could think of nothing worse than holding this old man's nicotine stained and dirt encrusted hand… EVERY DAY! What am I thinking… Just shut up!

But Bill did as he promised and, for the next year, he visited Arthur every single day. As near as he could tell, during that entire year, he was the only visitor Arthur ever had.

It didn't get any easier. Bill spent a bit of his visit each day picking up disgusting things from the floor and trying to make things a little cleaner. It was a losing battle, though. Arthur's house needed to be bull dozed… The carpet looked like tar paper from all the spills and ground in dirt. Flies were a constant presence, buzzing around… The cockroach continued to be king… The smells merged with one another - beer, stale pizza, smoke, sweat, stale air...

A few months later, when Arthur got sick, it was no big surprise. It looked to Bill like pneumonia, but he wasn't a doctor. Arthur wheezed and coughed… But Arthur was terrified of hospitals and doctors and absolutely refused to go. "People die in those places and I ain't ready to die just yet. I'll go when the good Lord insists and not a minute before." And all Bill's pleadings fell on deaf ears.

Bill didn't know what to do. But he knew what he had to do. He knew what he *still* hated to do – to visit Arthur, to care for Arthur, to be in that filthy environment, to be around this most foul man every day for what seemed like forever. He had promised.

Then came the days of Arthur's incontinence and incapacity. He could no longer get up from his chair, not even to pass urine which was welcomed into the musty old chair and made the air almost unbreathable. Bill urged, pleaded, begged Arthur to let him take him to the hospital – that this simply could no longer go on. Arthur adamantly refused.

Bill arrived one day with a few groceries to discover Arthur's solution to wearing those stinking, urine stained clothes. He had taken them off. He greeted Bill with a little smile and a totally naked body. Bill was mortified. He didn't know what to say so he ignored Arthur's nudity and said nothing, trying not to look at the old man's flabby, wrinkled, droopy skin and his privates…

"Bill, go to the cupboard over there and fetch that bottle of wine. Open that loaf of bread you brought. Give me communion."

It was the first time since Bill had been visiting that Arthur had wanted anything to do with spiritual things – at least in a positive way. But giving communion to a naked man seemed grossly sacrilegious.

"Arthur, how about you getting dressed first?"

"I thought you'd say that. But you know I'll just soil the clean clothes, don't you?"

Nevertheless, Bill helped Arthur put on a pair of underwear and pants and a shirt. It was painful for both of them. Arthur because every movement hurt him. Bill because touching the dirty, naked flesh of an old man was just about as uncomfortable as he had ever been.

"Owww. Be gentle. That hurts…"

And when Arthur was finally dressed, Bill poured the wine and broke the bread and, together, they shared the sacred meal. Bill didn't know how Arthur felt, but to him it may have been one of the most deeply sacred and special moments of his life. Here was a man he had come to love (even in the midst of revulsion). Here was a man who had felt abandoned by God and was now eating Jesus' flesh and drinking his blood and remembering his love…

A week later Bill came into Arthur's house and found him lying on the floor (naked of course). He was too weak to get up or to fight… Bill called an ambulance. While they were coming, Bill found some clean clothes and dressed Arthur. He hated to hear the groans, knowing the pain Arthur was going through, but didn't want the ambulance drivers nor the doctors to find him in such a humiliating state…

Arthur was only semi-conscious when he was checked into a room at the hospital. He was clearly dying. Bill took his hand and spoke lovingly to him. "Arthur, you're in the hospital. But it will be alright. I am here with you and won't leave your side for even a minute. Don't be afraid."

Arthur looked straight at Bill with a puzzled yet pleased expression on his face. "I see Jesus," he said. "I see Jesus."

"It's only me – It's only me, Bill" said Bill.

"You – Bill – I see Jesus." And those were the last words Arthur ever spoke.

At the funeral there were four people present: the minister, the undertaker and Bill Robinson. And, somewhere in the crowd, Jesus.

Plain Congregational Church is real. It is, indeed, a beautiful little church out on Poe Road in Plain Township, Ohio. The minister who inspired so many, Rev. Tom Witzel, was the most amazing man I've ever met. However all references to the town of Plain in this series are fictional.

A PLAIN STORY: THE BUZZARD BUZZ
Matthew 28:18-20.

Do you know what the word "Plain" means. Unadorned. Without elegance. No embellishment. Ordinary. Simple. Normal.... And when you live in a town named "Plain" you have to work very hard to overcome some of the natural assumptions that everyone makes about you and the place you live. So many Plain residents have worked very hard to not be ordinary – to not be "plain." So the town is filled with characters – some flamboyant, some creative, some overly outspoken, some artistic, some radical in their ideas and, of course, some who are, truly, just plain people like the rest of us.

Here's what I mean when I say that they tend to go out of their way not to be plain… They built a new high school a few years ago. Obviously the name would be "Plain High School." But they wanted to juice it up a bit so they named their athletic teams "The Plain Truths." But everyone knows that any time truth is espoused there are some who question it – they hold firmly to the idea that there is, really, no absolute truth. So these argued that naming their school "truth" is inappropriate.

And it's true. You can't say that the grass is green without someone pointing out that some grass has a blue tinge to it or that dry grass is a withered brown color. You can't say that ice is cold because there are degrees of coldness and ice at 32 degrees would actually be warm if you compared it to ice that was minus 32 degrees…. You can't say that God exists because, even though there is overwhelming circumstantial evidence, there is no empirical proof. They (these skeptics) are absolutely certain that there is no absolute truth.

Society has tended to give those "no truth" proponents a lot of credence and has failed to call them on their narrow and foolish perspective. We've said, "OK, you've got a point. But *I* believe such and such." And we receive their knowing smirks at how foolish we are – thinking themselves wise for not being hood-winked into thinking anything is wholly true.

The people of Plain had quite a debate about the whole "truth" thing. It went on for weeks. But no one could actually come up with a more creative name for their teams than "The Plain Truths." "Plain Chargers" – no. "Plain Bulldogs" – no. "Plain Pistons" – no. So the team was dubbed, officially, "The Plain Truths." But they compromised with those who didn't believe in truth and had a special mascot costume made. At games you couldn't miss their mascot – a guy dressed, going around trying to pump up the crowd, as a giant question mark.

Jane Livingstone grew up in Plain. She could never figure out why her parents didn't see it coming when they named her Jane. Living anywhere else it would be a perfectly fine name, but... She hated it when her out-of-town relatives would greet her, "Why, if it isn't Jane from Plain – Hello, Plain Jane." Jane grew up before they built the high school so she had to be bussed into Bowling Green for school and, on stormy days, she would invariably be greeted by friends and, sometimes teachers, with "Jane – how's the rain in Plain?" How lame is that?

But that was all in the past. Jane grew up and became one of Plain's leading citizens. She's been on the city council now for almost a decade. Everyone in town knows her and she is well respected as one of the bright lights of Plain. She went to the university and majored in Business. Her specialty was advertising and promotion.

Having grown up a Plain girl, Jane wanted desperately to overcome the stigma of living in a town with such a "Plain" name. Being creative, she came up with a plan…. She needed to capitalize on one thing that was unique to Plain and make a really big deal of it. She needed to make Plain known for something other than its strange name. She decided on Buzzards. Northwestern Ohio has lots of Buzzards. They can be seen every day over the corn fields of Plain. Hinkley, Ohio had capitalized on it for years - since 1957. They have a "Buzzard Sunday" around the time when the buzzards return from their winter home. They have a friendly competition to see who spots the first Buzzard flying in. But that's way over by Cleveland. Jane was pretty sure they could pull it off in Plain…. Buzzards… They would do it up right and make the world forget about Hinkley, Ohio and start to think of Plain as the Buzzard capital of the world.

Ever since Jane was a little girl she had been fascinated with Buzzards. She and her friends would watch them circle high in the sky in those ever-so-graceful quarter mile circles, catching updrafts and almost never flapping a wing. She and her friends did what all northwestern Ohio kids do in the boredom of summer. They would go out into a field and lay perfectly still as though they were dead until they attracted a buzzard to see if they could get it to land. There isn't a child anywhere who can lay still enough long enough to actually get a buzzard to land, I don't think, so no one actually knew what a buzzard would do if he did land and find you weren't dead. He probably wouldn't be very happy... But no one ever found out.

Jane took her idea to the city council. She would call it "Buzzard Buzz." It would be a weekend of buzzard mania. They would promote the weekend hard. They would have a parade and booths and rides and funnel cake carts and games for the kids. Maybe they'd have the mayor make a speech and a bandstand playing Souza and patriotic music all afternoon... Early Sunday morning they'd put out some kind of dead animal – maybe several – out of sight of festivity visitors and see if they might actually have a little buzzard show in the sky above. It would be an easy trick to get half a dozen buzzards circling Plain all morning and into the afternoon.

The council bought into the idea – they thought it was great. It would be the perfect thing to put Plain on the map and get scads of visitors to come into town – buying things – supporting the economy – finding out how much fun Plain folk can be.

The only concern they had was that they had no money. The township had no budget wiggle-room. There wasn't a dime they could spend to publicize such an event. And, if nothing else, Plain people are pretty fiscally responsible. There was no way they were going to spend money they didn't have. "Buzzard Buzz, Jane, is a no-go."

Jane was not daunted. She said she was simply seeking their blessing and support, not their money. "Really! You don't want any money for publicity? You'll take care of it all without it costing the township anything?... You're on! Go for it girl and good luck."

Jane started her campaign by going to the churches in town. She went to the Catholic church and the Methodist Church and the Pentecostal Church and the Congregational Church and the little Jewish synagogue and told them what she wanted to do and that, without their help, it would not be possible... She shared her vision and the possibilities for Plain. She gave each one the best pitch of her life.

The Catholics were hesitant. It didn't seem very dignified to proclaim the glories of vultures. They didn't think they would be able to participate. The Methodists didn't think much of it either. They said they'd make mention of it but not to expect too much. The Congregationalists had an easy out – they are, as I mentioned last week, without a minister right now. They really couldn't commit. The Rabbi thought the idea rather bizarre. But he liked it. Unfortunately, northwestern Ohio isn't rife with Jews and his congregation boasted about fifteen adults on any given Shabbat. The Pentecostals thought Jane's idea the strangest and most wonderful idea to come along since they didn't know when... They would certainly participate. They LOVED the idea. The minister warned her that they only had 120 members so their impact may not be all that she was hoping for. She assured them that 120 could rock the world.

There is no local newspaper in Plain, so localized news is mostly by word of mouth. But that's OK. In small towns, news travels much faster than it ever could in newspapers anyway. Word of the notice in the Pentecostal church bulletin made it onto the grapevine: "The first ever 'Plain Buzzard Buzz' will take place on June 12. The mayor has declared it the duty of every Plain citizen to get the word out. No citizen will be welcome within the town limits on the 12th of June of this year without an out-of-town visitor in tow. Not inviting your friends is not an option. Fun will be had by all."

Well, let me tell you, those Pentecostals spread the word. By Sunday evening 90% of Plain had heard the dictum from the Mayor and the buzz was on. Even Jane was amazed at how people responded when presented with a wonderful idea. Immediately the creative juices started flowing. Mel, over at Mel's Diner had a special sign made for his restaurant for the Buzzard weekend Buzz. For those two days, his restaurant would be renamed "Carrion Café." Hearing what Mel was planning, Joe, the barber, started advertising "Buzz Cuts." The antique shop in town added a tag-line to their website: "Joan's Antiques: Cleaning Up After the Dead." (Just about everyone thought that was in bad taste). Even the postmaster got into the act. It was probably illegal and would get him into trouble, but he planned to rename the Post Office for the weekend: "United States Buzzard Service." Even the kids caught buzzard fever. Someone managed to get a box full of buzzard head masks and kids all over town walked around looking pretty gruesome... Ever seen the face on a buzzard? No a pretty sight.

And it happened. People were so excited about the possibilities and the fun and the challenge of it all that they really did invite their friends. "Hey, Charlie – Jeannie - Mike, come with me to Plain's Buzzard Buzz. You'll love it. In fact, if you don't go with me, I can't go. The mayor told us to go out and bring people in and if we didn't we couldn't be Plain people that weekend. But if you can't go, just say so. I'll find someone else. I'm going to be there. This is the best thing that's hit Plain in – like - forever."

Some Charlies and Jeannies and Mikes went. Some didn't. But something happened to everyone who was invited. Their imaginations were ignited by the idea and by the enthusiasm of their friend. Whether they would end up going or not, the idea stuck with them. Buzzards – how strangely cool... People getting excited about what most of us take for granted... Taking the ordinary and making it extraordinary... "Maybe I'll go...."

Most people had never experienced anything quite like the passion Plain people were expressing for their new-found love for those circling birds... They wondered if they could ever have that kind of fire inside for something. And, whether they were a Charlie, a Jean or a Mike who went or one who didn't, almost universally they did something Jane never expected. They told their friends. "Sally – have you heard what's going on over in the little town of Plain on the weekend of June 12? It's the most bizarre thing. They're having a buzzard festival. Can you imagine?! And some Sally's chuckled and some asked where Plain was. They probably wouldn't go, of course, just curious... (some went).

The mayor knew he probably wouldn't get re-elected. It is not within a mayor's authority to tell his constituents that they can't come into town without a guest. But he REALLY wanted this thing to work and his little dictum was all he could think of. If it worked, it would be worth his job. If it worked, it would be wonderful for everyone.

Plain has a population of 1800 people – adults and children included. God gave Plain an unadorned, simple, ordinary day that weekend - a "Plain" day. The sun shone in a cloudless sky. Spring had fully sprung. The temperature was about as average as it can get – 74 degrees. A light breeze was blowing. ...And over 10,000 people showed up for the Buzzard Buzz in little Plain, Ohio. It was, without question, the greatest day of the little town's existence... The face painters were painting, the balloon makers were blowing, the fried dough vats were popping, the barbeque pits were sending out the most tantalizing of smells. There were jugglers and unicyclists and men on stilts and dogs on leashes everywhere... There were clowns and hot dogs and a general feeling of great fun.

The parade started at 11:00 and the first float after the Plain Truth High School marching band was a float in the shape of a buzzard – rather ugly, really – built by the Pentecostals and the Jews. After the Boy Scouts and the clowns came other floats, several extoling the wonders of a clean environment, recycling, living in peace – and every one of them had on it, somewhere, the visage of a buzzard. The kids of Plain marched along in a pack behind one of the floats on their bicycles with their buzzard masks on – circling, of course...

The parade ended at the bandstand and, although there was a lot of commotion and chatter, the mayor made his speech. He said, "What you see here is a profound truth. You see people who cared enough to tell you where Plain is. You see here the magnificence of multiplication. We did no publicity for this event. We didn't spend a cent to get the word out. Jane Livingstone told two people. Those two told 130. Those 130 told 1800 and those 1800 each told a couple others and those couple others sometimes told others and today you see what can happen. Our Chief of Police has estimated that today in Plain, there are 10,000 of us! 10,000 from one! Citizens of Plain and all of our friends – remember the power of telling others. Witness what can and does happen when people believe in a cause enough to share it. Now go out there. Have fun…. But come back tomorrow for part two."

There are no hotels in Plain, but every room in Bowling Green was taken that evening – there were no vacancies as far as Perrysburg in every direction.

Nothing was scheduled – not even allowed – at the Buzzard Buzz on Sunday before noon. That was church time and all the good Catholics and Methodists and Congregationalist and Pentecostals went to their various places of worship.

But something was different that morning. The Catholics seemed less dignified, the Methodists more certain, the Congregationalists less stressed, and the Pentecostals – well the Pentecostals are always expecting the best – and they felt they had gotten it.

And when churches were letting out and people were filling the streets for a second day of fun, something rather amazing happened. Everyone got quiet and looked up, following the pointing finger of a young boy. There, a thousand feet up, were twelve buzzards circling, each in his own path, looking – watching – waiting – to see what good can come from all those people down there who had heard – who had come – who had believed that what their friend said was true. Wondering what they would do when they left town – what they would think of buzzards after today – how their lives might have been changed – and wondering what would be left for them to scavenge.

A PLAIN STORY: FATHER JESÚS
Matthew 9: 9-13

"Napoleon" is the name of a town in Ohio not too far from Bowling Green and Bowling Green isn't too far from the little town of Plain, where our stories originate this summer. In Napoleon is a Campbell Soup factory where I spent one summer trying to make enough money for college for the next school year. My job was to work out on the receiving dock where, every morning, a dozen or so large flat-bed truckloads of tomatoes would arrive. We would unload the trucks – hard work – thousands of pounds of tomatoes every day... We'd be finished by noon so got to go inside and shovel barley into stainless steel buckets, measuring out the proper amount to be dumped into 300 gallon vats of soup... To this day I can't imagine who eats all that soup.

The tomato fields were populated by migrant workers – men and women and, sometimes, children coming up from Mexico to the tomato and beet and potato fields of the Midwest. It was an incredibly long journey for jobs that paid so little and housing that was worse than most city slums. But obviously that life was better than staying in Mexico where their families were about to starve unless they could bring home some money. But it's not easy to get all those migrants to go back home once they've experienced the luxury of living in America – especially if they should happen to realize the wonderful squalor they lived in as migrant workers is the bottom of the heap here and that life can only get better.

So Napoleon and environs had a growing Mexican population even after the growing season when they were scheduled to go home... If the Mexicans were smart, they stayed away from the cities and anywhere where immigration agents might find ample work. The safest places were small towns – like Plain. The nearest immigration office was in Toledo, almost 30 miles away and Plain really is pretty isolated.

The one question one never asked in Plain was: "Is he/she a legal?" The Mexicans were hard workers. They were gentle. They didn't bother anyone. Yes, they liked to drink, but they were usually pleasant drunks and not obnoxious or angry or violent. And when it comes to inebriation that really is a pretty important consideration.

The Catholics really try hard to place priests in parishes where they will fit and minister appropriately to the community. In Plain there was a pretty active Catholic church. It was actually the largest church in town – 245 families – nearly 175 people in attendance for a

Sunday mass. Their priest is of Spanish descent. His name is Jesús Menendez. He has been at the church now for eight or ten years... People love him. He is tall (for a Mexican) and handsome. He is in his early 40's and he loves his people and they love him. Every morning he gets up for the early mass and says it for the half-a-dozen old women who show up. Then he goes to his office and prays and works on various pastoral projects. He does research for his next Sunday's sermon... In the afternoon he often goes into Bowling Green to visit the hospital or one of the nursing homes or he visits some of the elderly in their homes. Every Tuesday evening he teaches catechism and meets with his trustees or deacons or teachers or social action committee. He easily puts in a sixty hour week. But being a priest in a small town is lonely. After the mass is said and the church administered and the classes taught and the infirm visited there are still hours and hours and hours – almost every day – hours when there is nothing to do but stare at the four walls of the manse.

Father Jesús is not one to do a lot of sitting around watching TV. He is a people person. He NEEDS companionship – he NEEDS friends. But it's not the Catholic way to be friends with your priest. Jesús likes the other ministers in town but they all have families – they don't want him hanging around all the time... (If you should happen to know a priest, invite him to dinner from time to time – the celibate, priestly life can be a bit overwhelming. Having to be on that pedestal really can be rather lonely).

So what do you do when you are a single guy (not looking to NOT be single) in a small town? Where do you find people? Where do you build relationships? Where can you find people who will accept you for yourself? Where can you go where you are not "Father Jesús" all the time – where you can be just plain Jesús?

For better or worse, Father Jesús found the same place so many others find friends and welcome and enjoyment and fellowship. Father Jesus found the local bar.

The "Buzzard's Nest" sits right in the middle of town – on Main Street down near the traffic light. It used to be called "The Plain Bar and Grill" but was renamed during the days of the famous "Buzzard Buzz" a couple years ago.

Jesus wasn't much of a drinker. He would have a glass of red wine every now and then, but he certainly didn't drink enough to warrant going to a bar three nights a week and often on Saturday nights, too. He went because the people he played cards with, the people he shot pool with, the people he swapped bad jokes with, didn't care if he was a priest or not. Oh, they knew. And at first it was a bit of a turn-off. But when they got to know him, they realized that he wasn't out to convert them. He just wanted to be friends. He never condemned their lifestyle. He never gave them disapproving looks. He never withheld hearty laughter if something was funny.

It is true that the place became a bit more civilized because of Jesús being around so much. The crude jokes became more and more rare, the salty language was severely curtailed, with only an occasional swear word springing to someone's lips. They didn't restrain themselves because Jesús was a priest. They did it because he never took part in it and they figured he didn't like it much and they all liked him very much. If this great guy could live life without being crude and profane, they probably could, too. A few even asked themselves, in the privacy of their own minds, just why they use foul language and couldn't come up with a good answer and a couple actually concluded it was a lack of civility and stopped using profanity even when Father Jesús wasn't around.

There were several others who were as regular at the Buzzard's Nest as Jesús and they became quite close:

Mike Tracy, a mechanic, was a borderline alcoholic. Fifty. Divorced. A bit bitter about life.

Steve Parker, a young guy in his mid twenties, floating from job to job, did a lot of pot smoking - quite funny when he was high – way too serious when he wasn't.

Sandy (Jesús never could remember his last name) – a guy so stereotypically gay that it was almost embarrassing – but he'd do anything for you. Sandy hated being homosexual, but there it is…

Then there was Talia Spence. Jesús could never figure out just what kind of work she was in – she was always a bit evasive – but he had his suspicions. She always wore expensive clothes and lots of makeup and was only at the bar in the early parts of their evenings.

There were others, too, of course, but those four were the most colorful. Whenever those four and Jesús were present, everyone in the bar had a great time – always a lot of laughter, lots of fun, lots of lies flying around and outrageous stories and jokes…

Being a small town, Jesús' little outings – especially when they became so frequent – became known by everybody. His parish was philosophical about it. They figured it was the sort of thing the real Jesus would do so Father Jesús doing it might be alright. They didn't go so far as to endorse or defend what he was doing, but they tacitly decided to overlook it.

Last February the Buzzard's Nest sponsored a poker tournament. Gambling for money is illegal, of course, so they offered non-monetary prizes for round winners and winners of the whole tournament. The owners came up with a whole raft of prizes: One winner could buy (free) a round of beer for everyone in the bar. One prize was a reserved bar seat for a month. Another was for a burger basket a day for a week. Then they trod a bit on Father Jesús' territory. The winner could sleep in on Sundays for a month while all the losers would have to go to church.

Father Jesus didn't think this was a good idea at all. He said it sounded like compulsory religion and he was against that. But everyone laughed, and each said they would play especially well so as not to have to go to church while all the rest of the losers did – for a month! (Jesús figured that what was going on was a healthy curiosity – they wanted to know what a guy like him did over at the Catholic church but didn't want to ask and showing up without some excuse was just too awkward). When that prize came up for play, it was interesting how many jumped into the game – all of them knowing that they (unless they won) would be required to go to church every Sunday for a month.

When the game ended, Jason O'day had won. Six others had lost. Mike, Steve, Sandy, Talia, Dave and Pete would be going to church for a month... I've got to tell you, there was a lot of joking going around for the rest of the evening about church and religion and losers going to church. Three or four others who weren't even in the game said they'd tag along just for the fun of it. (Father Jesús had never thought of anyone going to church "for the fun of it" before – maybe that would be his new tag line – "Go to church this Sunday – just for the fun of it!" Interestingly, their revelry at the bar ended uncharacteristically early that night. The next morning was Sunday – no sleeping in for anyone but Jason...

Eight of Father Jesús' bar friends showed up for mass the next morning. They knew they should be as reverent as possible, but it was just too funny. They didn't know when to kneel, when to get up from kneeling, how to genuflect (or even whether they were supposed to nor when). They kept glancing at one another to see if any of the others had any idea whatsoever where in the book Father Jesús was. They got a kick out of his chanting – the Father didn't have a great voice. They did enjoy the congregational singing. They picked up the melodies pretty quickly and all eight sang out like they were gathered around the piano bar singing drinking songs. They didn't notice that everyone was looking at them and rolling their eyes. Good Catholics, as we all know, NEVER sing out and certainly not loudly enough for one another to hear...

All in all, they made a bit of a spectacle of themselves. But Father Jesús was as proud of them as he could be. They showed up. They tried to take part. They sang with enthusiasm. One of them knew enough about Catholics to know that they weren't allowed to take the Eucharist unless they were Catholics in good standing, so there weren't any awkward moments with that.

The eight had lunch back at the Buzzard's Nest after church. Father Jesús joined them after everyone was gone. "Well – what did you think?" asked Jesús. "Man, we love you," says Mike, "but we felt way out of sync with everything that was going on there. Sitting and standing and kneeling and bowing and all that reading from God knows where. Everyone seemed to know what was going on, but I've got to say, we were way lost."

Steve says, "We've been talking. The penalty for losing at poker the other night was attending church for a month. Does it have to be your church? I mean, you're great, but seeing you up there with all that formal stuff it seemed like you were someone else, you know? It was just weird."

"Hey, I understand," says Jesús. "If you didn't grow up Catholic, its got to seem pretty foreign. Our church is not exactly 'user friendly.'"

"So we decided we'd try each of the other churches in Plain. There are four and four Sundays in the month so that works out just right," says Talia.

Jesús was a bit hurt, but he understood. He supposed that going to church somewhere was better than nowhere. He'd love to have them all be Catholics, but what can you do?

So the following Sunday the six (the two who were just going for the fun of it decided it wasn't really all that much fun) went to the Pentecostal church.

Seldom do outgoing, gregarious people – people who had practically made a spectacle of themselves at St. Anthony's – feel shy, but they really did at the Pentecostal church. They couldn't believe what they experienced. Everyone was talking while the minister was talking – "Amen!" "Preach it brother!" "That's right!" "Praise Jesus!" so much so that they had no idea what he was saying and they doubted that the talkers did either. Even during the prayers everyone was talking. Even bar people know you are supposed to be quiet during a prayer. Very uncomfortable. Some were even talking in French or Arabic or something… During the singing people were swaying and raising their hands and crying and shouting. Some even fell over like trees – fortunately there was always someone there to catch them before they bashed their heads on the floor. They had seen some of these people around town. Out there they seemed pretty normal. But here they all seemed like they were a bit batty… They wouldn't be going back there any time soon…

They were going to go to the Congregational church but they had heard they didn't even have a minister right now, so they decided to give that one a pass. The Methodist church was next on their schedule. Truly nice people there. They were greeted by a smiling couple at the front door. They were ushered to their seats (pretty classy). They were handed a program. The sermon was good. The service itself made some sense to them – easy to follow along in the program. It was a bit dry – the sermon and the service itself, but that's what church is supposed to be, they thought. The singing was pretty good. Old stuff mostly. The kind of songs they sing in church scenes in old westerns...

The minister had invited everyone to their fellowship hour. It was about lunch time but Father Jesús wouldn't be at the Nest for another hour or so, so they went. What a shock. It seemed that everyone was standing around in little groups talking and laughing like long-lost buddies. Some would cast a side-long glance at them and keep talking. No one approached them. No one took them to get some coffee or offer them a cookie. "Well, this is awkward," said Sandy. "I wish we hadn't come back here. How do we make a graceful exit?"

They stayed a few minutes, talking among themselves as they slowly made their way to the door...

"Listen guys," Father Jesús said. "Think about it. They all know one another and the six of you together may have been a bit intimidating. Talia – maybe you shouldn't wear something with so much cleavage and with a bit longer hem. Church people tend to be pretty conservative. And Sandy, gays are still a big question mark in many people's minds. You know that. Methodists are pretty traditional. Give them a break. Give them another chance."

So they did. They went back to Plain Methodist their last obligation Sunday. The service was surprisingly like last weeks. They even recognized some of the people. They had decided that they would split up during the fellowship hour to see if they could get any better results. These seemed like nice, wholesome people. Maybe getting to know some of them would be a good thing.

They each had their individual strategy. Mike decided he would hang out at the cookie table to see if, maybe, a cookie could be a conversation starter. People said 'hi' as he met their eye, but then moved on.

Steve, the 20-something marijuana smoker approached a group of girls and tried to join in. Within minutes, two of their dads joined the group, too – clearly keeping an eye on him...

Sandy just stood there. He was used to being looked at with derision – being judged for what he was, but he had never, in his life, felt ignored so powerfully as he did that morning. He had apparently put on his invisibility cloak. It was as though he didn't exist to anyone there…

Talia was dressed much more conservatively today, but she so loved her high boots and heavy makeup and short skirts and fishnet stockings. She felt like the positive end of a magnet. As she walked across the big room, it was like the seas parting. People got out of her way as if by magic. She could have put her arms out in both directions as she walked and not touched anyone. It was like she had the plague and everyone knew it. It was like they knew, for a certainty, all about her and were repelled by her very existence. It was one of the most humiliating few minutes of her life and, under her breath, she swore she'd never come back here again.

Lunch that day was a relief. No more church. They had seen it all. They laughed about their experiences and some of the people they met or didn't meet. They told Jesús, when he came in, that they loved him like anything, but they didn't love his people and that his people, obviously, didn't love them. "Forget them," said Mike. "THIS is our church. We have our own fellowship hour and it's a lot better and more welcoming and certainly more fun than theirs."

And Father Jesus felt like a weight had been tied around his neck and was bending his back. He had hoped. He had prayed. He had been working for just this - his friends meeting God's family and feeling welcome and a part. Now he would have to begin again.

"Hey, Sam. Draw me a draft! And one for all my friends."

A PLAIN STORY: MAYOR JAKE
John 21:18-19

Forty years ago Jake Winslow was the mayor of Plain. Forty years! Can you imagine saying you were at the top of your game 40 years ago – back when you were 62?

Jake could remember when Plain was nothing but corn fields. Now it is a nice enough little town with four churches, a bar, a gas station, a small grocery store, a grain elevator, and one traffic light (two four-way stops, one at each end of town) – surrounded by corn fields. The post office closed a decade ago. There used to be a doctor in town, but he found more sick people in Bowling Green so he opened an office there and closed his office in Plain. It had never really been a "prosperous" town, but Jake loved it. Oh, yes, there is a nursing home in Plain, too. That's where Jake lives. He is Plain's oldest and longest resident – this next September he will turn 103 years old.

Jake grew up on a farm just west of what is now Plain. He inherited a fifth of the farm along with his siblings when his parents died. It was a small farm and dividing it five ways left each of them with not enough to farm but too much to do nothing with. He sold his 45 acres for $4500 back in 1965 and moved into town. He had a little house where he and Mary had lived and raised their three kids.

The kids didn't stick around after they graduated from High School. One headed out west - Oklahoma. One went south. One east. Janet died of cancer in 2000. Tom of a heart attack in 2005. Gretchen, the oldest, lived the longest. She died at 81. Jake always thought it one of the peculiar cruelties of life that a parent should outlive his children.

Jake has seven grandchildren, 15 great grandkids and 2 great-great grandkids. They almost never visit. They have their own lives - they live dozens of miles away - some hundreds of miles - and Jake understands that there is really little reason for most people to ever be in northwestern Ohio unless they've come specifically for family - him... But if they should happen to visit, he can't offer them anything. He has no capacity to offer hospitality or even a cold drink. They'd have to stay in a hotel and eat their meals at restaurants and that gets expensive in a hurry... And even if they visited just a couple of hours a day, what would they do the rest of the time?

But Jake is so terribly lonely at Twin Oaks. He's gotten used to it, of course, but it hits him especially hard when some of the other residents have family visit - some almost every day. They laugh and talk and catch up with family news... Sometimes they take grandma or grandpa (or mom or dad - whichever it might be) out for lunch... That must be nice. Sometimes the little ones will play a game of checkers with the oldsters or listen to a story that grandma or grandpa tell them or read to them... Jake hasn't hugged or been hugged by a child for over two decades. Other than the sweet nurses at Twin Oaks he hasn't had any physical contact with anyone for more than a year...

Well, that isn't strictly true. Pastor Roy, the interim minister at Plain Congregational, stops by every couple of weeks or so. He has this thing about touching. He once told Jake that Jesus was a toucher - that somehow even non-Jesus types bring about healing through touching the sick and the lonely and the depressed and those in need. Jake always thought that was a bunch of nonsense - poppycock - placebo-effect kind of stuff - until recent years. He started to notice that he DID feel better when Pastor Roy touched him on the shoulder or held his hand. He felt better when one of the nurses took his wrist and felt for his pulse or even inadvertently touched him when helping him get dressed. There IS something special about one person physically touching another. No explanation - there just is...

Pastor Roy isn't Jake's only regular visitor. There are a couple of teenagers that started visiting him about six months ago. They, too, were from that Plain Church ("there must be some caring people there," he thought). Jim and Betsy. They were juniors at Plain High when they started coming. They just showed up one day looking for him. Someone had done a report in one of their classes about the history of Plain and Mayor Jake was mentioned and it came out that the old man was still alive living at Twin Oaks - that he was a centenarian. Betsy's mother worked there so she got permission to visit with her friend, Jim.

It was a bit awkward at first. What do a 102 year old man and two 17 year olds have in common? But they were pretty smart. They honed in on asking questions about the past (and that was a good thing, because Jake couldn't remember much about the present - his short term memory was truly short). They asked about what Plain was like when he was young... what he did for fun when he was a teen... how he met Mary - "What was she like?" - about raising a family - about their church (Jake had been a member at Plain) and what it was like back then - how he felt about all the changes he'd seen - about how it feels to be the oldest person most people have ever met...

Betsy and Jim visit almost every week (except this summer when they have jobs and vacation with family - they've only visited twice so far - and one of those times only Betsy was able to come).

Teens aren't touchers. Even after they had gotten quite acquainted, he didn't remember them ever trying to give him a hug or a kiss or anything more than shaking hands - and even that only the first time they met... Maybe he had bad breath or something. But those two healed him far more than Rev. Roy ever could hope to through his touching. They were young, so he felt young. They were interested so he felt interesting. They wanted to read to him or play cards or tell bad jokes or listen to his stories or take him for walks in his wheelchair or they would bring him a Big Mac or a milkshake and he felt valued. Once, even, they got very serious and asked him what he thought about a couple of very private matters - issues weighing on their minds (which I can't tell you about because the conversation was confidential)... and he felt wise. Last spring, when the world was coming to life, they had a very serious conversation about dying. They wanted to know how he felt about it. It was no secret that he couldn't have too many more years...

He grew to love those two and to cherish their visits. Most of the nursing home staff assumed they were his grandchildren. When they asked him whether they were or not he always pretended he didn't hear the question. He just couldn't say "No. They are just kids. We aren't related." He felt that wouldn't be entirely true. Betsy and Jim were his friends. He loved them - dare he say it - even more than his real grandkids or great grandkids...

Jake knew that they would be graduating in another year and probably going away to school (although he could never figure that out - there is a very fine university just a few miles away in Bowling Green - why would anyone want to go somewhere else). But it wasn't terribly unlikely that he, too, would be leaving sometime in the next year. Maybe he'd beat them to it and they'd miss him instead of him missing them...

Even though Jake was forgetful, he was still sharp. He had a lot of time to think and he did a lot of thinking. He thought a lot about his life and about God and how it all fits together. Why would God keep him here so long (although it didn't seem so long ago that he was Betsy and Jim's age)? 102 years! Why would God have him weep at Mary's grave and then Tom's and Janet's and then Gretchen's - his children... Why had God broken his heart so many times when his friends all died - Sam and Herald and Fred and Jeannie and Sal? Everyone dear to him was gone and he was still healthy as a horse. Well, at least an old, broken down horse.

And he thought about the world. He couldn't remember what was on the news this morning but he knew that things were getting bad. People were hurting one another - they were lying, cheating and stealing, killing, raping, scamming... It was good not to be able to remember the details... And this was another way Betsy and Jim worked their healing wonders. They showed him that there is still hope and goodness and kindness and joy in the world... He hoped that what he saw in them was more typical than what he saw on TV. He suspected it might be.

Jake has a roommate. Alex Smithfield. They've become friends. They talk about some of the big issues of the world - and a lot of other things. Alex is still sharp, too. He is just a young guy – 87. They talk politics and philosophy and religion and, like all people in their age bracket, about all their aches and pains.

Alex could, sometimes, be one of those pains in the you-know-where for Jake… Alex is quite opinionated on everything… Not to say that Jake isn't. He certainly is. But Jake grew up in the Congregational tradition and knows how to hold his own view and still respect and allow and interact with those of others without being judgmental or condescending. Alex – not so much. But one of the things they've always agreed on, and commented often about, was something that everyone in their station in life has observed: The days drag on and on and the hours seem endless, but the years simply fly by.

Jake is adored by the nursing staff. Some of the older ones remember him from when he was mayor. The younger ones love to hear the stories of his exploits as he, apparently, almost single-handedly pulled Plain into the 20th century in dozens of ways. And Jake is a real charmer - a bit of a flirt, truth be known. But they all agreed - there is something sweet about being flirted with by a gentleman of one hundred years.

And, of course, just listening to Jake and Alex' conversations is entertaining. Both have fairly severe hearing loss, so their conversations are anything but private...

"Jake – I've been thinking about these gol'darn politicians in Washington. What's wrong with them? Are they stupid or something? They don't seem to know the first thing about getting along. One says something is 'black' and the other will insist it's 'white.' Unless HE says it's 'black' – then the other will say it's 'white.' Fools!"

"You sound like a fool yourself, you ol' coot. They're all just trying to get re-elected. That's what politicians do. Just stop listening to them. They're all looking out for #1. Their care for the country is secondary – their concern for you and me is way down on their list. But you are right – they are fools. I wouldn't vote for any of them. Now give me Ike. There was a man who knew what he was doing. You vote for him?"

"Vote for him? I headed up his Toledo campaign headquarters! Any man who fought in that war was a hero to me. You fight, Jake?"

"No. I was already too old to serve. I stayed home. Not a bad place to be. Mary and I got married and started our family. Scary times - that war... "

Their conversations were sometimes serious - sometimes not, but always at full volume. And they seldom carry on their conversations in the privacy of their room. They prefer to hang out in common areas and put up with all the old folks trying to shush them so they can watch their soaps. Both are philosophically opposed to television - they always hoped some of the others would join in their conversations and abandon the boob-tube but that was rare.

Life in the nursing home is a small universe. You see the same people every day. Each day looks almost identical to the one before. Your sight, your hearing, your immobility, your forgetfulness, all close you in. Add to these the fact that you are at the mercy of a dozen people – nurses and aides and therapists and meal-makers and activities directors – and your life becomes less and less your own. You are told when to eat and what. You are awakened in the morning and told when to go to bed. You are wheeled in your wheel-chair from here to there wherever someone thinks you ought to be - they never ask whether you want to be there or not. When the activities director thinks you need exercise you are wheeled down to the lounge and play games that wouldn't keep a 4 year old's interest - tossing a beach ball back and forth - what a stupid game for adults to play. Even the clothes you wear. You struggle into whatever some aide is kind enough to put out for you. She combs your hair – often not bothering to notice which side you like your part on… Life – Liberty – the Pursuit of Happiness – that's what Jake remembered but it all seemed like a dream to him now…

But he could remember. Not so much yesterday or this morning, but He could remember when he was just a young man. He was mayor of Plain for 17 years. He stepped down when he turned 70. He had had respect and influence and everyone in town knew him and liked him. Now it was a revelation to Betsy and Jim's high school civics class that he was even still alive. ...How times change.

Something happened that was rather astounding for a 102 year old man a few months ago. Jake found himself. He didn't know he had been lost, but certainly knew, beyond doubt, that he had been found. It was Betsy and Jim's visits as they intermeshed with Pastor

Roy's talking about the healing power of touch and the love of God that did it. Jake was inspired to believe that his life still had purpose and meaning. All of his life that came before was history - he didn't regret it - not any of it - but he knew that the rest of his life - whatever God yet allowed him - would be the best years (months, weeks, days?) of his life. He decided to do what Pastor Roy was doing - touch people - healing - letting them know he cared. So many of these old folks were more lonely than he had ever been. He decided that he would become known as the man who touches others - who holds their hands - who puts an arm around them as best he can - who listens to their complaints (not hearing very well might make that easier). And he'd take Betsy and Jim's tack. He would ask questions about their lives - the past and their families and their friends who are gone. He would let them talk about themselves... He would read to those who had poor vision, he would joke with those who were depressed, he would sit at meals with those who weren't eating, he would know names and call out to whomever he saw from across the room with a friendly greeting. He would be to these poor souls what Betsy and Jim and Pastor Roy were to him. As he saw it, they were replicas of Jesus. He wondered why he had never seen this before – the "ministry of presence" to others – affirming their value – letting them know that God cares and that he does, too! What a wonderful calling in life… And over the ensuing months Mayor Jake became a more important man in his little world at the nursing home than he had ever been as Mayor of Plain.

    I don't know how much longer Mayor Jake has in this world. Can't be much longer, one would think. But wouldn't God be proud of him? He is living every day of his life fully - ministering to those in need - showing compassion and helping - loving (and in return being loved), reaching out, touching.... truly being Christian in all he is and yet has.

A PLAIN STORY: THE LOURDES HOUSE
John 4: 7-14

Some aspects of small town culture tend to be a bit peculiar to suburbanites. Traditions and ways of doing things and the way corporate history is captured and remembered are unique. I'm not sure that even the residents of the communities themselves, if pressed, could give a good reason for some of the traditions and "ways" that develop...

Try to visualize Plain. There is a main street that is about ten or twelve blocks long - that's about a mile. At each end of main street - east and west - is a four-way stop before the speed limit returns to 65 mph and heads out through the corn fields and farms and open countryside. Along Main Street you will see businesses - but only on Main Street. Streets off of Main Street are only residential - no business establishments at all... As you travel down Main you'll see the little grocery store, a used car lot, the Buzzard's Nest, the barber shop/beauty parlor (mostly beauty parlor because most Plain men won't go into any place that smells of hair color and women's shampoo). There is a Sunoco station. The grain elevator. The hardware store. A tiny bank. There are at least three empty storefronts along the way (one used to be the post office) and, at the far western edge of town are the schools - an older elementary and the new high school. The only traffic light in town is right in the middle, at the intersection of Main and Elm Street.

They've done an interesting thing in the naming of their side streets. They are all named after trees in alphabetical order from east to west: Ash, Birch, Chestnut, Dogwood, Elm, Fig, Gorse, Honeysuckle, Ivy and Juniper. Oddly enough, none of those trees exist in Plain. The only species of tree in town are Maple and Cottonwood and some Cedar planted as windbreaks. There used to be some Ash and Elm but you know how those have disappeared due to foreign insects and disease...

But the naming of streets after trees that don't exist in the town isn't the thing you and I would find odd (after all, I live on Quail Run Drive and there hasn't been a Quail around there for decades). One of the peculiar things you find in small communities is the naming of houses. "Oh, you live over in the Grant house!"

"OK... I've lived there for six years - bought it from a family named Owen who had lived there for fifteen years and I know they bought it from a family named Atkins... I'm not sure why it's called the 'Grant House.'"

"Well, that's because Gary Grant lived there. He was the Postmaster back in 1967."

"Did he build the house?"

"Oh, no. It was built back in the 40's - long before Gary lived there."

"Then why do you call it the 'Grant House'?"

"Because that's what it is. It's always been the 'Grant House.'"

There really is no rhyme nor reason to it, but houses somehow take on the name of some former resident - not necessarily the first resident or the immediate past resident - just someone that everyone seems to have known at some point in history... When you refer to the 'Grant House' or the 'Tate House' or the 'Ryder House,' everyone knows what house you are talking about even though there aren't any Grants or Tates or Ryders in town and haven't been for twenty years or more.

On Elm Street is a house that has been known, for as long as anyone can remember, as the "Lourdes House." (spelled L-o-u-r-d-e-s - like the village in France where Bernadette saw the virgin Mary). At some point in time, the Lourdes family lived there even though there is no one in town who remembers the family nor anything about them. People remember the Blake family who lived there for a few years and the Setter's and the Cheney's. Most recently the Priest family lived there. The Priests were an amazing family. They were some of the most compassionate people you'd ever want to meet. They regularly took in foster kids. They put together the Plain Potluck every year for the town. They organized outings over at the nursing home for any of the old folks who could get around. They always went on the Mission Trips that the Congregational church sponsored.

But tragedy struck the Priests. Judy Priest was in a car accident and broke an arm, several ribs, and fractured her skull. She would be hospitalized for weeks. About the same time Peter lost his job and couldn't pay the bills. They were under water on their mortgage and they lost the house. Within four months they disappeared from Plain - it was a terrible thing - they had been such an important part of the community... So well loved.

So there sat the "Lourdes House" - sitting empty. It's not a large house. A ranch house built probably in the '50's. About 1500 square feet. Brick. Nothing much exceptional about it. Just an empty house.

Most Plain people have one thing in common. They think that everything happens for a reason. It may not be immediately clear, but it is our job to figure it out and give it validation... It's a philosophy of hope. If everything happens for a purpose, then whatever happens can't be thought to be too terrible. I suppose EVERYONE in town isn't that way, but it seems to be somewhat common.

That's the way Sally Fuller thought. Sally drove by the Lourdes house one day and was struck with an idea. The Priest family was gone but that house still held the vibes of good people doing good things. She wondered if it could be continued.

That very afternoon Sally stopped in to see Mr. Booker, the banker. "Mr. Booker, that house the bank owns over on Elm Street is empty. It won't take long for the windows to be broken by kids and weeds to grow up in the lawn and sidewalk cracks and begin to look terrible. I live just down the block and I just won't have it. What are your plans?"

"Oh, you mean the old Lourdes house? Yes, it was too bad about the Priests. I hated to see them go - nice family. But what can you do? We'll try to keep the house up, Sally. But times are tough, you know. We're not going to put any money into it other than, maybe, boarding up the windows and keeping the weeds down. Chances of it selling any time soon with this housing market are pretty slim."

"Not acceptable," says Sally. "I won't have a boarded up house in my neighborhood. You should be ashamed of yourself for even suggesting such a thing. Do you want Plain to start looking like some slum?"

"Now Sally, what would you have me do? ... Wait... You've got something up your sleeve, don't you?"

"Well, I was thinking, John, why don't you go ahead and try to sell it. But you're right, it's not going to sell - we both know that. But how about, while you're trying, you let me have the keys. I'll take care of it. I'll mow the lawn. I'll pay the bills. I'll make sure it doesn't become derelict. I want to open a food pantry in it... more than a food pantry, really. I want to call it, "The Lourdes Table" and have it be a place to give away food to anyone who wants it - a place where people can bring in clothing items for give away - where people can come, no matter if they are rich or poor or hungry or full, and get free food if they want it and look through coats and shirts and slacks and dresses and take freely whatever they need. I'll be in charge and will recruit volunteers from the churches in town. I'll solicit financial donations from wherever I can. I'll find people who will mend some of the clothing that needs mending and handymen who will keep the house up. This is something that is desperately needed in Plain. In fact, I'm pretty sure there isn't anything like this even in Bowling

Green or Toledo. I can see students from the university coming and volunteering and others coming for food and clothing (not all of them can really afford all that college costs). I can see people coming from miles around who are in desperate circumstances and getting a little of what they need and a little hope along with it... And, John, just think what such a thing would do for your bank's reputation which, by the way, isn't so great with all the foreclosures you've been doing in the past couple of years.." And Sal stopped, waiting expectantly for Mr. Booker's reply...

"Well, Ms. Fuller" (she knew that him calling her by her formal name wasn't a good sign), "that's all well and good and you make a good case, but still... Charity is not the line of work I'm in. I'm a banker. My job is to make money and solid financial decisions. I won't even take your request to my board of directors. I would be laughed out of the room. I'm afraid your request is completely out of the question. I'm sorry."

"Oh. ...Well then...," Sally stammered, almost on the verge of tears, "I guess I'll have to pray about it. I believed this was something God wanted. I really thought you'd jump on it - that old house has been called the 'Lourdes House' for decades. I just thought... I thought that maybe even the name was a sign..."

Whenever you have the wind taken out of your sails, you feel pretty helpless. Sally certainly did. She had never been more excited about anything in her life. She just KNEW God was in it somewhere. Why the roadblock? Why did the idea come to her so crystal clearly if it was to come to nothing? There was no explanation. She could SEE it! She KNEW it was needed and that she could help so many. "God, I've done what I can. What else is there? What more can I do?"

God has a way of changing people's minds. No one really knows what happened in John Booker's life during the next twenty-four hours but it must have been something pretty dramatic. The next day he walked up Sally's walk and knocked briskly on the door and when she opened it to him he simply handed her the keys. No explanation. Not one word spoken. He just handed her the keys, turned on his heels, walked to his car, and drove off. Sally thought he looked a little pale, but that might have just been her imagination.

She got to work right away. Went in and painted everything, scrubbed the floors, washed the windows, hung curtains, got tables and clothes hanging racks and posters with encouraging words to hang on the walls. She got a blank book for beside the front door, not for people to register, but for people to leave little notes to others who might come in - to encourage - to give hope - to say 'thank you' to all the donors. She had a big sign made for the front lawn - "The Lourdes

House - Come Freely and Be Filled - Be Blessed" and a sign for inside the house: "Whatever You Find in This Place is Freely Yours - Including Our Love."

As you know, the town of Plain really is a close-knit community. The people in town rallied to Sal's cause in amazing ways. They collected food - put out boxes for on-going contributions at places of business. The churches put out donation baskets and asked their people to give generously and to stop by "The Lourdes Table" to sign up for a volunteer slot on a regular basis. Restaurants in Bowling Green heard about the project and offered their leftover food (there is no "Forgotten Harvest" in Bowling Green but all of them had heard of the concept). A department store in Toledo sent one of their trucks to Plain with a load of brand-new last years model clothing. Even the Buzzard's Nest made a contribution - although a bit odd. When Father Jesús started as a regular customer and only drank wine, others started drinking wine too, but that was short-lived and they went back to beer, but Pat, the owner had ordered a dozen cases of red wine which nobody except the Father was drinking, so he gave ten cases to "The Lourdes Table." They weren't sure if they could legally give out wine at the pantry or not (obviously not to minors), but an attorney looked into it and apparently it was OK so long as it wasn't being sold...

Everything was ready for doing business by the first Sunday in August. That was the day scheduled to be their "Grand Opening." It was a great day. The mayor made a speech on the front steps and cut the ribbon, the clergy were all present, the city council served cookies and punch, Pastor Roy, from the Congregational Church, gave a prayer of blessing and, it seemed, the whole town took a tour of the little house. It was a great day for Plain.

Later in the day, after everyone was home and settling in for the evening, some saw the irony of the day. In the midst of opening a food and clothing distribution house - in the midst of celebrating what a great thing was beginning - in the hoopla of community pride - no food was actually given away to anyone in need. Not a pair of socks, not a pair of shorts, not a scarf or a coat... not a can of soup or a box of cereal... even though everything in the house was free, no one took anything... no one there had a need. Sally knew this would happen. It was the grand opening only in the sense that the community wanted to launch it AS a community. Most of the people who would use it would be rather anonymous, as they should be. TOMORROW the needy would begin to come...

But no one did. The Lourdes Table was open for a week and no one came. Sal was a bit discouraged, of course (maybe a little more than a bit), and sat down with some friends to do some evaluation to figure out what was going on. They looked at all the preparation that had gone into the project - all the time and work and energy and prayers - at all the community interest in helping and reaching out to those in need - all the donations and volunteers and money coming in...

Mark Simons was the first to see it. He started to laugh. Once he said it out loud, everyone began to laugh in embarrassment. Laughing, he said, "I'm looking over all we've done to get this place ready and it occurs to me that we may have overlooked one essential element. We haven't told the needy about it." How embarrassing... Everyone just assumed those who most needed the Lourdes Table would know about it since, it seemed, everyone else did and would simply come and take of the food given freely and would be encouraged and have their hope in the world renewed... But, oddly, everyone in town failed to tell the hungry where the food was - where warm clothing could be had - where the Lourdes House was at... "You know," said Mark, "unless someone tells people, they can't possibly know how great this place is or what it has to offer. We forgot to tell the hungry where to get food... What an odd oversight..."

So they began another campaign. This time to find those in need and to make sure they knew where food was available. They passed out fliers in the poorer neighborhoods of Bowling Green and put them in mail boxes out in the countryside. They went to the local radio station and asked for some public service announcements to be made. They put up posters in the grocery stores and in the schools. They advertised "Grand Opening II - Free Bread and Wine and Love to All Who Will Come." And Sal made another sign to be hung on the living room wall. It said: "Come and Eat and Drink. Never Be Hungry or Thirsty Again." And people did come. They came by the dozens - by carloads and walking - they came from Plain and from Bowling Green and Perrysburg and Napoleon. And everyone who came, everyone who ate Sal's food and drank Sal's wine was satisfied. There was no doubt that they would be back. They had been the recipients of amazing grace. They had received hope. They knew, many of them for the first time in their lives that, so long as the Lourdes Table was available, they would, truly, never hunger nor thirst again.

Aren't you glad someone told you? Go – tell others.

A Plain Story - The Him Sing
Psalm 71:22-24

There is a small, exclusive group that meets on a regular basis in Plain. Most of us wouldn't have much interest in joining. Their meetings are pretty profession centric. It is the Plain Minister's Society (lovingly referred to as the "PMS"). The members are: Father Jesús, the Catholic priest (whom we've met), Pastor Roy Barry, the interim minister at Plain Congregational, Rev. Roger Sunquist, at First Methodist, and Rev. Jake Charis, pastor at the Plain Pentecostal Church. From time to time Rev. Andrews from nearby Tontogany and Rev. Thomas from Weston will join in, but generally not. It is almost always just the four of them. And they have actually become quite good friends. Jesús had been in Plain for almost ten years, Sunquist for 4, Charis for nine and Pastor Barry for only two and a half. But Roy Barry is the kind of man that everyone loves from their first exposure to him. His smile captures you. His warmth makes him feel like an old friend, his exuberance is contagious... But all four of them were very aware that Roy's time was drawing to a close. They hadn't had any official word from the pulpit search committee, but hints dropped here and there indicated that they are closing in on the person of God's choosing for their new minister. When he or she is called, Roy will be on his way. But a minister's life is one of moves. The average tenure of a minister is 5 to 7 years. An interim is typically about a year or eighteen months. Roy has already been in town for two and a half years.

Over the years they have discussed various theological topics - baptism and transubstantiation and funeral protocol and Biblical interpretation and Lectionary issues... Sounds interesting, doesn't it? Believe it or not, if you are a minister, it is...

Today Roy brought up an idea: "You know, we haven't done anything together as churches in Plain for a long time. I think we should. You know, just letting each of our congregations know that they aren't the only Christians in town. I've kind of let you guys do all that kind of thing because I've been the new-comer and only an interim... but I want to spearhead something before they kick me out of town.... As you know, I'm Welsh. Ahhh, Wales – 'the land of song.' We Welsh love to sing and there is nothing that brings a community together like singing. I would like to sponsor an old fashioned hymn sing.... We used to have them weekly when I was growing up in Ruthin, Denbighshire. And, oh can the Welsh sing! The power 'o God was in that place when the old pipe organ played and those who loved the Lord showed it with their voices... What 'd you think? Would it work in Plain?"

The other three kind of looked away, not knowing exactly what to say. A hymn sing? Could there be anything as old-fashioned as that? How would you get people to go? In this modern world of ipods and MP3 and hi-tech musical mixing anything "old fashioned" would be seen as somewhat.... old fashioned.

Father Jesus was the first to speak: "Roy, that's a marvelous idea, but I'm not sure it is for Plain. We've never done anything like that before and I'm not sure anyone would come. I know that we over at St. Anthony's are really bad at singing. You've attended a mass. Can you see Plain Catholics belting out hymns? I'd certainly invite them, but I'm not at all sure anyone would show up."

Jake Charis said, "We haven't sung a hymn over at our church for twenty years. They are such dirges. Modern people much prefer the modern choruses - they move you emotionally. Although I suppose many of our young people would think a hymn is something new and different. They've never heard most of them. But our older people have and they won't like the idea. If you do this, if you want any Pentecostals to come you'd better name it something other than 'Hymn Sing.' Maybe you can make it appeal to those of us more into worship by calling it a 'H-i-m Sing' - you know, like singing to Him - Jesus. "

"That's kind of corny," piped in Sunquist. "But if that's what it takes to get you 'holy rollers' in, I guess it's OK with me. Now, we Methodists love the old hymns. Charles Wesley was our founder, you know. He wrote the words or music or both for eight thousand hymns. I would presume you'll be singing some of those.... I think I can get some of my people to come."

"Well, I know that the Congregational church is into their own history - the Pilgrims and all that - and they do love to sing.... sometimes. I've never quite figured it out. Some Sunday mornings I'd swear we have a bunch of Welshmen and other Sundays a bunch of Catholics (no offense intended, Jesús). It's a mystery to me, but I truly think that if they know people from other churches will be there, they'll open their voices and sing out.

"If it's OK with you, I'd like to hold the thing at Plain Congregational. We have a small enough sanctuary that people won't feel lost in all the space like over at Jesus' church and our facility is a lot more 'church-like' than your place, Jake, traditionally speaking, of course. Besides, it's kind of like my swan song - a big event as I ride off into the sunset."

"Plus the fact that, if it's a bust, you won't be around too long to be embarrassed by it," said Rog Sunquist.   "OK... So here is the plan," says Roy. "So as not to mess with any of your sermon schedules, let's have the 'Him Sing' (that is bit corny, Jake), in the summer - we all need a Sunday away from the pulpit anyway. I propose to have it on August 14. Now, I've already been thinking this thing through and I'd like to share my vision with you. I want you all to walk through it with me to see how it all fits together..."

[Think of the next hour as Roy's vision - and you are all part of it...]

"When everyone gets there - at about 9:30 in the morning - the first thing I'll do is welcome everyone - *It's great to have you all here this morning to sing praises to our great God. Most of you know one another even though we are from different congregations. We've come here to sing and I do hope you'll sing for all your worth. The next hour will be one that will inspire you and you'll leave here knowing you've been in the presence of the angels.... Let's start out with a prayer.....* [pray].

"Now, *first of all, everyone should have a Him Book or a Him Booklet. No sharing this morning. Yours is yours. Second thing - could I have everyone who has ever sung in a choir stand up... You folks are key to our little Him Sing this morning. We're all depending on you to inspire us to sing well. So sing out! You are the section leaders."*

"*Our first two Hymns this morning are great ones. Both written by Charles Wesley, founder of Methodism and probably the greatest song writer of all times. The 'Guinness Book of World Records' lists Paul McCartney as being the most prolific song writer of all time. He wrote more than 3000 songs. But someone they forgot Charles Wesley. Wesley wrote 6000 songs and the lyrics for another 2000! Let's sing one of his greatest - a song of passion for God so overwhelming that he feels inadequate in his single, squeaky little voice... Stand and sing with me - 'O For a Thousand Tongues to Sing My Great Redeemers Praise..."* page 76

"*You see, the first thing you want to do in a hymn sing is to give people a feeling of power with a powerful melody with a powerful message. People will begin to feel that their one voice IS inadequate but will see that together - maybe a thousand - might come close....*

"*Another of Wesley's greatest hits is one that Pastor Steve Schafer, up in a Congregational church in Michigan, heard for the first time and fell in love with right here in Bowling Green. He once told me that he rarely has it sung at his church because if they don't do it justice he is disappointed. He wants it sung at his funeral... You can't sit down for this one either. 'And Can It Be?' page 203.* [sit following]

"Do you see what is happening? People are asking the big questions in song: 'Can it be that I can approach God's throne? Can my sin-imprisoned soul be released? Did Jesus sacrifice do what it was intended to do? Sorry, Jake, you just don't get those kinds of questions in your modern choruses... AMAZING love!!! ...how vast and free... Then we take that overwhelming understanding of who God is and have a prayer of consecration of ourselves... 'May the Mind of Christ, My Savior.' This is one of those hymns with way too many verses. I'll ask the people to sing only the first four...

"Then we'll sing this one as a prayer. "*Consider the words. Mean the words you sing and your life will never be the same again...*" "May the Mind of Christ, My Savior" page 390 - verses 1-4.

"Then I'll tell a hymn story. Every great hymn has a story... *Back in the mid-1800's there lived a young man named Samuel Francis in the great nation of Wales. He was a troubled young man and one evening he was crossing the Hungerford Bridge near the Thames in London when he stopped and looked at the roiling water below. He says he heard a voice in his head, 'Make an end to all this misery in your life...' He says he drew back at the evil thought. Then he heard another voice, a small, whispery one: "Do you believe in the Lord Jesus Christ?" He immediately answered, "I do believe!" and his life was forever changed. He wrote this next hymn thinking of that water and the depths of Jesus' love. The tune is often called, "Ton-Y-Botel" which means "Tune in a Bottle" - Myth has it that it was washed up on the Welch coast... It is not a dirge - let us not sing it as one... visualize the swells of the ocean as you sing... This hymn is one of the great ones...* "O the Deep, Deep Love of Jesus" p. 211.

"*Joseph Scriven's fiancé drowned the day before they were to be married in Dublin, Ireland. Reeling from heartbreak and grief he gathered his things and sailed for Canada. A few years later he found another love of his life, Eliza Roche, and they were to be married. But she contracted tuberculosis and died before walking the aisle. Joseph wrote the words, a broken but not a faithless man, to* "What a Friend We Have in Jesus." *We will sing it today to a melody you have never heard. Notice how these old familiar words take on new meaning with a new melody. It is printed in your program.*

"Next we're going to sing a hymn that was banned from the Methodist hymnal by John Wesley himself. The Rev. Edward Perronet had travelled with the Wesley brothers for several years, proclaiming the gospel with them side-by-side. But they had some sort of falling out. John tore his hymn from their hymnal - perhaps wishing **he** had penned the words to one of the greatest hymns ever written. And doubtless the best men's part in any hymn ever - AND the best women's part. If you can sing parts - this hymn was written for you: "All Hail the Power of Jesus' Name" page 96 - we MUST stand for a hymn like this one... Then remain standing for the one following...

By the way - Pastor Sunquist assures me that this great hymn has been in the Methodist Hymnal now for a long time... As you all know, the Barry family traces its ancestry back to Wales. We do love to sing in Wales. We've been called be, 'the land of song.' This next one is from Wales. The powerful, "Immortal, Invisible, God Only Wise." Page 25.

"SIT. 'Tis time to take a break and give your vocal cords a rest. You can't come into a church - in Plain or anywhere else - without having an offering. 'Dear God - Thank you for the bounty which you pour into our laps. This day we give a bit back to you. Teach us always to be grateful and always to be generous. Amen.... Let the ushers come... Ms. Laura Murphy will grace us with some truly Godly music - From Mozart - his Fantasy in D minor.

"So many of the great hymns are great because they talk about commitment to Christ and Christ alone. They don't have to be barn-burners. They are beautiful in their simplicity and in their message... in their love for Jesus and love for the life He gives... "My Faith Has Found a Resting Place" page 405. And can anyone not be moved by "Fairest Lord Jesus"? Page 88.

"The flaw in so many of the modern songs written is narcissism. They tend to be about "ME." The hymns tend to be about... "HIM." But even when they are about ME, HE is strongly present... Stand with me and sing "Who Is On the Lord's Side," page 484. Sorry - once again we must stand... not that you could fall asleep with this hymn...

"You may sit. Language changes over the years. Not so much old men like me. "Come, Thou Fount of Every Blessing" (page 2) has had a face-lift and, if you would, for an old man, would you sing it the old way? Take a look. The second verse reads "Hither to Thy love has blest me; Thou hast bro't me to this place." They changed it because people didn't know what the original meant. Nobody in the modern world knows what an "Ebenezer" is. 'Tis a shame. An Ebenezer is a stone of help. At the end of a dark period in Israel's history, Samuel took a large, flat stone and stood it on end as a symbol of renewal - starting over - of God's help. It was called an "Ebenezer. Let us sing verse 2 as it was originally written. " If you can't remember the phrase, you'll find it printed in your program where this hymn is listed.

"Our God is incomprehensible to our puny little minds. Hymn writers have used images to try to convey a tiny bit of the divine character... A Strong Deliverer and a Mighty Fortress: "Guide Me, O Thou Great Jehovah" page 51 and then "A Mighty Fortress Is Our God" page 26.

"Patrick was born in the year 373 in Scotland, son of a deacon and grandson of a priest. When he was 16 he was captured by pirates and sold into slavery. After a few years he escaped and had a vision rather like St. Paul's convincing him of his need for Jesus. At age 30 he picked up his Bible and headed back to the place he had been imprisoned and preached the gospel - to the Druids and the pagans of rural Ireland. He established 200 churches and baptized 100,000 converts. A follower wrote a poem asking God to be his Vision, his Wisdom, his best thought. In 1905 it was set to music – the tune named for the place the Druids inhabited - Slane. Soak up the words of this hymn - let the passion of St. Patrick become your own. "Be Thou My Vision" page 382.

"So - Jake, Rog, Jesús - what do you think? Can we do it? Can we have a Him Sing?"

"I can SO see it," says Jake. I don't know if my Pentecostals will come but I'll do everything I can to get them there. Thank you, Roy, you've given me a new appreciation for some of the great music of the church."

"I still don't know if my people will come," says Jesús. "I'll try. Some of those hymns aren't in our tradition but I know them all. Great stuff! Maybe you'll transform our parish into singers."

Rog says, "Will you do one for me, Roy? So many times we forget that all of us are in this together - Catholics, Methodists, Pentecostals, Congregationalists - and have been for a very long time. We're in it with people from all ages throughout the world. Do you think you can end the whole thing with 'For all the Saints?' Have people stand, sing, have a closing prayer and blessing. I think, then, the morning will be just about perfect."

"Of course I'll do it," says Roy. "A thousand generations of people of faith have come before us and, depending on when the Lord returns, perhaps a thousand after us. Let us remember them and us in their midst - Stand - With all that is within you, sing "For All the Saints" page 546." Amen.

A PLAIN STORY: HAZLET POND
John 5: 1-9

Water. What a wonderful thing. Have you ever thought about it? Without water there could be no life on earth - no plants, no animals - nothing but rock. Our bodies are 60% water - more than ANYTHING else, we are water! 46% of the earth's surface is water - 65.3 MILLION square miles of water! Have you ever sat beside a large body of water and just looked at it for a while? It's soothing and refreshing and renewing... Most of us remember the first time we saw a body of water that we couldn't see across. You look out and you see where the water meets the sky, you see the curvature of the earth. You can't help but to think, "If I got in a boat and sailed straight that direction for 3000 miles I'd get to England. Incredible - water.... Whoever invented it ought to be praised... What an incredible thing water is.

10,000 years ago, during the ice age, glaciers scraped across this part of the world, making hills and valleys, scraping topsoils from some areas and depositing them in others. When it got to what is now northwest Ohio, the glaciers scraped it flat, creating the "Black Swamp." Over the centuries the swamp dried up and solidified into the plain it is today.

When you live on a plain where all the hills have been scraped away by the glaciers thousands of years ago, you find that you miss something most of the world takes for granted. If you or I want to go to the beach, we get into our car and go a few miles east to Lake St. Claire or a short way south to Belleville or north to Walled Lake or Orchard Lake or Union Lake or a dozen or so other beautiful water spots. Although we can't swim in it, we all routinely pass Newburgh Lake right here in Livonia... I've heard that there isn't anywhere in Michigan where you are more than five miles from some kind of lake. But not so in northwest Ohio. No lakes. To get to even a small lake you have to travel north into Michigan or all the way over into Indiana. Ohio does have Lake Erie, but people in Plain would have to travel further than you or me to get to it - not easily accessible...

So in and around Plain - and maybe in other flat areas of the country, too, a phenomena has occurred - farm ponds. I think the idea of farm ponds came with the advent of freeway overpasses. To get enough dirt to make a ramp high enough and dense enough for traffic, you have to haul in huge quantities of dirt. To cut corners a bit, contractors got permission to invent the freeway slough - a pond created by the hauling of dirt from a location right next to the overpass ramp. The depression fills with water and makes a somewhat attractive little pond.

Farmers, who tend to have quite large parcels of property around their houses, took the idea home with them and began to build farm ponds. They would get a bulldozer and carve out a dish in the land, line it with rocks or maybe even a plastic liner, allow God to fill it with water, and they would have a place to cool off after a long day tending the fields right there in their own back yard. More appealing than a swimming pool because it, somehow, seems more natural. My brother has one. It's really quite appealing on a hot August day. To keep them aerated to avoid bad stuff growing in them, they almost always have a fountain in the middle. That in itself is a fun feature when cooling off.

Barney Hazlet has a farm a mile or so outside of Plain and he has a farm pond. He is a deacon at Plain Congregational and every spring, after the ice melts and the water has had a chance to warm up a bit, the church holds a baptismal service in Barney's pond. They've been doing it ever since the pond was built - for more than twenty years.

Baptism is a curious ceremony. No one really knows why we do it. Paul suggests that it is a symbolic following in the progression of Jesus' life - death (when we confess our sins), burial - (when we are buried in the water), and resurrection to new life (when we emerge from the water with Christ in our lives) (Romans 6:1-5). For John the Baptist baptism meant that a person was cleansed from his or her sins - except when he baptized Jesus. Then it was an initiation into his heavenly ministry on earth - an endorsement of God's blessing. Philip, when baptizing the Ethiopian, did it, clearly, as a sign or regeneration - new life.

Early on the church began baptizing babies as a replacement for the Jewish rite of circumcision - a physical sign of a spiritual covenant with God - made by the parents on behalf of their child - with the hope that the child would acknowledge the covenant when he or she grew older.

Jesus' last words on earth were "Go into all the world making disciples, baptizing them in the name of the Father and the Son and the Holy Spirit, teaching them to obey everything I have commanded..." He didn't say why. Maybe it is sufficient that we baptize for no other reason than that Jesus said to... We don't have to understand it. We just do it as an act of obedience no matter what other meanings we place on it.

The Hazlet pond is such a beautiful setting. Barney and Ethyl have done a wonderful job of planning it out, landscaping it and maintaining it... Whenever Pastor Roy or any of the other previous Plain Church ministers have had a baptismal service there everyone thinks it just wonderful. He, of course, being a Congregationalist, will either immerse a person or pour the baptismal water - whatever they prefer... Last year, though, something happened at one of the baptismal services that changed everything.

The Methodists and the Pentecostals have started using the pond. Plain is a small town and every time a Congregationalist told a friend about what a beautiful service they have at Hazlet's pond, that person would tell their minister and, before long, Pastor Charis and Pastor Sunquist both approached Barney to see if they might have a service for their respective churches at the pond.

Rog Sunquist's Methodists gathered on the banks of the pond on the first of June. Methodists seldom baptize adults, but there were more than a dozen who wanted to be "re-baptized" in the pond. There is something about deciding oneself about being baptized that seems important. They wanted their commitment to Christ to be public and self-determined. Now, of course, you can do that in any number of ways - you can TELL of your faith to others - you can BE Christian in all you do and say - you can reach out and DO things in the name of Christ to others... But these twelve chose public baptism...

Again it was a lovely ceremony. It was one no one attending will ever forget. Pastor Sunquist even baptized three babies in the pond that day (not by immersion, of course), and it was just thrilling to experience.... emotional and awesome and wonderful...

On August 28 last year, the Pentecostals had a baptismal service scheduled. Jake Charis had 7 people tell him they wanted to be baptized by water and by the Holy Ghost. There was Pete Johnson and Emily Tracey and Joe Heath and Stacey Jay and Malcolm Price. The sixth one to be baptized was Mike Sunday... This one was going to be a very special one because Mike had lived quite a checkered life and only become a Christian the year before. And Mike was handicapped. He had been in a terrible automobile accident a few years ago on his way home from a bar and smashed up his body something awful. He broke ribs and punctured a lung - he fractured his skull and was in a coma for two weeks - he broke his left leg in three places and would always need crutches to walk - the leg giving him constant pain... Seeing this young man turn his life over to Jesus and to now have him be baptized was a point of great pride in the congregation (not pride in any sinful sort of way - they were just touched and moved by the transformation of his life and were so proud of him for following Jesus).

    Barney had been having trouble with his pond fountain pump since mid-July. For some reason it wouldn't spout the water as it should. It was steadily losing power. No longer would it shoot a spout fifteen feet into the air as it was designed to do. The spout got shorter and shorter until, the week before the baptismal service, it was spouting only a few inches and starting and stopping altogether more or less at will. He had tried everything he knew how to do. He'd have to do more research to figure out what was wrong with the thing.

    In the meantime, he was a bit concerned about algae growth without the water being properly aerated. He certainly didn't want anyone getting sick following being in his water. Jake told him not to worry about it. He would instruct those being baptized to hold their noses and keep their mouths closed and to shower when they got home. Everyone would be just fine. Barney wasn't so sure but he hoped so. He had warned them...

    August 28 was one of the most beautiful days of the summer. The sun was shining, big cumulous clouds floated lazily across the sky, the temperature was about 74 degrees. It was the perfect day in every way so Jake's people turned out in large numbers. There must have been a hundred and fifty there. They brought their lawn chairs and blankets to sit on the shore. Some of the ladies brought parasols to keep the sun off. The baptees were dressed in white gowns as they, together, filed into the pond to await their turn. It really was quite picturesque. Beautiful day, beautiful setting, white robes, people singing songs of praise lead by the music director on her guitar...

    Pete Johnson was first. Pastor Jake invited him, by name, to obey Christ. "Peter Johnson, you have come today to be baptized into the family of God. You have come here to tell the whole world that you are a follower of Jesus Christ. Do you, this day renounce your sins? - Do you publicly seek the forgiveness of God and your fellow man? - Do you desire to be cleansed and forgiven and live life as a free man?" Pete quietly says 'yes' to each question.

    Jake holds out his right hand for Pete to take, his other hand holds onto Jake's arm. Jake puts his left hand on the back of Pete's neck and tilts him backward.

    "Peter Allen Johnson, I baptize you now in the name of the Father and the Son and the Holy Ghost." And Pete comes up with the most glorious smile on his face you could ever imagine. He had said "YES" to Jesus in the most blatant way possible. He had been obedient to the command...

Then it was Emily's turn. Jake used slightly different words with her, but essentially the same... The same with Joe and with Stacey and with Malcolm. And always the same results. Their smiles, when they came out of the water, were beatific and all the spectators were so glad they had come to witness this glorious day.

Now it was Mike's turn. He hobbled over to Jake - not easy without his crutches but, of course, you can't use crutches very well in a pond. The next person in line, Carolyn Spencer, helped him. She let him put his arm around her and use her like a crutch... When Jake had him safely, Carolyn stepped back. And Jake began his litany. Mike responded: "Yes I renounce my sins. Yes, I seek the forgiveness of God and of anyone I have harmed or offended. Yes, I desire to be cleansed and live as a free man."

Right in the middle of Mike's affirmations, the old pond pump decided to kick on. It was weaker now, however, and there was not even a two inch spout of water shooting up. It was all under the surface. It gurgled and tried its best, but nothing much happened other than stirring up the otherwise glass-smooth surface of the pond. And just as Jake tipped Mike back into the water the first ripples of the surface disturbance got to them and Mike went under. Two seconds later he was raised back up but the smile on his face was not like the smile on Peter or Emily or Joe or Stacey or Malcolm. His expression was one of utter astonishment. The others had each said the prescribed words when they came out of the water, "Praise be to God." Mike said, instead, "It doesn't hurt! My leg! It doesn't hurt! I've been healed! I've been healed! **I've been healed**!"

Pentecostals are prone to believing that sort of thing. They believe God heals the sick. He heals their sorrows. He heals cancer and diseases and works miracles on a regular basis. Healing is no big deal to Pentccostals. It's standard fare for God. But Mike's leg was broken in three places. He has hobbled on crutches for the past year. He has winced in pain every time they've seen him move. He had applied for and gotten Social Security disability... This is something somehow more physical than cancer or disease or sorrow. Those you can't see. They are microscopic dangers within the body. They are regularly mis-diagnosed. That's how God works. He gives the doctors an "out" - the cancer is gone? "Our tests must have been wrong." The disease is no longer in the body? "Sometimes these things just happen." But broken, mangled limbs? That just doesn't happen – not even in Pentecostal circles.

Yet it just did. No one could deny it. There was Mike. Walking in the muck at the bottom of the pond steadily. Grinning and laughing and splashing and praising God and generally acting like an ecstatic fool.

The rest of the baptisms were a bit anti-climactic except for those being baptized, but it would be a day nobody who was there would ever forget...

But something like a miraculous healing doesn't go unnoticed by anyone in a small community like Plain. Before the next morning everyone in town had heard all about it and Pastor Roy and Pastor Rog and Father Jesús were getting calls. Even Jake was getting calls from some of his congregation who hadn't attended, wanting to know exactly what happened and how and why...

The ministers met on Monday over lunch in a small, out-of-the-way restaurant in Bowling Green - away from Plain. "I can't explain it," said Charis. I didn't pray for Mike's healing. I don't think even Mike prayed for it. His bones were shattered. I don't have any explanation for what happened."

Pastor Roy said, "The pond aeration pump kicked on. It wasn't the Holy Spirit stirring up the water. It was a mechanical failure. I don't think Briggs and Stratton are in the healing business."

"I was really taken off guard, Jake," says Roger. "You should have called us and told us what happened so we could come up with something to tell our people when they called. I felt like a fool not knowing what to tell them."

"There isn't much to tell," says Jake. "A miraculous healing took place out at Hazlet Pond. It was something God wanted to do and He did it. I don't know why. I don't know how. I don't know anything other than something truly astounding happened and that no one can deny that it happened."

"But what do we tell our people when they ask why MIKE was healed and not them or their parent or their child?" says Roy. "Mike isn't any more deserving than some of my people who are hurting - maybe less so. I've been in ministry for 40 years and have never seen anything like this."

"We see healings all the time in our Pentecostal services. Healing isn't all that uncommon. This one, of course, is a lot more verifiable than most. I don't know what you should tell your people. I'm not even sure what to tell mine other than 'Praise the Lord. Halleluiah'"

"We have an annual healing service," says Roy. "It's designed for people who have a problem that we can all join in prayer for. I don't know that anyone is directly healed through it but a lot of people feel the presence of God in their lives as their family and friends gather around them seeking God's grace. THAT'S healing as far as I'm concerned."

"Yeah. We believe in healing too," says Pastor Sunquist. "But come on. Bones being knit back together instantaneously? That's a bit much, don't you think?"

"I've known Mike ever since the accident," says Jake. "I've seen the x-rays. I've sat with him through rehab. I've taken him to check-ups. I've witnessed his constant pain. A lot of us have. He's not faking it. This really happened. He was a broken man and now isn't."

"Has anyone seen him since the service?" Sonquist asks.

"I saw him myself," says Jake. "I went to see him this morning and he was walking around as well as you or me. He's got an appointment with the orthopedic doc in a couple of days. That may shed some light on some of this."

Father Jesús had been uncharacteristically quiet. He had never met Mike - never even heard of him except for the newspaper report of the accident last year. He didn't go for this "pond baptism" thing people were doing these days. A holy sacrament shouldn't be taken in such a cavalier manner. Like the others he was skeptical, but he said, "We are discounting the most powerful force of the universe, gentlemen. We don't understand it. It makes us a bit nervous. Even the four of us have a hard time with it. Faith. You see, it didn't matter what was prayed for. It didn't matter what the cause of the ripples in the water. It didn't matter who was deserving or not.

Mike, as an unblemished new Christian, had no doubt heard about the story of Jesus at the pool of Bethsaida. He had heard that the pool had miraculous healing properties when the water was disturbed. He had just confessed his sins, sought forgiveness, committed himself to a righteous life - as pure in that instant than a person can ever in this life be - and he saw the disturbed water with no earthly explanation that he knew of. His faith, fresh and new and untarnished by skepticism, simply believed and he was healed because of that faith. You and I know it is impossible. We have seen good people suffer and die - faithful people. We have become people who proclaim limited faith in an unlimited God while calling what we proclaim unlimited. Roy - Rog - Jake - it really is. Faith can move REAL mountains. Faith can quell REAL storms. Faith can do far more than we can fathom... and we all know it. That's who we are. The waters of baptism contain a power that is beyond our small minds to comprehend. Those waters, when stirred up, have healing and power and hope and grace and ...God."

I don't think any of the Plain ministers have ever been the same since the Hazlet Pond healing. Their preaching has been filled with more wonder - with more expectation - with more doubt questioning - and with a lot more belief in the God who is able to stir the waters and make miracles.

The people of Plain have been changed too, I suppose. But we tend to move pretty quickly on to the next thing on our agenda. Miracles, after all, happen all the time.

A PLAIN STORY: PROM '07
Matthew 7: 24-29.

Many of us grew up in small towns like Plain. Some of us in towns just slightly larger - few in towns smaller. And we know that when something happens in a community that size it is almost instantly known by everyone. But more significantly, when something happens in a small town, it AFFECTS everyone. It's not that everyone is related to everyone else (although many are related to one another). And it's not that everyone even KNOWS everyone else. But somehow the sense of community is far more profound than we suburbanites can comprehend. It has to do with what sociologists call "Degrees of Separation." When something happens in Livonia we probably know someone who knows someone who knows someone who was involved. In a small town everyone knows someone who knows someone who was involved.

If there is an armed robbery in Livonia - or corruption in City Hall or the Police Department - or even a murder - we all know about it and we have a feeling of insecurity or betrayal or fear because it affects all of us in an indirect way. But in little towns like Plain, Ohio, those kinds of things feel as though they happened to you or to one of your loved ones. In a small town you never grieve alone. You never rejoice alone. You never experience life in isolation... You share a common history and a common present and a common future. What happens to your neighbor really does happen to you. And so Prom Night of 2007 was a night that made its mark on the people of Plain - a night none of the fine citizens would ever forget.

Jacob Swecker was a typical High School student. And by typical I mean totally ordinary in every way. He stood 5' 9" and 120 pounds - thin, he had sandy brown hair that was a bit unmanageable. He had a few freckles, but these were not too noticeable because he had a case of teenage acne - not too severe - just enough to notice. Academically he was not a great student - but not terrible either. He didn't study much and got by with "B's" and "C's" and he was satisfied with that. His parents always thought he could do better if he tried, but they hadn't a clue how to make him try or care. He didn't worry about grades. He was doing just fine. He would graduate and go on to college maybe or join the Navy. He'd figure it out as he went along... He didn't seem to care much what others thought and, really, no one knew much of what he was thinking...

Jacob was not overly athletic. He wanted to be though. He tried out for the basketball team but he didn't make the cut. Same with football. He wasn't tall enough for basketball and not dense enough or fast enough for football. A lot of teens fall into those categories and don't make the teams, but Jacob felt especially bad about not making it. After all, Plain High was not like our Stephenson or Franklin or Churchill where the choice of players is from hundreds and MOST kids don't make the teams. Plain, even though a consolidated school, was still pretty small. Not making the team there probably meant you really weren't very good at all. And that, thought Jacob, stunk.

Jacob did make the track team. After all, anyone can run. But he wasn't fast and throughout his High School career he never did come in first at any track meet. Once he was in second place, but usually further back in the pack. Maybe he should have/could have been faster, but even he knew he didn't have that fire in his gut that makes an athlete a winner. He didn't LIKE to lose, but he was never devastated by it like some of his teammates.

Jacob was well-liked though. And, perhaps, that is where he was not entirely "ordinary." He had an easy smile and he could call just about everyone in the hallways at school by name. He could laugh and joke and punch and tease with the best of them. He didn't have a "best" friend, but that's how guys are. He wasn't a loner exactly. Quite the opposite. He was friends with everyone. Except girls. He liked to look but he almost never spoke to one. Whenever a girl was around his mind simply went blank. He couldn't think of a thing to say no matter how hard he tried and the harder he tried the more stupid he felt and the more locked up his mind became. Obviously he never dated. WAY too shy for that. He had a younger sister and he could talk to her - he could argue and poke and make her life as miserable as she made his. But teen girls? - No way. They seemed to be made of something entirely different than his little sister.

Jacob's father worked for the township. He was in charge of cemetery maintenance. He worked a hard physical kind of job and came home exhausted every day. His mother was a nurse. She, too, worked long hours and would come home tired. But somehow they managed to recoup for weekends and almost always the family would take off for somewhere - usually a lake over in Angola, Indiana. They had a boat docked there so they would go for the weekend and spend a glorious two days swimming and fishing and skiing and getting a sunburn. In the winter, they mounted up on their two snowmobiles and headed out across the Plains of Plain whooping and hollering and having a great time, coming home at dusk for hot chocolate and family time watching a video...

    Church never crossed the Swecker family's minds. Joe and Chloe, Jacob's parents, had gone to church as children but it was so boring that they stopped as soon as their parents allowed it. They had never taken Jacob or Susan to church in Plain or anywhere else. Like so many of their classmates, Jacob and Susan had never actually even been inside of a church. They hadn't been invited to family weddings because they were kids. None of their close relatives had died so there were no funerals to attend. They believed in God in some vague, ethereal, self-defined way, but formal religion was as unknown to them as the Great Wall of China is to you or me - we know it exists but it in no way impacts our lives...

    Amanda Brown's High School experience was different than Jacob's. She was moderately pretty. She was a good student - not straight "A's" but "A's" and "B's" pretty consistently. She was likeable - approachable - kind - had a great personality. In terms of popularity, she was on the "B" team - not likely to ever be the Prom Queen but probably would easily have a date for the Prom. She was known to be "religious." Most didn't know exactly what that meant. She was certainly not a Bible thumper. She never tried to convert anyone. She didn't talk about Jesus all the time. It was simply known that she attended that little Congregational church just out of town - never missed. She was there every Sunday and even on Sunday evenings for youth group. And it was known that she was a genuinely good person. Everyone liked Amanda - the popular kids liked her, the nerds liked her, the jocks liked her, the retards liked her, the cheer-leaders liked her. There was just nothing about Amanda not to like...

    You've all seen the title of today's story - "Prom 07." You don't have to be a seer to know where I'm going. Somehow, in their senior year, Jacob and Amanda end up going to the Prom together. We don't have time this morning to get into all the details, but suffice it to say that it all had to do with a lot of text messages going around among Amanda's friends and Jacob's friends and finally between Amanda and Jacob themselves and by the time they actually got around to talking face-to-face, Jacob found that he could, in fact, talk to Amanda and even enjoy doing so. He was pretty sure this was what love was - being able to talk to a girl - an attractive, wonderful girl - and taking her to the Prom. He had never been happier in his life.

    The Prom was the most magical event Jacob had ever been to. The crepe paper streamers and the turning mirror ball and the beautifully decorated tables and the soft light and the band playing and everyone dressed up looking like well-to-do adults. Sitting down to a meal served from the left with everyone using manners they had seen in movies... The dancing - the sheer joy of the event was an emotional overload. And to be with Amanda and to look into her eyes and see that she really liked him. And she was gorgeous that night - breathtakingly beautiful. And it was obvious that she was enjoying the event every bit as much as he was. Jacob was the happiest young man on the face of the earth.

But all things come to an end and when the MC announced the last dance they danced and Jacob was sure he was in love... They stayed as long as they could, but eventually the magic ends and its time to go home... Jacob drove Amanda around Bowling Green for a while, just cruising, not wanting the evening to end, and then they finally headed out Poe Road toward Plain. Teen passions run hot - especially on Prom night - and Jacob asked if they might pull in somewhere and enjoy the evening and talk. Amanda said that would be nice.

They happened to be passing the Congregational church just then so Jacob pulled into the parking lot and turned off the engine and they talked for a bit. Then they kissed - and kissed some more - and then they kissed a lot. Then Jacob, feeling that he was getting certain signals, tried to do more than kiss and Amanda stopped him.

"I can't, Jacob. I never have and I'm not going to until I get married."

"That's a bit old fashioned, don't you think?"

"I am a Christian and it would be wrong. God would not be pleased."

"God? You've got to be kidding! You think God cares about you and what you do?"

"I do. God knows and God cares. I love God and wouldn't do anything to offend Him."

"Amanda - we're in Nowheresville, Ohio. You and I are less than specks on a speck in the universe. Do you really think God cares for YOU? That's absurd."

"No. It's not. I have experienced the love of God. I know His forgiveness and his compassion and that He watches over me in everything I do."

"That's a bit creepy, don't you think? I've got to say, I don't WANT someone knowing everything I do - watching and monitoring my every move. It sounds like your God is some kind of peeping-Tom pervert..."

Amanda didn't know what to say to that. She knew it wasn't like that at all, but she was flummoxed. "Take me home, Jacob. It's getting very late. I've got church tomorrow..."

So Jacob took Amanda home. They kissed good-night just as Amanda's father turned on the porch light and Prom Night was, sadly, over. Or so everyone thought.

At 7:00 the next morning, Amanda's mother came into her room and woke her. "Amanda.... Amanda wake up. Put on your robe and come into the kitchen. Right away." Something obviously being wrong, Amanda got up immediately, grabbed her robe and headed downstairs. There in the kitchen was Jerry McKay, one of the Plain police officers. Jerry said, "Amanda, I'm afraid something terrible has happened. Jacob Swecker's parents called the police station at about 4:00 this morning saying their son hadn't come home last night. He had a curfew of 2AM because of Prom. I'm so sorry to tell you but a little while ago we found his body at the base of the water tower. I understand that you were his date last night. Had he been drinking?"

Amanda felt faint. She pulled out a chair and sat down, in utter shock. Tears sprang to her eyes. "No. Nothing. He brought me home at about 1:00. No. We had nothing at all to drink."

"Did he seem upset about anything? Did he indicate that he was depressed or distraught?"

Amanda's mother said, "What do you mean? Do you think it wasn't an accident? Do you think he might have jumped?"

"Ma'am, we don't know. We know that a lot of the high school boys go up there to smoke and sometimes drink. We try to chase them off, but it's pretty attractive. And that catwalk that is around it makes it pretty safe. It would be somewhat difficult to fall unless you were quite drunk."

And thus the event that changed Plain forever.

Jacob's parents were beside themselves with grief. They steadfastly denied that Jacob could have jumped. "He was such a good boy," they said. He wasn't depressed that they knew of.

"He was about to graduate. Everyone liked him. He was about to begin the rest of his life. Why would he? Why should he? He didn't. He fell. We know he fell... "

And they kept telling themselves that until they almost believed it. They didn't know why. They had no idea why. He was so full of life and possibilities... But deep down, inside, they knew. They just didn't know why...

Pastor Roy knew Jacob's father from doing funerals at the cemetery. He called the deacons and asked them to conduct the service without him that morning. He had to go to be with the Sweckers. It wasn't easy. Even though he was a seasoned minister, one never knows what to say at times like that. He said a prayer with Joe and put his arm around his shoulder. Joe was so profoundly sad that he couldn't speak. Pastor Roy stayed with him for a few minutes and then silently went to find Chloe (for some reason they were not even in the same room of the house - as though they needed to each have their space to sort out their feelings and grieve). He did the same with her. He put his arm around her and, after a time of silence, asked if he might have a prayer...

"Why?! Are you going to ask God to bring back my boy? Didn't God just kill him? What kind of a capricious God can take a young man's life like that? He could have saved him. He could have prevented him from falling from that blasted water tower. He could have brought him home to his family... I can't stand your God! I can't stand you. Get out of my house!..."

That evening there was a prayer service at Plain Congregational. There hadn't been so many people in the little church for decades. Pastor Roy spoke. He talked about guilt and love, compassion and peace, and healing and God's grace.... About guilt he confessed his own feelings - that he should have somehow reached out to the Swecker family and to Jacob specifically. He acknowledged that it was an insidious kind of guilt - a guilt that everyone in Plain would have in the days to come. "If only I had done such and such... maybe this wouldn't have happened."

"That's not how life works," Pastor Roy said. "We do our best and we trust God. The guilt we all will feel is the commonality that connects the human family. We feel that if it happened to someone we know, it could happen to us and that makes us want to DO something... What we need to do is to trust God and entrust our loved ones into His care... and our own lives into His will. We cannot control what happens in life. We are responsible only for what WE do... Our task is simply to love one another..."

He talked about compassion and peace and suggested that we, as a community, surround the Swecker family with love. "We cannot know what they are going through unless we have gone through it. But we, as humans, can care and we can share the suffering and ease the pain. We can be Christ to the Swecker family - Joe and Chloe and young Sarah. We can pray for them and write notes and call and, if you know them, visit. Talk about Jacob and share a tear..."

Plain ceased to be a plain little town in the spring of 2007. It became a community where love came alive. The Swecker family was so overwhelmed with the caring of so many people that they actually began taking Sarah to the Congregational church - those people had reached out in so many ways. They didn't start immediately, but in the fall. Sarah liked it. She couldn't understand why her parents had always told her church was boring. The other kids - the great adults - the classes and fun times - church was great, she thought. Later that year she gave her life to Jesus.

Obviously the Sweckers were never the same again. Joe stopped making jokes so easily around the graves he and his team were digging. They understood.

Chloe's heart was always compassionate, but the extra care she now gave - especially to the families of terminal patients that she nursed at the hospital was noticed by everyone.

Amanda went away to college in the fall, a little less naive about life but even more committed to living the life God wants her to. Knowing what community can be like after witnessing what started that night after Prom in her little country church.

KRISTOFF YERUSHALIIM
Matthew 4: 1-11

"Did you hear about the new guy?" That's Campbell St. James down at Dina's Diner. ...Talking to a cadre of 5 friends who meet there every morning at 8:00 for coffee and a sweet roll. Jesse Johnson, Michael Tracy, Nat Story and Tony Snavely are the others. Every small town has its town gossips. Sometimes they are women. Sometimes they are men. But every community has them. In Telhum this little group of five is the designated peddler of town rumor and news, mixed together in a unique brew of fact and fiction. Nothing in town goes on without a thorough airing by what is affectionately called "the Dina's Club," but never to their faces.

"You mean that fellow who bought Rafe's woodworking shop?" says Jesse. " I don't know what the fool wants that for. Rafe tried to make a go of it for years and never made a dime. Nobody out here wants that fancy-Dan handmade furniture. You go down to Walmart and you can pick up something ever' bit as good at a quarter the price. That's what I say. Mark my words - that guy'll be gone in six months. Besides, he's some kind of foreigner or something, ain't he?"

"Worse," says Nat. "He's a foreigner AND a city guy. I hear he moved up here from down near Detroit - town called Inkster. Never been there, but I've heard stories. It's a place you don't want to live if you want to stay healthy. Don't know what brought him up here. Telhum ain't for him, that's for sure. I sure hope he doesn't bring any of his homies to town and start trouble."

"I don't even like the way he *looks*," says Campbell. "Swarthy little guy. What do you think - he even 5' 6"? And I've always hated tattoos. Did you see that one on his bicep? The holy virgin! Sacrilegious, I say. Well, at least he ain't one of those Arabs."

Michael pipes in, "Six months? Heck, he won't last one. He's got to pull all those permits over at city hall. He'll need a business license, a DBA, a building permit, inspections.... He hasn't met Stan yet. He's no lover of newbies - unless they've got some scratch."

All five laugh at Michael's observation. It's true. County supervisor Stan Quin is known for being pretty tough. He's been around for nearly forever and he's a man you just don't cross. And it's suspected (although never proven) that he is a bit crooked - maybe a lot crooked. Rumor has it that, to get anything at all out of him, you have to grease his palm pretty well - not that anyone has ever reported anything illegal or threatening. It's just something everyone seems to know without saying out loud.

Kristoff Yerushaliim did, in fact, come from Inkster - born and raised there. He might even agree - living there isn't always so good for your health. That's one reason he left and decided to take up residence in this small town in the thumb area of Michigan. He wanted a better life - less hustle and bustle - less crime - better air - more opportunities to build relationships and to belong. And, living in a town on the banks of beautiful Lake Huron was about as good as it gets.

The fact of the matter is that he rather LIKED living in Inkster - the mixture of poverty and solid middle-class values - a city desperately trying to make it in a complex and difficult world. But he also longed to be nearer nature - to build relationships with solid, stable people. He wanted to be able to look up at night and actually SEE the millions of stars God put up there - to walk along the beach on a sunny day - to sit out on a boulder on the bay and watch the world go by. And besides, Kristoff, by trade, is a master furniture maker and there was a fully equipped shop for sale at a good price. He is nothing if not practical.

Kristoff (lets call him 'Kris' - he far prefers that to his given name) - Kris is a second generation American. His parents were both born in Greece. They immigrated here in search of a better life. A year after they arrived Kris was born and, a couple years later his brother, Jim. Life worked out for Kris, but Jim got involved with the wrong crowd and left home when he was sixteen and broke off all communication with the family. Kris is one of his "friends" on Facebook, but doesn't know anything about where he is nor his life - just that he's still alive out there somewhere, into who-knows-what. Kris's parents found life in America almost as hard as it was in Greece. His father struggled to find work and keep food on the table all his life. He had no skills. He spoke broken English.

Society isn't kind to people like him...

Both of his parents are gone now. This world was just too difficult for them. It beat them down until their health failed and they passed, one one year, the other the next... Kris misses them. But their being gone gave him permission to move on with his life - to begin again - in Telhum.

You can see why Kris wanted to start over - to have a bit more open space - away from the troubles of the city - away from memories of tough times... He suspected that no matter how tough life in Telhum might be, neighbors would stand by you, help you out - be encouraging - and no one slept in the gutter in Telhum no matter how down and out they might be. If there was poverty, it was a better kind of poverty than in metro Detroit...

He was right, to an extent. But those great small town benefits don't always apply to newcomers. They have to fight hard for acceptance - for approval - for membership into the community. Sometimes that takes years - sometimes generations - sometimes it simply never happens at all.

Kris moved in about a month ago. It felt right - good. He was already starting to feel like a new man. The beauty of this place!! Really something. And the people he had met so far had been very nice. Everyone wanted to know about his nationality - such an unusual family name. Everyone has a national heritage, of course, but most Telhumites didn't have one just one generation old. Friendly, gracious people. He liked them.

His first Monday in town he decide it was time to get down to business. He had freshly painted his sign and hung it out. He had customized the shop to make it just the way he wanted it for maximum efficiency. He had dusted the cobwebs and cleaned the windows. He was ready to get started on his new life. All he had to do was get the proper paperwork. So off to the county courthouse he went.

Kris got there just after noon. As he was going up the steps of the ancient brick building he was saying to himself what a beautiful day it was. He was just... happy. He looked on the office roster sign and found the office to which he needed to go and headed down the hall. Then he ran into Stan Quin. Literally. They were each walking down hallways that were perpendicular to one another and they got to the corner at exactly the same time and they collided. Stan was carrying an armful of file folders and when the collision occurred they went flying everywhere. Stan began immediately to curse and swear at Kris while Kris apologized profusely and stooped to help pick up the spilled papers. Stan was still furious as he grabbed the papers out of Chris' hands. "Idiot! You don't know which folders these go in. Just give them to me and let me sort the whole mess out! Get out of my way!" Kris continued to apologize and sheepishly arose and continued down the hall.

When he got to the office he told the receptionist he'd like to see Mr. Quin for permit papers. She said he had just stepped out but would be back soon. Kris could wait "right over there." So Kris took a chair and picked up a magazine to wait.

Fifteen minutes later the man he had collided with came in and walked to an office and went inside. Kris felt his stomach sink. That MUST be Mr. Quin. And, of course, it was. "You may go in now," says the receptionist. "Great," thought Chris. "This is going to be interesting."

"Hello, sir. My name is Kristoff Yerushaliim. I'm new in town and starting up a business and need the permit packet."

"So you are. And a bit of a klutz, aren't you? You could have killed me."

"I WAS very excited to get here and get the paperwork filled out - again, sorry about the mess I made and so glad you weren't hurt - I was just excited to start my new life in Telhum and took that blind corner too short."

"New life! I've heard about you. New guy. City slicker. You think you can just march in here and own the place. But let me tell you something right now. *I* own this town. *I* own this whole county. And you ain't gett'in it unless I give it to you. And I'm not gonna."

"Oh, I don't think I own anything, sir. But, to be honest, neither do you. In fact, if you remember the philosophy of some of the native Americans who lived here long before us, they taught and believed that none of us own anything. We are just the custodians while we live on earth. They were right. God owns it - every blade of grass and every stone along the shoreline - every flower in the meadow and every cloud in the sky. It's all His."

"Don't preach to me, young man. You don't seem to know who you're dealing with. I have the power to issue these permits or not to. I have the power to make you starve to death while waiting for them if I want to - to go broke waiting for my approval if I want to."

"Mr. Quin. I must humbly disagree with you. You don't have that power. Have you looked out your window lately. There is a vast Great Lake out there. There is enough fish in that sea to feed this entire village for as long as it exists - a massive abundance... God put those fish there. God makes the crops grow or not. God gives us health or allows our diseases. In the greater scheme of things, you - or I - or any of us - have no power at all. Whatever semblance of authority we may have comes from God - always."

"Why, you impudent little twerp - I OWN this community I tell you. I can pass it to my heirs. I can withhold it from others. I can shut this town down - this whole county - with the stroke of a pen!"

"You may be able to do that (at least in theory) but you won't. There is too much self-preservation inside to allow you to overstep your authority and that would be WAY overstepping. People may let you get away with some pretty outrageous power things, but they won't let you destroy them. Neither will I."

"Let's make a deal, Mr. Yerushaliim. I'll let you live and prosper in our fair community for a price. The permits you need have a fee of $358. I'll push them through for you - you'll have them by this afternoon, expidited - for a flat $2000. Take it or leave it."

"That's pretty tempting, but I'll leave it, thank you. Let me write you a check for the $358 - make it out to Helmer County? I'll fill out the forms and leave them with your secretary." And Kris stood and walked out of Mr. Quin's office, filled out the forms, paid the fee, and walked home. Mr. Quin was furious but the permits arrived in his mailbox three days later and the very next day he flipped over his window sign to now say "OPEN."

Telhum is a small town and news travels at the speed of sound. Nobody knew exactly what happened in Mr. Quin's office, but they knew there must have been something quite extraordinary. No one had ever had their permits approved in three days. The new guy must really know how to play the system... or he had paid through the nose.

Everyone in town was curious about Mr. Kristoff Yerushaliim. Everyone had seen him around town but few had actually had a conversation with him. It's a bit awkward just walking into a furniture store if you aren't looking for something... Tony Snavely was the first to get some real information. Tony is the mail carrier for Telhum so has the opportunity to stop at every house in town nearly every day. And, since Telhum is a small town, the route doesn't really take all day so Tony has never had any problem stopping and chatting with the neighbors if they happen to be out (most avoid being out when Tony comes around because he is in that infamous "Dina's Club" gossip group down at the cafe and they'd rather not be the topic of idle talk).

Kris didn't know about not getting caught up with Tony or telling him things unless you wanted the whole town to know. So when Tony came by to deliver his mail, Kris happened to be out on his front porch. "Hey there, Mr. Yerushaliim - how you doing today?"

"I'm doing fine. Please - call me Kris. How are you today Mr. Snavely?"

Tony was impressed. This guy knew his name without having ever been introduced. "You can call me Tony. I see you've hung out the "OPEN" sign. Congratulations for getting all that paperwork through the system so quickly. Usually old man Quin drags his feet with newcomers."

"Yes. The shop is open. Haven't had any customers yet. Want to come in and be my first browser?"

"I'd love to!" As they went inside, Tony said, "You've really fixed the place up nice. Old Rafe kind of let it run down - not much business around here. How do you think you'll do - er, I mean 'what are you going to do that Rafe didn't to make a go of the place?'"

"Well, first of all, the store section here is mostly just a showroom. I'm not expecting the bulk of my business being from Telhum or even from up here in the thumb. I'm hoping to spread the word of what I do far and wide. I think people everywhere want quality workmanship if they can find it. I'll do mail order and internet sales. I'm hoping eventually to be busy enough to have word-of-mouth be my advertising... Let me take you back into the workshop. I think it's come out just about perfect."

And it was. It smelled of sawdust and turpentine and mineral oils. "A good smell," thought Tony. The hand tools were all mounted on pegboards, the screwdrivers and chisels lined up on a rack with holes. The power tools neat and clean - obviously much used but clearly well cared for. Tom noted the air filtration system and loved the whole atmosphere of the place. He said to Chris, "I'd love to work in a place like this - it is so cool - except I don't know the first thing about woodworking."

"Come by some time. I'll show you. I'll work and you watch then I'll let you do some things and I'll watch and teach you. If you think you'd like woodworking chances are you really will when you get into it. Hey, it's a bit early, but do you want to stay for lunch? I'm not having much - just some pita and humus and a glass of wine. But if that's OK with you, you're certainly welcome."

So Tony had lunch with Chris, pumping him for information and enjoying their time together... and couldn't wait to get back to Dina's (the "club" was scheduled to have lunch today). Tony was a bit late getting there, but that was exactly as he wanted it. When he arrived, they were talking about the town librarian, Millie, who had recently undergone a bit of a transformation. She went from frumpy librarian to a real looker. No doubt there was a new man in her life. They were all making guesses as to who it might be. "Tony - you old scoundrel - you're late. We've already ordered. Where've you been?"

"Unlike the rest of you jokers, I've got a job. I work for Uncle Sam. Besides, I've already eaten. I ate over at the furniture store."

"THE FURNITURE STORE! NO KIDDING! You ate with the new guy? Give us the scoop."

"Well, I've got to say, I really like him. He isn't like everyone else in town - he's clearly not from here - but there is just something about him that is appealing. He's not at all like I thought he'd be. He invited me in, he showed me around, he fed me (not much but it filled me up - you guys go ahead and start eating). He served some kind of flat bread and hummus and poured a glass of great tasting wine - I need to ask him what kind it was. But just as I was about to reach for the bread he looked up at the ceiling and started to pray out loud (I've never seen anyone look up instead of down to pray - very strange, but that's just what he did). Then he said a very bizarre prayer. Something like, "Thank you dad for all you do. Thank you Holy Father for this bread and this wine that nourishes and fills our body and soul. Thank you for Tony and all who know him and all whom he knows." That's it. He doesn't say "amen" or anything. He just smiles and pours the wine. We talked a bit about Telhum and what it was like growing up here and how the town has changed. He told me about why he came here - "to find peace and to make peace" he said. But he said it so mater-of-factly that I didn't feel I could ask him what he meant... Just before I left he said something else that confused me. He said, 'I'd love to meet the "Dina's Club" members. I've heard about your little group of friends. Why don't you tell them to stop by. I'd like to get to know them.'

What's the "Dina's Club?" Jesse asks.

"It's us, you old coot," says Campbell. "That's what the whole town calls us. Where've you been?"

"Why does he want to meet us?" Michael asks.

"I think he just does," says Tony. "We need to take him up on it. You guys need to meet Chris. He's great. Tomorrow afternoon - lets go over while the invitation is still good."

The next day they did go to the Yerushaliim furniture shop. They met Kris and, like Tom, they liked him more than they thought they would. They agreed, he isn't like everyone else in Telhum. He has a sense of inner peace that none of them could exactly describe. Like with Tony, he invited them to sit with him and have a glass of wine and a bit of bread with some dip. Again he said that strange prayer in his unique way - looking up. He called God "dad" just like Tony said. Who does that!? But he didn't seem to be putting on aires. It just seemed to be what he was used to.

Before they left, Kris asked them to do him a huge favor - to help him out. Before he even told them what it was he wanted them to do they told him they'd do anything he wanted. None of them hesitated. Of course they would. He had mesmerized them - he had won their trust - amazingly, in minutes! Later they would reflect back on that simple request and realize that their consenting to it was the defining moment of their lives. None of them would ever be the same again. Simply saying "yes" to Kris - not even knowing exactly what they were saying "yes" to made all the difference.

THE GRAND OPENING
Matthew 14: 14-21

    Kris Yerushaliim opened his furniture shop for business last week. Do you know how many customers he had in his first seven days? None. It's not that the people of Telhum didn't want to see the new place and to meet Chris, they most certainly did. He was the new guy in town EVERYONE wanted to meet him. They had heard all about him from the "Dina's Club" - the biggest gossips in town. He had worked some kind of magic with ol' Stan Quin in the county permit office. He was all licensed and ready to go in record time. Supposedly he had fixed up Rafe Tracy's old place real nice. They'd LOVE to see it. But the people of Telhum are not the sort who would go snooping around just to snoop. If they weren't actually looking for a piece of furniture, they figured they had no business going into the new furniture shop. And they were all pretty committed to NOT buying any custom made furniture. The Walmart, over in Bad Axe had furniture good enough for their needs. The savings were worth the 15 mile drive. So no one from Telhum jingled the bell at the top of Chris' door for a week.

    Not to say that he didn't have visitors. Tony Snavely, the mail carrier, had had lunch with him one day and the very next day all five of the Dina's Club members showed up - at Kris' open invitation to Tony and Tony's insistence they go soon before the invitation was forgotten. They got along famously. Like with Tony, Kris offered them pita bread and hummus and wine for lunch. "That must be all the guy ever eats," thought Tom. The guys discovered that Kris had a quick wit and a great sense of humor. They laughed and joked around (a bit of the camaraderie may have been the most excellent red wine he had served them) and, as strange as it may seem, after about an hour they all felt they had known Kris all their lives. He just... "fit" and this new guy could easily be a part of their close-knit group. Tony was glad Kris had invited them and that he had gotten them together.

    Just before they were about to head out, Kris, who obviously felt the same closeness to them as they did to him, got serious and said, "Guys, I need a favor from you, if you would. I need your help in a big way."

    "Hey! Anything, big guy." says Campbell. "Whatever you need, if we can do it, we will."

"Campbell - watch what you're promising. Kris may ask us to rob a bank or something. We don't know him that well yet," chides Jesse.

Michael chimes in, "I don't think he's that kind of guy. You saw how he prays didn't you? He looks up as though he and God are pretty tight. I don't think robbing a bank is in his nature."

"No. No. No. Really," says Khris, "what I want you to do isn't anything illegal or immoral or even too physically taxing. What I need is a little help publicizing this place - you know, a little advertising. I seem to be invisible around here so I thought we should have a grand opening so people can come in and see what I've got and what I do - maybe buy a few pieces so I can pay the light bill. It's no good having a store that nobody comes to, you know. I'll go broke in no time. I've got my website all set up but it will take a while for people to find it."

"So what can we do?" asks Michael. "None of us are really much into advertising or even business. I was an accountant. Nat here was a school teacher. Campbell a fisherman and Tony a mailman. I'm not sure what we can do for you."

"Oh, I'm not asking you to do any advertising like that. I just need some grunt work done. I've printed off about a zillion fliers and I need to distribute them - you know, house to house, post them in businesses around town - maybe over in Bad Axe and other communities in the area. I'd do a mass mailing but I really can't afford it - sorry Tony, I know mail is your thing, but the rates for even bulk mail would kill me."

"I'm not sure what Uncle Sam would say about me walking the route delivering things for anyone but him," says Tony. "But what the heck - I'll do it on my own time - can't deliver your fliers with the mail, though."

"Oh, I wouldn't dream of asking you to do anything unethical, Tom. But you're the one who best knows how to do this kind of thing, so if you could share the technique for efficiency with the others that would be great."

"I'd be glad to. How many fliers do you actually have?"

"I got carried away. The printer had a good price per thousand, but if you bought more the price dropped - and it dropped even more the more you bought. I ended up with ten thousand..."

"TEN THOUSAND! There are only 450 people in town - men, women and children! What were you thinking, Kris! What are we going to do with TEN THOUSAND!?"

"I really don't know. But that's what I've got. I'd rather not have nine thousand sheets of scrap paper, but..."

"**We'll do it!**" Nat says. "I don't know how, but we'll find a place for every one of those fliers, Kris. You just leave it to us. Where are they? Let's each take a couple cartons and head over to my garage and put a strategy together."

So that's what they did. But think about it. If there are only 450 people in town, each person would have to get at least 20 copies to have them all distributed. Campbell and Jesse and Michael and Nat and Tony decided that EVERY house would get one - all 100 homes in Telhum. And then they would get another one the next week just before the open house. There you are - 200 distributed! Only nine thousand eight hundred to go. But these five men were committed to keeping Kris in town and in business. Spreading the word was the only way to do that. They WOULD distribute all ten thousand fliers.

They decided that the only way such a mass distribution would be possible would be to get them to neighboring towns, so they agreed with one another to take their families - wives, children, children's friends and even cousins, if possible - to every town in the area and pass these things out. Campbell went to Bad Axe and Pigeon, Jesse went to Ruth and Snover and Sandusky and Cass City, Michael headed for Caro and Vassar, Nat took the long drive to Bay City and Tony, since he knew best how to do it, took his family for a little delivery outing to Saginaw. House to house, business bulletin board to business bulletin board until, eventually their cartons were empty and they had passed out every one of that massive printing. They were exhausted - and pretty excited that they had done such a mammoth job in such a short time.

For the next two weeks, everywhere you looked in Telhum and in every neighboring town were those fliers. It was a paper blitz. They were on people's refrigerators, on telephone poles, on bulletin boards, on shop counters, on windshields - everywhere you looked you saw one. But no one minded because Kris had done something that seemed almost impossible with his advertising campaign. On every flier, at the bottom, he had written the address of some scripture passage - **on every one of the ten thousand!** And it wasn't always the same verse. In fact, it became a craze around town to try to find someone who had the same verse as you had - and no one knew anyone who had found duplicates! People could be seen carrying their Bibles around, looking up verses on the fliers they encountered to see what the message was. Most knew by heart the message they had received on their own, but were curious to see if the others were as personally meaningful. You see, as improbable - as impossible - as strange as it may seem, everyone's verse said exactly what they needed to hear at that time in their lives... For instance, Betty Snow had Jeremiah 29:11 on her flier. She looked it up. It said, "*For I know the plans I have for you, declares the LORD, plans to prosper you and not to harm you, plans to give you hope and a future.*" Betty had just gotten word that she has cancer. She needed to know God has a plan for her and that she had a future.

Jake Epp got Isaiah 41:10. His read, "*So do not be afraid. I am with you. Do not be terrified. I am your God. I will make you strong and help you. My powerful right hand will take good care of you. I always do what is right.*" Jake had been anxious about his farm. The debts were piling up and it looked bleak. His verse really helped him to get perspective and believe God would give him help.

1 Corinthians 10:13 was on Don Phillips flier. He was contemplating an affair. But his verse said, "*You are tempted in the same way all other human beings are. God is faithful. He will not let you be tempted any more than you can take. But when you are tempted, God will give you a way out so that you can stand up under it.*"

And this went on and on and on. Becky Brown, a senior at Saginaw Valley got Psalm 32:8 - "*I will guide you and teach you the way you should go. I will give you good advice and watch over you.*" She'd been struggling with what career path to choose. Now she knew what to do - it was so simple - ask God.

Reba Hawn had just lost her husband of 45 years. She got Revelation 21:4 - "*He will wipe away every tear from their eyes, and death shall be no more, neither shall there be mourning, nor crying, nor pain anymore, for the former things have passed away.*" And she was touched and encouraged and the healing started.

I could tell you story after story about how these verses found their mark but that was only the beginning. Somehow those verses touching people drew entire communities together. Often people don't even know their neighbor more than to say "hi" when they are both out, but people wanted to share what their verse said and how pointed it was to their situation and when that happened, people began to realize that their neighbors all struggled through life just like they did - had some of the same issues and frustrations and fears and hopes...

I don't know how he did it. I don't know how anyone could have the stamina or the time or the ability to write on 10,000 fliers. I don't know how the right flier seemed to land in the hands of the person who needed that particular message. But somehow it did and Chris' little ad campaign made more of a stir than anyone could have imagined.

The Dina's Club crew were whipped. They were glad they helped Kris out but they hadn't realized how big a job it would be -

how time consuming and energy sapping and really, really boring. The most excitement any of them had was being chased by a couple of unfriendly dogs who didn't like strangers in their master's space and one man put the fear of God into Jesse when he came to the door with a shotgun, telling them to get off his property. But it was done. They hoped it would bring some people to the shop on June 10, Grand Opening day for the Yerushaliim Furniture Shop, but certainly no guarantee. How effective can that kind of advertising be - a bit low-tech... As they met there at Dina's they were totally oblivious to the buzz they had caused with their distribution of Kris' fliers and his little hand-written scripture references. They had seen the verses, of course, and thought it a gargantuan task that Kris had undertaken to hand write all of them, but they didn't think much of it. But they were listeners and they began to hear little snippets of conversation from other customers at the diner. People were talking about the fliers! "What's the deal?" they all thought. Other than those little verse references all the flier said was: "The Yerushaliim Furniture Store announces it's Grand Opening. Come and browse - look - take a tour of the workshop - enjoy appetizers and cider. 10:00 until 5:00 June 10 - One mile south of Talham, MI on route 53."

"Shhh. Let's hear what these people are saying."

What they picked up was that somehow people were "touched" by the fliers. Somehow their receiving a flier seemed personal. It didn't make any sense but they decided they had better tell Kris. No telling what might happen at the Grand Opening...

"Kris," says Tony," we delivered them all - all ten thousand. But something is going on and we think you had better prepare for a larger crowd than you expect."

"Oh, I've got it covered. I've got five gallon of cider and about a dozen boxes of assorted frozen appetizers from that warehouse store. I think that will be plenty. I borrowed a few tables for serving from the Congregational Church. I'll just set up the tables outside and people can help themselves."

Well, people started arriving at 9:30 - before Kris had even opened the doors. He let them in, of course. It makes no sense to turn people away. That's the whole point of the day. He showed them around the store and took them into the back room where his woodworking shop was. But he still had to finish setting up. The early arrivals offered to help, so the tables were set up and the first round of appetizers and cider was set out in plenty of time. By 10:00 there were fifty people on Kris' front lawn. By 11:00 a hundred and fifty. By noon there were, by Ken's count - no exaggeration - over five hundred people milling around, eating appetizers and drinking cider, taking tours, admiring the merchandise, chatting with Kris. FIVE HUNDRED! There are only 450 people in Talham! People were coming from all over just to see the shop, to meet Kris, to eat his food, and to enjoy the beautiful day. Little kids were running around playing tag. Teens were throwing Frisbees. Families were laying out blankets under the shade trees... And Kris was eating it up. He tried hard to meet every person - to hug or shake hands or to have a brief conversation or to, at least, greet them. He probably didn't get to everyone but it wasn't uncommon to see him mesmerizing a group here or another over there all day long. This was his thing. He didn't belong in the solitary woodworking shop. He ought to be a politician or something. People just loved him - and it was clear that he loved them.

  Jesse and Tony and Michael and Campbell and Nat were continually busy keeping the tables cleaned off and fresh appetizers put out and punch bowls filled and trash collected. Man, could these people eat! It was clear to the Dina's Club that Kris had gotten a lot more than a dozen boxes of appetizers and five gallons of cider. All day long they restocked the tables and brought out more cider and they never ran short - this must have cost a fortun! No wonder Kris couldn't afford to mail the fliers. He spent all his money on food. This shindig would probably cost him more than he'd make in a year. Towards the end of the day it even looked as though he was going to have a ton left over.

  No one was ever certain how many people actually came through that day. Tom said there must have been a total of 5 or 6 thousand. Matt guessed 7 or 8. But crowds coming and going are pretty hard to estimate so who knows. All everyone knew was that this was, probably, the biggest event Telhum had seen in years - maybe ever. No one knew whether the memory of it would last in people's minds or not but Kris and the Dina's Club crew knew they would never forget it.

  And the day did turn things around for Kris. People knew about him now and every day dozens of people from all over the region stopped in at the shop. Some to buy, some to place an order for something custom made, some just to talk to Kris. He always had time for everyone who came in and took his time with them to discuss whatever they needed or wanted - usually about home furnishings, but often about personal matters. Somehow people trusted him and opened up to him in rather frightening ways.

  One of the casualties of Kris' Grand Opening was Dina's Cafe. The five who had made the day a success adopted one of Kris' round tables in his showroom and, from that day on they met there every morning instead of at the diner. Kris always had a pot of coffee brewing and they were most certainly always welcome. Between customers he'd sit with them and during especially busy times, one of more of them would jump in and help with the customers, taking Kris' lead. Sell them something if they were in the market, but just as important, just let people talk and share their lives and love them.

The gossip stopped, of course. Kris didn't even have to do anything to stop it. Somehow they all just knew that talking about people behind their backs would not be something Kris would participate in nor care to have in his house or shop. And because the gossip stopped, their reputations improved and other guys would join them on occasion just to share stories of their lives and their hopes and dreams for the future - to share pictures of their children and wives - to talk sports...

Do you remember from last week that Tony found the idea of woodworking appealing? Kris taught him to use the router a bit and for his first project Tony made a wooden sign for over the round table that everyone sat at. It wasn't really a craftsman quality job, but that didn't matter to anyone. What Tony put on the sign was the words to a song that kept going through his mind every time he sat at the table. The sign said:

Making your way in the world today
Takes everything you got
Taking a break from all your worries
Sure would help a lot
Wouldn't you like to get away?
Sometimes you want to go
Where everybody knows your name,
and they're always glad you came.
You wanna be where you can see
our troubles are all the same
You wanna be where everybody knows
Your name.[1]

And then, as a jibe at Chris, he put a scripture reference as the last line.
He put "Isaiah 40: 29-31." You'll want to look it up to see if it applies to you today.

---

[1] *The theme song from the TV series "Cheers" written by Gary Portnoy and Judy Hart Angelo.*

OUT ON A LIMB
Luke 19: 1-10

Gossip in any small town is a way of life and although the "Dina's Club" took on a new name, "Chris's Round Table" and had given up the gossip trade, gossip in the town didn't end. And whether you are a participant in it or not, you hear things. Wisdom says you need to have the ability to discern what is true and what is false and then to listen to only about half of even what it true and, if you do, you still learn quite a bit about your fellow citizens.

Kris had heard about one particular fellow in town who, it seemed, nobody liked – I mean <u>nobody</u>. Even the children would run around him and taunt him as he walked down the street. *"Hey, old baldy, whatcha doin'? Where you goin'? What's that ugly thing on your neck? Oh – that's your head!" "Hey, shorty, my little sister is taller than you... How come you're so tiny?"* And, while parents would never tolerate their children acting this way to anyone else, they just smiled when they did it to Zachariah Taylor.

Zachariah Taylor had worked for the IRS for years as an auditor. That, of course, is never a popular job to have but he was very good at it and was able to make those he audited sweat as he squeezed every penny out of them that he possibly, legally, could. He had even had a special self-inking rubber stamp made that he relished using while he did audits. He'd be leafing through someone's tax return and he just loved to stamp on as many deductions as he could, "DISALLOWED." In bold red ink, of course. He made life miserable for everyone he worked with.

Zachariah was the consummate IRS agent. He constantly watched for people living a higher standard of living than he thought they should be able to afford and he'd submit their names for an audit. And, since he was local, he was the one always assigned to audit his neighbors. He saw it as nothing more than doing his job. The people of Telhum saw it as an invasion of their privacy and they hated him for it.

Zachariah had started with the IRS as soon as he finished High School. That was pretty unusual. Usually the IRS requires some kind of college education or at least some specialized training to be among their ranks but he was a wizard with numbers and single-minded in whatever he undertook. He started at 18 and had his thirty years in by the time he was 48. He retired with a full pension but way to young to sit in a rocking chair the rest of his life. So he put together some money – a lot of it really - (he had a lot because he had never married nor had any children to support) and so he bought the Telhum Savings Bank – the only bank in town

    The citizens of Telhum had always been afraid of an audit by Zachariah. I mean, really. NO ONE knows for certain that they haven't made errors on their tax returns – some in their own favor and some in the governments (they knew that errors that favored the government would never be pointed out but not so much the other direction). All they knew was that they had been meticulous for years for fear of red flags triggering an audit by Zachariah. Now that he wasn't with the IRS any more didn't really give them much comfort. He could still report them if he so much as suspected. But they were even more afraid of him now, because now he was in a position to see exactly how much every one of them owed on their houses, how many times they had been late, what their equity was, their credit scores… personal things not anyone's business but their own and the bank. Zachariah was privy to all of it. And, because he owned the bank, HE often owned more of their houses than they did.

    When he discovered that a dozen or so Telhum residents were upside down on their mortgages, Zachariah put together a personalized form letter he sent to each of them telling them that, while it is unfortunate that they owe more on their houses than they are worth, it makes no difference concerning their obligation to pay the bank. He outlined what walking away does to your credit history and the dire consequences of foreclosure.

    Since Telhum Savings was the only bank for miles around, HE held the paper on just about everybody's home. Every new mortgage application that came in he poured over for weaknesses and always reject them if he could, but if it seemed that the borrower could make the payments he socked them with the highest interest rate allowed by law and had them sign the papers. He was becoming a very rich man.

    Kris had gotten his mortgage someplace down in the metro area before he moved to the thumb so he had never had any contact with Zachariah. He had only heard of him from various sources. He rather felt sorry for the poor guy. No family. No friends. No apparent enjoyment in life. All he had was his money and his housekeeper, Millie, living in that big house up on the hill with the magnificent view of the bay.

    On Saturday afternoons Kris had started giving woodworking workshops. He was inspired by how much Tony enjoyed it once he had learned a few of the basics. One Saturday he would teach joinery. Another session would be glues. He had one on types of wood for different projects. These workshops had become quite popular – so popular, in fact, that they outgrew his workshop pretty quickly. Each Saturday morning he would drag the needed equipment out under one of his large shade trees and set up shop there. But Chris' classes weren't just about furniture making. They were about that, but he also inserted a fair amount of philosophy and life wisdom in such a warm and wonderful way that people were drawn to his classes. After all, how many people really want to know how to make a chair or ever will? But learning how to cope with life? That struck a chord with just about everyone…

Kris was a master at it. He would take the most common things and draw profound meaning from them. Once an ant had climbed up on his workbench and was carrying away a chunk of sawdust. He said, "Look at that ant. We can learn a lot from this little guy. Ever watch an ant? They may be the most industrious little creatures on God's green earth. They work hard – don't have to be prodded to do so. They build their homes as a team. When some big human comes along and steps on it they attack even though they know it is futile and then they immediately begin building again. We need to be more like that – indestructible – unstoppable – hard workers – play as a team. I think that is what God wants for all of us…" (Proverbs 6:6) Then he picked up his shaping tool and told them, "Do you think the wood suffers when it is cut and shaped the way we want it to be? If it had feelings it probably would hurt quite a lot. Turning into something beautiful or useful is often a painful experience. Some of us have gone through a lot of pain in our lives – lost loved ones, experienced betrayal, setbacks, shattered dreams. When these happen God is shaping you into something you can't imagine – something beautiful and good and useful to His kingdom and to your world. So when bad things happen – when you hurt – when life dumps on you – when you fear – know these can be used by the master craftsman to make you into something beautiful. Endure and you will be astounded at what God makes of you." (Isaiah 64: 8)

Another time he made quite a good observation about language when one of his students hit his thumb with a hammer. He said it is a shame that the words that come out of our mouths are often punctuated with profanity (although the young man who hit is thumb didn't utter any profanity, he just screamed in pain). He said that what comes out of the mouth reveals what is in the heart. He said that the words we use show our intelligence or our ignorance. And if we are ignorant wouldn't it be better to keep our words to ourselves and be thought idea-less than to try to cover our ignorance by vulgarity and shout to everyone that we are, truly ignorant? Good language, he said, is a gift from God. Bad language comes from hell. (James 1:26; 3:5)

This whole little folk-wisdom/woodworking cadre gathered every fair-weather Saturday for about a month and a half before everyone in town knew about it and had been to at least one of Chris' classes. Zachariah, too, had heard about it and was more than a little curious as to what this woodworker's attraction was. But he didn't dare go see. He brought out the worst in the Telhumites. He might hold the papers to their homes but they didn't have to like him or, it seemed, even treat him as a human being.

Yesterday Kris was having a class on staining and finishing so he had a variety of stains spread out on the tables and samples of several varieties of wood so his class could see how different stains look so much different on different kinds of media. He found staining the most satisfying part of woodworking. Stain seemed to bring out the best in the wood and make it come alive. His lesson could have been predicted. It was about the stains we gather in our lives. Not uniform stains like on wood but stains of failure and resentment and sins of various different kinds. He picked up an old piece of barn siding – weathered, beaten up, probably a hundred years old. He said, "Watch what happens when I apply stain to this wood. Before you came I applied a little pre-stain – a coat that prevents the stain from sinking into the wood too much." He applied a rich cherry stain and his students ooh'd and ahh'd. The piece of rough-looking wood was transformed, before their eyes, into something beautiful. With a little sanding and this kind of stain applied, it would make something great. "You see, we are all beaten up and marred. We all have the scars of life etched into our souls. God can make you into something beautiful if you will let him. All you have to do is soak up HIS spirit and let it permeate who you are to the very depths of your being…"

Then there was a commotion at the back of the crowd, "What you doing up there old man? Spying? Leave us alone! Go back to your counting house and count your money you old reprobate!" Everyone turned to see what was going on, of course. It seems that Zachariah had come up to the group after Chris' class started and couldn't hear nor see what was going on. Although he was in his 50's he was a spry little guy so he climbed up the tree to see over the crowd. His plan was to watch and listen and then, when it was all over to wait until everyone left and come down. But someone had spotted him and was making a scene. This was humiliating beyond anything he could imagine

Kris smiled and made his way to a spot just below and in front of Zachariah. Everyone was gathered 'round looking into the tree at the little man. "What are you doing up there Zachariah?" he asked. People were laughing now, saying rather snide things under their breaths to one another. Zachariah got so flustered that he didn't know what to do – so much so that he lost his balance and came crashing down at Chris' feet, falling flat onto his back. The laughter came from the entire 360 degrees around him. His face was red. He was mortified – didn't know what to do. "Zachariah – I don't believe we've ever met," reaching down and giving him a hand up, "I'm Kristoff Yerushaliim. I'd love it if you'd invite me to your house for dinner tonight. We can get acquainted a bit. Call Millie and let her know you'll be having a guest."

Kris' students were shocked. NO ONE treated Zachariah Taylor with anything other than disdain. What was Kris doing, acting like he was a friend and a great guy – inviting himself to the mansion for dinner? Was Kris not what he appeared to be? Was he really just a social climber and would turn out to be a scoundrel like Taylor? He, himself, had once said that we become like the people we associate with… This was not a good sign.

"Class is over for the day. See you all next week!"

"We'll see about that," thought Mel Snyder.

"Doesn't seem likely if he's going to buddy up with that creep," said Karyn Jones to her boyfriend.

"La-de-da! Fancy dinner for Kris tonight!" said Louie See. And the crowd dispersed, leaving Kris and Zachariah there alone. "Make the call. I'll clean up here and be along around 5:00. See you then."

Millie was nonplused. She had worked for Zachary Taylor for over twenty five years and he had NEVER had a guest other than his mother and sister years ago before they died. Did she still have the silver polish around here somewhere? Should she get flowers? Should she use the Royal Dalton or the Lenox china? What kind of music should she put on? 5:00!? That's three hours. This will be impossible!!!

Kris was never late to anything. He banged the door knocker just as the Grandfather Clock started to chime 5:00. Millie was all atwitter. A guest! A real guest! and someone so interesting as the new guy in town. Everyone was talking about him - how kind he is and charming and wise - people just loved him. Like everyone else in town, she couldn't imagine why he would want to associate with Zachariah. Even after two decades of working for the man she still found him hard to be around. If he didn't pay her so well she'd have been gone years ago.

Millie had been anxious to meet this "Kris" but didn't know when she'd get the chance - and now here he was, coming to her dining room... She hoped he was a charming and wonderful as she had heard. She hoped he would like what she had prepared.

She answered the door and ushered him into the den where she offered him a drink - he declined - and said Mr. Taylor would be right down. "Oh, Mr. Yershaliim, it is SO nice to meet you. I hope you are settling in nicely and enjoying Telhum. We have such a nice little town here."

"Thank you, Ms. Talbot, I agree. Telhum is a wonderful little town. I'm enjoying life here immensely. I hope your family is doing well..."

"He knew my name!" she thought. "We've never met. We've never laid eyes on one another and yet he knew my name! How extraordinary. How wonderful..."

Dinner was pleasant enough. Millie hadn't had much time to prepare but she came through with a royal feast for the two men. They chatted amiably about current events and the weather and how the Lions might do next season. After dinner they retired to the den while Millie cleaned up.

"Zachariah, that was quite a little scene in my front yard this morning. What were you doing in that tree?" said Kris.

"Please, call me Zack. All my friends do." Kris just smiled at that. He knew that Zachariah Taylor had no friends. "Well, you see, I'm a bit vertically challenged and I couldn't see what you were up to. The tree gave me a visual advantage to see you and learn about what you were teaching."

"That's not the only reason, though, is it, Zack?" asked Kris.

"What on earth do you mean? ...Well... no. I suppose not. I'm not very well liked around town. People tend to bristle whenever I'm around. I thought that being in that tree would give me a bit of invisibility and I wouldn't have to put up with their taunts - you saw what they were like - that worked out just great, didn't it? You saw what happened when they spotted me."

"Why do they hate you so much?"

"Because I'm rich and they aren't. They're jealous. They hate me because I'm successful and they wish they had what I have."

"Really? Do you really believe that is the reason?" asked Kris.

"I don't know. How can I know what goes on in their little brains?"

"You do know... They resent you - and you're right - some hate you because of how you got what you have. What you've got is

175

their sweat and tears - their fears - their hopes - you have them under your thumb and there's nothing they can do about it. You've cheated them out of their savings. You've made them mortgage their futures at exorbitant rates. You've gotten rich off their backs. And what do you have to show for it? You've got a beautiful house. You've got a servant. But who really calls you Zack?"

There was silence for what seemed an eternity. Kris looked at Zachary and Zachary hung his head... Then Zachary spoke, "No one calls me Zack. I haven't a friend in the entire world. When I die no one will mourn. The only ones who will come to my funeral will be those who want to make sure I'm dead. Chris, I'm the loneliest man in the world. I would give anything to be loved - to have even one friend who makes me laugh... to have people look up to me and not look out for me coming down the street. You've done all that in a month and a half here in Telhum. How?"

"Zack - you've got to love people if you want them to love you. It's really just that simple. Your usury enriched you but enraged them. Your threats scared them. Your cruelty (or what they see as cruelty) has repelled them. It would be hard for even God to love all that."

"You're right. I've wasted my life..." Tears began rolling down Zachariah's face. My wealth is worthless... I've been a fool. If you think it'll help, I'll give half of what I own to charity - to the church - to the food pantry - to the homeless shelter in Flint. I'll cut people's mortgage rates in half. I'll pay back those I've cheated with interest. I don't want this life anymore. I need so much to have friends before I die. I need so much to have people smile when they see me coming instead of crossing to the other side of the street. I want God to look at me and not see me as a wretch."

"Zachary, as you do those things you will find peace. You will find a new respect. You will discover the life you were created to live. You can't undo the past but you have the ability to form the future and make it a wonderful thing. This very day, I believe, you've made God smile on you. You've begun to understand what life is really all about."

The very next day Zachary began his transformation. He sold the big house. He gave the equity to Millie. He wouldn't be needing her any more. Now she could retire secure. He sent out letters to all his mortgagees telling them that they were all automatically being refinanced for the same term as they had contracted but with the lowest rate allowed by law. He sent letters to all those who were upside down and told them he would forgive their loan to the amount of their being under water so they could at least start from -0-. He called everyone he had reported to the IRS over the years and apologized and asked them to send him their legal bill statements from the audits. He would send them four times what they paid just to make it right. He sold half his investments (he was an outstanding investor so even selling half he was still the richest man in town) and he gave a third to the Congregational Church in Telhum, a third to Flint's Salvation Army Post, and a third to Forgotten Harvest in Detroit. Then he re-wrote his will such that all he had left would support missionaries and inner city children and the poor wherever they might be. And he left a chunk to Kris, but he knew Kris probably wouldn't keep it. He would just pass it on to those who might need it most.

CRAZY LOUIE
Luke 4: 31-37

I'm pretty sure Livonia has one or more. Westland does. Farmington does. Redford does. Every town has at least one person who is known widely as the town drunk. But I've lived in Livonia for a long time and I can't tell you who that person or who those persons are in our community. But I'm quite sure they are here. Every town has them. But one of the facts of small town life is that you DO know that person and, if there are more than one in the category, you know who excels among them. You know who THE town drunk is - the one who outshines (so to speak) all the others. Telhum had one - - probably more than one but one specific man whom, if asked, everyone would name. Everyone called him Crazy Louie. They didn't just call him that behind his back - that is what everyone called him even to his face. He didn't seem to mind. Crazy Louie was, of course, unemployed - couldn't hold a job because of his drinking problem. He lived in an abandoned shack that someone had once owned. They moved out long ago - couldn't make a living way up there in the thumb and couldn't sell the property so they just left it. The city now owned it, I suppose (or maybe the bank), but whomever owns it apparently has no intention of doing anything with it - too expensive to tear down - too expensive to fix up. Nobody was buying anything in the current market. So it has just sat there empty, waiting for Louie. The previous owners had left several cords of fire wood along the back property line so Louie could live there even in the winter in relative comfort. Each year it fell into greater and greater disrepair and eventually even Louie wouldn't be able to live there, but it wasn't there yet... Louie had some time. He had already been there for four years.

Not only was Crazy Louie the town drunk, he was also the town panhandler. If you didn't want to give him your spare change, you had better cross to the other side of the street when you saw him. He was always somewhere in town asking for handouts - except when he wasn't - then you knew he was most surely drinking those he had gotten over at Telhum's sports bar, named "Lions and Tigers and Beers."[1] (*Oh, my*)

But Crazy Louie didn't get his nickname from all the drinking he did. He got it because everyone knew he was, in fact, crazy. ...That isn't the politically correct term, of course, for what Louie had, but that's what everyone called him. Louie was a schizophrenic. When he was sober NO ONE wanted to be around him. He was obnoxious in things he said and rather frightening in the things he did. He had never really been violent with anyone but he always seemed on the edge of it. He would argue vehemently with some invisible person - swearing at them and yelling and physically fighting them off... or he would approach you and say something totally inappropriate and you didn't know what to say or do - very awkward... or he would start crying - weeping uncontrollably, for no apparent reason - and that made everyone quite uncomfortable. One time he climbed to the top of city hall and stood on the edge and pelted everyone walking on the street below with profanity. Louie had some very serious psychological problems. In fact, THAT is the reason he drank. When he was drunk he didn't hear the voices so clearly, he didn't feel the invisible people touching him all the time, he didn't smell all those intermingling, nauseating smells everywhere he went. He wasn't as afraid of others and the world seemed to stop broadcasting his every thought... but only until he sobered up.

Although drinking made him incoherent, it at least gave him some peace - a respite from all the psychological issues he had. Louie had been institutionalized for a few years down in Northville, but when they closed that facility and sent the patients into the world to fend for themselves Louie put out his thumb and somehow made his way to Telhum and made it his home.

So although people got tired of giving their change to Louie. Having him drunk around town was far better than having him crazy around town. It seemed worth the investment. "Hey Louie, here's two bucks. Buy yourself some booze!" It was a bit of a taunt, but Louie never refused it. He loved to be medicated...

Kristoff Yerushaliim has been in Telhum for about three months now. He had bought the furniture shop for a song and was learning to enjoy the slower pace of small town living. He taught classes in woodworking on Saturday mornings interspersed with a bit of folk wisdom and some intriguing ideas about God. He never got preachy but it was clear he was a true believer. He talked about God the way some people talk about what they had for lunch. It was just a part of who he was. No apology. No backing off. No insistence that others believe like he did. People liked Kris as much as he liked them. Wherever he went people would greet him with a wave and a "hey." He had made a few close friends in town. Actually they had been friends with one another for years and sort of adopted Kris into their group whenever he was able to join them. And that was fairly often because they now hung out in his little showroom for a couple hours each morning as Kris served them coffee and sweet rolls. Kris had even started having little daily spiritual devotionals with them and they'd talk about the ideas for a while - sometimes most of the morning - debating, dissecting, making applications to 21st century life... Campbell and Jesse and Michael and Nat and Tony were always there. Johnny Anderson and Mattie Saint had been joining in for the past couple of weeks too. Free coffee and rolls always make for some good fellowship and, although they were much different from one another, they really did like each other.

Kris had heard about Crazy Louie (although he couldn't bring himself to call him that). But up until last Friday morning he had never actually been in direct contact with him. He had heard the stories. He had seen him at a distance panhandling. He hadn't intentionally avoided him, but just was never where he was in close proximity. Until Friday afternoon...

It seems that Louie had had a rough time getting the booze money he needed on Thursday - and Friday morning was never a good time to panhandle - too many people getting ready for the weekend and too busy to chance getting involved with him, so he was broke and starting to have problems. He needed a drink. Even when the locals didn't come through for him, he knew better than to go into any of the businesses or stores along Main Street and ask for money. He had been warned by Officer Roman to stay out and NEVER to ask for money in business establishments if he wanted to stay out of jail. But Louie was desperate. He NEEDED a drink before the voices started in earnest - before his senses were so heightened that he felt like jumping off a cliff. So he took the short walk - less than a mile - to the Yerushaliim Furniture Shop. Maybe, since it was technically outside the town corporation limits, he wouldn't get into trouble. Maybe the new guy would have pity on him and give him some money...

Walking wasn't good for Louie that morning - at least not out in the country. As soon as he left the city limits the trees started reaching out their branches to grab him or to smack him. But he was quick and they didn't get him. He had to keep bobbing and dodging.... And there was so much green out there that it hurt his eyes. He could hardly believe how powerful a color could be - he was pretty sure he was going to be sick to his stomach. And then there were the birds. They dived at him and pecked his head and hundreds of insects bit his arms and neck. He kept busy slapping at them, swatting away the crazy birds, and shielding his eyes from the blazing green of the trees and grass... The gravel road he walked on kept tilting and trying to make him fall into the ditch. It threw stones at him - they really hurt... the country - what a miserable place to be.

By the time Louie got to the furniture shop he was a wreck. He stumbled in through the front door, practically in tears. Kris immediately came over to him and asked him if he was alright. At that Louie actually did have tears. No one had asked about him for years. Now here was this stranger asking if he was alright. He wasn't alright. But did someone actually care?

"Come over here. Sit down. Tell me what's going on" Kris instructed.

Louie did as he was told. He sat. Then he began to rock - forward and back, forward and back. Kris didn't know exactly what to do. So he just sat with him in silence while Louie rocked. They sat like that for maybe ten minutes - Louie rocking and Kris just looking on.

"**NO!**" shouted Louie. "**GET AWAY FROM ME! I WON'T! DON'T YOU SAY THAT TO ME, YOU FILTHY MOUTHED SON OF THE DEVIL!**"

Kris just sat there, watching and listening. He didn't move nor did he respond. Whatever demons Louie was facing just then he couldn't imagine. Finally he spoke. "Louie, I'm here. I, in the name of God, love you."

"**AHHHHH!**" and Louie fell right off his chair and onto the floor, foaming at the mouth, his body jerking wildly. A seizure or something... Then the shaking suddenly stopped and Louie just lay there only about half conscious.

Kris got a bowl of water and a towel and cleaned Louie up. He put a cool compress on his forehead and put a pillow under his head... When Louie came to he looked rather sheepishly at Kris but Kris just smiled and gave him a hand up. "Are you alright now?"

"Yes. Yes I think so. I'm so sorry." Louie hangs his head. "My life has been so miserable for so long. I just want it all to end. I want all this to be over. I just want to live life like everyone else... Can you give me some money?"

"No. I won't give you any money. I'll offer you some food. I'll give you some clean clothes. I'll do what I can but I can't give you money for liquor. That only masks your problems - never solves them."

With this Louie got up from his chair and started pacing - walking around the showroom - telling Kris how miserable he was and what an unkind and uncharitable cur Kris was and clearly getting agitated again. "I could but I shouldn't" he quietly said. "It would be so peaceful, though, wouldn't it? Would it hurt? Really? You say I should but I'm scared" talking to no one visibly present....

Louie reached the display case Kris had in the showroom - mostly antique woodworking tools and pictures of how they were used. Louie reaches in and picks up a lathe gouge and starts fingering it sharp tip. "Where? Right here? **NO. I WON'T DO IT**" Louie screamed as he placed the tip of the gouge on his chest. He looked over at Kris with a mixture of desperation and despair on his face. "They want me to end it. They want me to do it right now. And why shouldn't I? What does this life have for me but suffering and pain? **Why shouldn't I end it?** ... **NO. I'LL DECIDE. LEAVE ME ALONE!!!**" and Louie began to cry again. Then he put the sharp edge of the gouge to his temple and clearly was about to plunge it in...

Kris got to Louie before he did and put his arms around him tightly so that he couldn't plunge the gouge anywhere, and as he held Louie, he looked up toward the ceiling and said, "Father of us all - Yahweh God - Holy One of the Universe - release this man from these demons - banish them from his life never to return. **Come out of him, I say. Be gone in the name of the Holy One.**"

And Louie dropped the gouge and slumped in Chris' arms and cried some more. But this time not a weeping of the same quality. Before it had been in desperation and frustration. Now it seemed more profound and emotional somehow, but free from the terrors of his disease. Louie had been healed and he knew it immediately.

"Kris- I don't know what just happened, but I feel different. The light is different. There is no rumbling. The air smells so sweet. Do you hear the silence? Isn't it wonderful?"

For the next hour Kris and Louie talked. They talked about Louie's childhood and some of the crisis' he faced in his young life - his own father had the same kind of mental illness that he had. They talked about the torture he had endured in these past years (it all seemed like a dream to Louie already). They talked about his future - what he would do now that he was free from his disease and, hopefully, his drinking. They talked about God's love and God's power to heal and power to sustain and power to overcome whatever life throws at us. They talked about God's continual presence even in threatening times...

Eventually the sun began to set. Louie needed to get going. Kris made a request of Louie before saying a final good-bye. "Louie, if you would, please don't say anything about any of this to anyone. I think it would be better if people didn't know just yet what happened here today." Louie said he wouldn't tell anyone...

But how do you keep the new Louie a secret? By ten o'clock the next morning everyone in town knew. Someone had seen Louie walking down the street clean and sober and sane and the news spread like wild-fire. Someone else had the courage to ask Louie what happened to him and all he said was that he had been rescued from hell and was now at peace. He said that God had saved him. No one knew exactly what that meant but no one could NOT be impressed with the massive change in Louie's life that was so instantaneous. Many wondered if it was just a brief remission. Later in the week Louie would go into the Red Owl and ask if they needed any help and he would be hired as a bagger. In the weeks ahead he would move out of the shack and share an apartment with a fellow he had met in the bar. And before long Crazy Louie became part of Telhum in a new way. He was just Louie now - some called him "Miraculous Louie" but most just Louie.

    Betsy Greenwood, John and Sarah's teen-aged daughter, had seen Louie making his way out of town on that Friday afternoon. She had been riding her bicycle and was amused at the way he was acting, dodging the trees and waving away the birds high in the sky and slapping at imaginary mosquitoes. She saw that he was heading toward the furniture shop - that's all that's along that road for several miles. But she got bored before long and rode on home. She told her parents what she saw and they wondered if whatever happened to Louie had anything to do with that new guy in town... who knows? Maybe. But what could He have done?

---

[1] The name "Lions and Tigers and Beers" is borrowed from an actual bar that recently burned in Wyandotte, MI.

THE MT. EREMOS SERMONS
Matthew 5

      Kristoff Yerushaliim is a church-a-holic. More than anything else in all his life he loved to go to church - he just liked going. I know, that's just weird. To those of us with super busy lives, we sometimes feel the OBLIGATION to go to church but, in reality, church is sometimes - often? - more of a bother than a blessing. But Kris didn't see it that way. He always remembered his catechism days back when he was in Confirmation classes. He remembered having to learn that list of 107 questions and answers in what was called the "Shorter Westminster Catechism." He remembered the between class conversations with the other teens - "if this is the shorter, what must the longer be like?" To this very day he could give the word-for-word answer to every one of those 107 questions. But the one that sank the deepest into his mind and soul and impacted his life the most and often came to his mind whenever he thought about life, was the very first one: "What is man's primary purpose?" That, to him was the biggest question in all the universe and he never could understand why everyone wasn't clamoring to know the answer - "Why am I here? Why are any of us here?" The answer, according to the catechism: "Man's primary purpose is to glorify God and enjoy Him forever."

      "What are we here for? What is the purpose of life? Why am *I* here?" - the biggest questions in the history of the human race - and he knew the answer. That felt pretty good. We are here to glorify God and to enjoy Him - both here on earth and then throughout eternity. It stood to reason to Kris that, if that really was the answer, then worship is the only way to legitimate and real peace and happiness in life - it is what we were meant to do. So he was a church-goer. Telhum has three churches (four if you count the Baptist church - it is about three miles out of town in the middle of the corn fields so, technically, it isn't a "town" church). Kris attended them all. If there had been a synagogue in town he would have attended that too, I"m sure. In fact he had when he lived in Inkster. There aren't any synagogues in Inkster, of course, so he had to go to Livonia's *Congregation Beit Kodesh* on Saturday evenings when they held them and then, on Sabbaths when they didn't, he'd go to Adat Shalom in Farmington. Then, back a day - on Friday's - he would often attend the Islamic Center service in Dearborn. So he was worshipping with

God's people on Friday nights, Saturday nights, Sundays - three out of the seven days of the week. And he loved it.

    Telhum had no synagogues - no mosques - only a Methodist Church, a Congregational Church, and a Catholic Church - and the Baptist one outside of town. The Methodists were trying to get more modern so they actually had two services. One they called "contemporary" (whatever that means) and the other "traditional." Now, you have to remember that Telhum only has 450 people with another 450 or so living in the surrounding countryside within drivable distance, so there were only a total of 900 people to draw from for all four churches. Nobody's congregation was very large. The Methodists had usually around 15 at their contemporary service (part of the problem was that they met at 8:30 in the morning and "contemporary" tends to appeal more to young people and getting them out of bed to be somewhere by 8:30 on a weekend morning - well, what were they thinking?) Their traditional service was attended by about 60 people. Worship time is 10:00. The Congregationalists have what they call a "blended service." That means they sing both the old time hymns and modern songs, trying to please everyone while, in fact, pleasing no one completely. Their worship time is 11:00. The Catholic Church is the largest in town with a congregation that averages 120 every Sunday morning. Masses are at 7:00, 8:00 and 9:00. So on any given Sunday morning Kris had a schedule. He would go to the 7:00 Mass at St. Stephen's, the 8:30 contemporary service at First Methodist, the 9:00 full Mass back at St. Stephen's, back to the Methodist Church for their 10:00 worship and then over to Pilgrim Congregational for their 11:00. He couldn't have done it most places, but in a small town where everything is only a few blocks away - and nothing actually started right on time, you could... THEN, on Sunday evenings, he headed out to Ebenezer Baptist for their evening service. If you were counting - that totals SIX HOURS of church time on a Sunday. Running from one church to the next didn't really allow him time to visit with others or to stay for fellowship hours, but that wasn't his purpose anyway. His purpose was to glorify God and Enjoy Him. And he did. He **LOVED** Sundays.

    One of the strange consequences of being a church-a-holic is that everyone in every church you attend regularly thinks you are a part of their congregation. You're there every Sunday. Your one of "us." But every minister knows you aren't really and wonders just what you're up to. Ministers talk. They all knew that Kris attended all of their churches - couldn't figure it out. The guy is a bit strange...

    Small towns get new ministers or priests every 2- 3 years or so. They are almost always young men (or women - the Methodists once had a female minister). The young ministers are usually fresh out of seminary and going into their first church before either moving on to something more prestigious or deciding giving up every weekend of their lives isn't something they want to do. The small town church is the boot camp for clergy rookies. They get all the first time ministerial mistakes and bad sermons and inventive but sometimes foolish programs.

But even rookies get vacation time, so when it came time for Mark Johanson over at Mt. Eremos Methodist Church (I've no idea why you would call anything "Mt." when there isn't so much as a hill in sight in any direction) - when it came time for the minister to take a couple of weeks away, it fell to the Board of Elders to fill the pulpit. Usually those were "Hymn Sing" Sundays. Everyone liked those (and, to be honest, Johansen was a boring preacher - way too intellectual for Telhumites - so him being away was a vacation for his congregation as well as for him and his family). And "Hymn Sing" seemed to be the consensus until Elder Nat Storey (of the former Dina's Club crowd) piped up: "How about getting Kristoff Yerushaliim in to preach. I think he'd do a great job. He's been attending here ever since he moved to town. Let's have a 'Layman's Sunday.'"

It was like a light went on. Sure - why not have one of their own - a man with obvious spiritual insight - deliver the sermon. "Nat - would you be willing to ask him? Be sure to tell him there is no honorarium involved - just his ministry to his church family. We don't have anything in our budget to pay him anything."

Later on that day Nat asked Kris.

"I've never done a sermon before" said Kris. "I really don't think standing up there at the pulpit and pontificating is really my thing. I'm more of an interactive kind of guy. Organized religion kind of scares me. And to be the one up there supposedly knowing it all - I don't know..."

"Come on, Kris. You'll be great. Hey - you do it all the time on Saturdays at your woodworking workshops - you just talk to those who are there - same thing. Just talk to the people. How hard can it be?"

"If it's so easy, why don't you do it, Nat?"

"I wouldn't know where to begin. But you....you've been ready for this all your life."

So with a bit of arm twisting, Nat got Kris to say he would give it a try.

The morning of his first sermon Kris was as nervous as he had ever been. It's one thing to be talking while you are filing a stile or staining oak, but all these people were looking directly at HIM, waiting for him to say something important - meaningful - moving - and to say it in such a way that it keeps their attention and keeps them from throwing rotten eggs at him... Just a bit stressful...

As it turned out, Kris was right. Public speaking wasn't his thing. Every minister has drilled into them that a good sermon has three main points. It is constructed in such a way that you tell them what you are going to say, you say it, and then you tell them what you said... But Kris hadn't been to seminary. He didn't know...

"A person who is beaten down - who is dumped on - who is a spiritual wreck - is a person God will truly bless eventually - his or her fortunes will be turned around.

"Are any of you hurting this morning? Put up your hands (he had heard that asking a question was a good device). The rest of you - gather around those who are hurting and give them a hug. Let them know you care. Go ahead, do it now. Hugs all around..." Only a couple did. Everyone else just sat there feeling uncomfortable. You don't go hugging people in the middle of the service.

Kris continued on, "People who are most needy will be most blessed by God - I'm confident of that.

"Anyone who wants to be a good person - **really** wants it - can be.

"If you are a tender-hearted person, chances are others will be tender-hearted to you. And that's pretty cool, don't you think?

"God truly loves people who go around in their daily lives making peace with others or between enemies. What higher calling could there be?

"Turn the other cheek. That is the credo of every Christian in the world, yet we are so ready to support wars and aggression and retribution. I don't get it. Can't we all just get along?"

And on and on he went. It was like a litany of proverbs. There wasn't any central theme anyone could discern. Just pithy little pieces of wisdom. Johanson's seminary preaching professor would have given Kris a failing grade... No central theme, no clear direction, no application...

But Christians are wonderful, gracious people. After the sermon was finally over (it was only about 14 minutes long but was so painful that it seemed like an hour), numerous people came up to Kris and told him how much they enjoyed it. Who knows, maybe they did get something out of his disconnected thoughts....

As Kris made his way to fellowship hall, he asked Nat, "How'd I do?" You're not supposed to lie in church, but Nat did - "You did great. I think you hit everyone right where they live. I know you were speaking directly to me a couple of times." Then Nat did something totally unplanned but it just popped out, "You know, Johanson is gone for another week - we've got another Sunday to fill..."

"I'd love to. I think I could really get into this sermon stuff" says Kris.

During the week Nat (and Tony and Michael - the other Methodists in their little group) hinted to Kris that he may need to focus a bit more and have more that applies to people's lives... Kris appreciated their feedback and worked on exactly that as he prepared for the next Sunday. They were all a bit apprehensive.

When Sunday morning rolled around, the church was full - rather amazing for a July Sunday - or any other Sunday for that matter. The Methodists seemed to each have a friend or neighbor in tow. And you could overhear the buzz: "*Last week's sermon kept coming back to me all week long*" said Sally Fuller. "*I think it subtly changed my way of thinking.*"

"*I wasn't here last week. I'm a Congregationalist, you know*" said Joan Abbott. "*But when I heard Kris was going to preach how could I stay away? He's such a wise man.*"

"*I hope he gives more of those easy-to-remember rules for living*" said Joe Turner...

But Kris' sermon was much different this second week. He wasn't quite so nervous - he knew better what to expect.

He began: "*You people are beacons of hope in this world. When people see your faith they have a little light shine into their souls and that little light illuminates a piece of them they didn't know existed. It is their own faith. But the other side of the coin exists, too. When people DON'T see your faith, no light shines into their souls and nothing happens. You and you and you and you - show your faith by demonstrating every day how much you love God and when you do that God is truly pleased and begins to illuminate the spirits of others. That's what our faith is all about - spreading God's love and the opportunity to be forgiven and to live forever...*

"*But here is what so often happens. We look so plastic in our faith to others. We try too hard to be good. We follow the rules too exactly. You know, if you truly want to follow the rules you have to also follow the principles behind the rules. For instance, you'd never kill anyone. But have you ever WANTED to? Then haven't you, in principle, broken the rule? You wouldn't have an affair with someone else's spouse. But have you WANTED to? Haven't you, in principle, then, broken the rule? Don't worry so much about the rules in life. Just live as righteously as you possibly can in every aspect of living.*

You still won't succeed, but that's where God's mercy comes in. If you ask him to forgive you, you will be forgiven. Then go back out there and try it again... and again and again.

"The key to the whole thing is to love others - your family, your friends, your neighbors, your work-mates, the stranger on the street - and even your enemies. When you can do that, God will smile on you in ways you can't even begin to imagine. Give to the needy. Pray for the hurting. Look to God for guidance."

It wasn't anything Johanson hadn't said. It wasn't anything the whole string of young whipper-snappers hadn't said during their tenures in Telhum, but somehow Kris' words were different. They weren't peppered with flowery allusions. He didn't have any captivating illustrations or stories. But somehow when he spoke those words it was like hearing them for the first time. Love - righteousness - forgiveness - grace... Everyone there sat in stunned silence, knowing they had heard the Word of God - the Word of God spoken as they had never heard it before... It had, truly, shined a light on their souls and they could literally FEEL different. It wasn't like being pumped up by some motivational speaker. It was a deep-seated peace and wonder and love that they experienced and, somehow they knew that they just may never be the same again.

Kris didn't get any compliments on his sermon that day. Somehow, gushing didn't seem appropriate as they left that morning and Kris greeted them at the back of the sanctuary. Instead, each person simply shook his hand and looked into his eyes and both spoke to one another without uttering a word...

Rev. Johanson returned on Tuesday. The first thing he did was to take a look at the attendance card for the past two weeks. The first was pretty typical. The second made him gasp. Was there some kind of mistake? There had NEVER been that many at Mt. Eremos on a July Sunday. In fact, almost ANY Sunday. This was not good. What had that new guy done? He was really going to look bad now if that Kris fellow was THAT good that people flocked to hear him. This was not good at all...

Several weeks later, at the monthly clergy meeting, they were chatting and Mark mentioned that they had half a dozen new people attending. "These people seem to be so happy. They seem to love to sing the hymns and they smile when the scripture lessons are being read - as though hearing a wonderful story for the first time. They are so filled with joy that I am thrilled to have them as a part of my congregation. Maybe some of you know them - the Mattson famly, the Parrett family, the Lauban family - oh, yes, the Kieth family, too - I guess there are more than a half dozen...

Father McCauley got a puzzled look on his face. "Really? Those same families have been attending my masses."

Rev. Johns, the Baptist minister said, "They've been to Ebenezer too."

"Oh, my!" said Smithers, "They've been over at the Congregational Church too. I wonder what's going on? No one can love church that much. Why would anyone want to go to church more than an hour on Sunday? And as soon as he said those words something popped into his mind. He didn't know why. He thought of the words he had learned so long ago and hadn't considered as anything more than something for adolescents to learn in Sunday School: *What is the chief purpose of man? The chief purpose of man is to love God and truly enjoy him in every conceivable way.... both now and forever?"*

TROUBLE IN SEA GULL HARBOR
Matthew 9: 1-9

    You can't make it in a small town as a fine furniture craftsman. The cost of living may be low, buying or leasing work space may be affordable, everything about the setting may be inspirational, but with such a small number of potential customers to draw from, unless you are able to advertise widely and ship long distances, you're going to be in trouble in a fairly short time. Thanks to the internet, Kristoff Yerushaliim was, indeed, able to make a go of his little furniture shop. He knew how to get the word out online – through rented mailing lists and search engine optimization and pay-per-click advertising and a beautiful website he was doing pretty well. Nevertheless, there was a fair amount of travel involved in what he did. Because his tables and chairs and hutches and bookcases were of the finest quality he was always searching for new and better sources of exquisite wood. He had a special penchant for exotic woods like Osage Orange, Hawaiian Mango, and Black and White Ebony. It wasn't uncommon for him to travel as far as central Indiana for a few board feet of Sassafras or to New York for a length of Bolivian Rosewood. And sometimes, if an order he had filled was especially large or not too far away he would load it up on his small flat-bed truck and deliver it to his customers in person. Of all the "business" side of his business, THAT was his favorite part. He had always thought that when he made something creative he was putting a part of himself into it – not just his time and effort and creativity and skill, but part of his very soul.

    That may sound strange to many of us who tend not to be very creative, but to you artistic types, you know just what I mean. I once knew a very accomplished artist who HAD to paint but kept all his completed pieces in cabinets in his basement. His walls were full of his work but he just couldn't bring himself to sell anything. He felt that taking money for his art, which contained a part of his very soul, he said, would be akin to prostitution. So he never did. He was employed at an advertising company drawing pictures of plastic storage-ware – pretty soulless work. Kris wasn't that guarded – after all, he had to make a living – but still, whenever he could meet his customers and maybe even see the homes in which his work would reside, it gave him great pleasure.

    There is a small community about 80 miles from Telhum named Sea Gull Harbor. It is a beautiful little town on the banks of Lake Huron. For the most part tourists haven't yet discovered it so it has always been a sleepy little town with great beauty. But the beauty of the town is only surface. There is a darkness about the town that the bright sunshine and the sparkling lake water just can't dissolve. It hasn't always been that way - only within the past 15 years. Up until that time it was, really, quite an idyllic place to live or visit. But a tragic event profoundly affected just about every member of the community a decade and a half ago.

For 27 years Jack Murphy had been the mayor of Sea Gull Harbor. He had been mayor that long because everyone loved him like a father. He was charming and insightful and he could get the job done. He literally knew every resident within the city limits and most in all the outlying countryside. He knew their children and what they did for a living and who their parents and grandparents were. He was not a politician even though he did, in fact, kiss the babies and ladies and slap the backs of all the men and tussle the hair of the boys. He didn't care about political party or religious preference or social status. He was just the best guy you ever want to meet. To even SEE him was to like him – he was that charismatic.

Jack's wife, Emma, was exactly the same. When she walked into a room, it lit up. People smiled. They felt honored when she spoke to them and thrilled when she called them by name. And she did that often because, like Jack, she liked people and easily remembered their names.

The Murphey's had two daughters and both of them had inherited the best of each of their parent's qualities. In ever so many ways, the Murphey's were royalty in "The Cove." Jack never had any serious competition in elections. Why would anyone vote for someone else when you have a prince of a man as a mayor? Mayor Murphey's years in office were golden years for Sea Gull Harbor. Everyone hoped they could go on forever.

But Camelot, with its bigger-than-life actors, if it ever really existed, always eventually comes to an end. And it did in this beautiful little town. On a warm July evening fifteen years ago Jack and Emma and Rhonda and Alison were returning from a shopping trip to Saginaw when a local man – Terry Jackson – was driving north on route 53 drunk. He was speeding upward of 95 miles per hour investigators said – he had a beer in his hand when he crossed the center line and smashed head on into the Murphey's car, killing all four of them instantly and breaking Terry up such that he was in critical condition for three months. And then, when he did eventually begin to respond, it was discovered that he had injured his spinal cord and he would, in all likelihood, never walk again. He had tons of therapy - even all these years later he had a weekly session, but nothing seemed to be happening.

Terry was charged with manslaughter. His court date was set for October but along the way something happened – to this day no one knows exactly what – but the charges against Terry were dropped and he was allowed to go home…

The Murphy's deaths devastated Sea Gull Harbor. They knew the truth of the matter – they would NEVER have another mayor and mayor's family like the beloved Mayor Jack. They would <u>never</u> know such lovely, gracious people like Emma and the girls. And it was all because of that lowly piece of scum, Terry Jackson. It seemed that the entire town hated this man. They hated what he had done. They hated what he had taken from them. They hated that they were expected to open doors for him when he wheeled into or out of a building. They hated everything about him and that hatred seemed practically unquenchable - and it seemed to be universal.

Ideally, Terry would have moved from Sea Gull Harbor. Staying in a place where people despise you is foolish if there is an alternative, but there didn't seem to be one for Terry. He had an elderly widowed father he couldn't leave. He had no money to uproot and start somewhere else. He was stuck in the town where he was despised and, as you can imagine, he was miserable. He seldom went out except for necessities. He knew he was hated. He hated himself. He hadn't so much as smelled liquor since the accident - but that changed nothing in his life... The Murphey's were still dead. He was still crippled. He was and ever would be hated...

Kris was in Sea Gull Harbor last Wednesday. He had come because he had heard that a farmer nearby had cut down four virgin cherry trees and he desperately wanted to make an offer for the wood. He was across the street, heading for Clara's General Store when he saw Terry trying to come out. There were several people around but none of them seemed inclined to help this poor, handicapped man. So Kris jogged across the street and opened the door and let Terry out. "I don't know what's going on," said Kris. "I'm so sorry no one wanted to help."

"Oh, that's not so uncommon," said Terry. "It happens all the time. They just don't much like me is all."

"Don't like you? What'd you do, kill their dog?"

"I wish. No. I really don't want to talk about it" said Terry.

"No problem. Anything I can do for you? Can I give you a lift somewhere? Open any other doors…?"

"No. That's alright. I'll be fine."

"Well, have a good day then. God bless you." And Kris started to walk away.

"Thank you, sir. You've been kind and that's rare around here" Terry called out, loud enough for those who hadn't helped him to hear. But they didn't care what Terry thought. They just stood there and stared at him with resentment and contempt... Can you imagine carrying that kind of hatred in your heart for fifteen years - letting it burn a hole in your soul - and for everyone around to think it acceptable?

Kris glanced back and saw the loathing in the eyes of those who were nearby. He couldn't help but wonder why people would so despise a handicapped man. Kris returned to Terry. "You know, I've discovered that people are really pretty good at their core. Flawed, but good. Every one of us are made in the image of God. That's pretty awesome. They may not open the door for a handicapped man, but I'll bet they'd come through in a pinch." Like Terry, Kris said it loud enough for those around to hear. He was trying to let his spectators know that he thought not helping a handicapped man – for whatever reason - was pretty low.

Terry saw the people on the sidewalk listening, so he made yet another attempt to say what he had said a hundred times over the years: "I'll tell you what I've done that makes them hate me. I've done the unforgivable. Fifteen years ago I killed the mayor and his beautiful family – his wife and daughters. They hate me because I was drunk and I got away with it. I don't blame them. Every day I live with what I did. I've said 'I'm sorry' a million times - and I'll say it a million times more if I have to, but they won't accept it. I'm the one who should have died, I know that. I'm the one who should be behind bars. I know that. I am sorry."

Kris reached out and touched Terry, "Young man, your sins are forgiven. God accepts your apology. God has forgiven you even if others won't."

Well, I can't tell you the reaction that couple of sentences caused. It was like someone had sucker punched them in the gut. They NEVER expected something like this little interchange. "Whoa there, mister," said one man. "Just who do you think you are - God or something? NOBODY in this town forgives this little so-and-so. He robbed all of us of something special - then he got away with it scott-free. He doesn't deserve getting so much as the time of day from any of us - not forgiveness, not understanding, not so much as help across the threshold of the 'Five and Dime.'"

Another in the little gathering piped in, "There's no way this guy's forgiven by God or anyone else. He was drunk. He was reckless. He killed people and walked away. He single-handedly ruined this town."

"Such evil in your hearts," replied Chris. Such unresolved and unhealed pain. I'm so sorry for you. But this man IS forgiven. He has confesses his sin. He has sought forgiveness. Just because you can't doesn't mean God can't. God does, in fact, forgive him. Look, which would be easier, to offer this man God's forgiveness or to make him walk?" You could see the confusion on their faces. What was he talking about? What does walking have to do with anything? That makes no sense.

"Terry, get up out of that wheelchair and go on home," said Kris..

Terry looked at Kris as though he was nuts but, as he looked, he saw a sincerity in his eyes that couldn't be mistaken. He meant it. He wanted him to push himself up out of that chair and try to walk. He knew he would make a fool of himself and end up being picked up off the sidewalk, but this guy had stood up for him. He had assured him, before everybody there, that he was forgiven. So he tried. Kris stood in front of him, putting his hands out for Terry to take to pull him up to a standing position, keeping his eyes locked on Terry's. About fifteen seconds later, Terry was standing. One of the younger men who was watching all this reached out with his foot and pushed the wheelchair away from Terry so that if he tried to sit back down he would end up on his rear end on the ground...

Terry smiled and tried lifting his leg. He never took his eyes off Kris. He found that he could, in fact, lift his foot off the ground. He put that foot down and lifted the other - just an inch or so - and he could. Kris put his arm now around Terry's waist and Terry put his arm around Chris' neck and together they began to walk. After a few steps Kris told Terry to let go. He did and he found that he could stand and even walk. He hadn't walked for fifteen years! It was impossible! But it was true. His gait was a bit halting but he proceeded to walk down the street and around the corner as they all watched...

Everyone was dumbfounded, of course. Someone even suggested that that wasn't really Terry - just an actor look-alike - that this was all some kind of little hoax. Terry would show up tomorrow as pathetic as he always was. Others wondered. Was this a miraculous act of God or was this some kind of voodoo magic straight out of hell? One man said, "I would never believe it if I hadn't seen it with my own two eyes. I'm pretty sure when I tell my wife and family about it they will all think I'm daft. But it did happen - didn't it? Didn't Terry Jackson just get up and walk?"

While they were talking all this over with one another, Kris just walked away. No one saw him go. Later they would tell people that he vanished into thin air after the incident, but really they had just been so blown away that they didn't notice him leave.

It didn't take long for the news to get around town - literally minutes. Within the hour 85% of the people of Sea Gull Harbor knew (I don't know whether anyone even remembered the "forgiveness of sins" thing - they were all so awestruck with the idea that Terry was healed that forgiveness seemed somewhat unimportant).

And they knew where Kris was. He was at the saw mill. A couple of dozen town folk headed in that direction. The mayor led the little parade. Two women brought their children - one had a heart murmur and the other asthma. MAYBE Kris could heal them like he had Terry... The rest of them just wanted to see this guy who, supposedly, put Terry Jackson back on his feet.

Kris was just completing his purchase when the little troupe got there. When he came out of the office he was greeted by two weeping, anxious mothers and the others wondering what he would say or do. "What's troubling you ma'am?" said Kris. "And you: Why are you crying?"

"We heard that you healed Terry Jackson. Would you heal our children? Sarah's heart is weak. Pete's got bad asthma. It's so scary. Can you do something? What do we need to do? We can pay."

"It would be a hard-hearted man who could say no to crying women and hurting children. Let me see them." Kris stooped down to the children's level. He put one arm around one and his other arm around the second. He looked up to heaven and said, "God - Your children. Every one of them is defective in some way. Some you choose to heal and others not. Your sovereign will is a mystery to the small mind of man. But here are two small children that I present for healing. Their mothers have come with the belief that I can...." Kris stopped speaking for a bit - maybe fifteen or twenty seconds. Then he said, "Thank you." And he sent the children back to their mothers. Did the heart of little Sarah stop its murmuring? Did Pete's lung capacity increase and his bronchial tubes dilate? No one could tell just then and if so what did it mean?

"Look, Mr. Yerushaliim," Mayor MacGeorge said, "we don't know who you are or what it is you are trying to do here, but you've stirred up Sea Gull Harbor's population pretty good already. I think it's time for you to finish up your business here and leave. I don't know how you did what you did to Terry, but I've got to say, it was not appreciated in these parts. Have a good day now. Let's all move along now..." And the Mayor turned and walked away as people began to disperse.

But not everyone left. The two mothers remained, as did a couple others who were intrigued and a bit awed by and a bit afraid of this man. The mothers said quiet thank-you's for what he did for their children - or what they hoped he had done - heart murmurs and clear lungs aren't too visible - and humbly turned and walked away. Gale and Dale Dudley, identical twins, were still there. Gale said, "Mr. Yerushaliim, the two of us have been waiting for you all our lives even though we didn't know it. We're members over at 'Open Arms Pentecostal Church.' We believe that you have some kind of special connection with God that we want to coattail. Could we become your apprentices? Could we learn to make chairs and cabinets and just learn all you have to teach? We're willing to leave Sea Gull Harbor and move to wherever you're from. We promise not to get in the way."

"So willing to jump into something you know nothing about," replied Kris. "You know, even wild animals out on the plains know where they will be spending the night. They need that security. But you - You're willing to give up your lives here for what you consider a mystery in some unknown place. Such rare and wondrous faith. But I've got to say, I have nothing to offer you. I have no funds for hiring anyone. I have no spare room for you to sleep in. All I have is sawdust and the smell of turpentine. If you want to apprentice with me, it won't be easy. But come to Telhum. I'll teach you to make a chair and we'll see where it goes from there."

So Gale and Dale went back to their Seagull Harbor home to prepare for their new life in Telhum - their new home, and awaited whatever adventures might come in their new lives, knowing that with Kris, truly anything seemed possible.

THE MAYOR'S DAUGHTER
Matthew 9: 18-26

As you may recall from last week, Kris basically got run out of the little town of Sea Gull Harbor. He had done the unthinkable and gotten into trouble for it. He told the town pariah that he was forgiven for the tragic accident of fifteen years ago in which Terry Jackson, drunk, smashed his car head-on into the car driven by the beloved town mayor and his great family, killing them all. Then, although he was paralyzed from the waist down due to a spinal cord injury during the accident, some kind of technicality allowed him to walk away (not literally) with no punishment or penalty of any kind - except for the ongoing knowledge that everybody in town despised him. Kris told him that, since he had confessed his wrong-doing and asked God and everyone else - everyone he met up with for the past decade and a half - that he was sorry, he was forgiven - that God forgave him even if the people of Sea Gull Harbor wouldn't or couldn't. It caused a fire-storm. People were furious about even the IDEA of forgiving this most-hated-man in town.

Later that day Kris was over at the sawmill and an unofficial delegation from town approached him with Mayor McGeorge in the lead. The mayor told Kris that he was disturbing the peace of their quiet little town and that he was no longer welcome there and that he had better be on his way.

But as it turned out, Kris couldn't leave town just then. He had purchased some Cherry wood from a local farmer and needed to wait around until it was milled - probably two days. He decided to lay low during that time and kind of stay out of sight. He certainly didn't want to stay somewhere where he wasn't welcome. He had a room at the Cherry Tree Inn so he decided to stay holed up there until his wood was ready. He'd only go out for meals. That was okay with him. He had been working too hard and figured he probably needed a couple days just to crash.

When he got back to the motel he flipped on the TV. There was nothing on that was worth paying for with an hour of his life on any of the 42 channels. He realized there probably wouldn't be later either so he opened the end table drawer and pulled out the Gideon Bible. He wondered how much of the Bible a person can read in two days, discounting time taken out for meals and the little naps one fell to when coming to some of the less exciting parts... He opened to the first page and was greeted by those wonderful first words in Genesis: "In the beginning, God..." That, he thought, was the whole thing. God

WAS from the very beginning. How awesome! How incomprehensible! Then his mind wondered to something he had once read about the wonder of the universe. It was so powerful a thought he could remember it almost word for word. "*Let's see... what did that author say? Something like 'Imagine you're on a huge beach. Imagine you pick up one tiny grain of sand. Just one. Then you look up and down this long beach that stretches in both directions for as far as the eye can see. Do you think our entire solar system is as small as that grain of sand is to that beach in comparison to the universe? Well, if you did, you'd be wrong. It is much, much smaller. Try this: Imagine you're still holding that tiny grain of sand. Now not just the beach you are on, but all the beaches all over the planet, all of them, all down the coast of California and the East Coast from Maine to Florida and on the Indian Ocean and off the coasts of Africa. Imagine all that sand, all those beaches everywhere in the world and now look at that grain of sand you're holding and still, STILL, our entire solar system - forget the individual planets - our entire solar system - is smaller than that compared to the rest of the universe.'* [1] *'In the beginning God created the heavens and earth.' Awesome.... What a wondrous - amazing - Heavenly Creator."*

  For the next day and a half Kris read the Bible. He read all the great stories in Genesis and then continuing into Exodus - how God lead and chastised and protected the Israelites... He skipped over some of the sections on dietary law in Leviticus - rather enjoyed the genealogy sections - into the Psalms and the Prophets... Mid afternoon on the second day the mill called telling him his wood was ready to ship.

  He didn't hesitate. He drove his truck to the mill, loaded it up, and headed for Telhum. He was anxious to get home. It would take a couple of hours. It seemed that this trip took more out of him than he had expected - although it was good to have those two down days reading and sleeping.

  He was about four miles north of Sea Gull Harbor when he saw flashing red lights behind him. He slowed down and pulled to the shoulder and stopped to let the police car coming up fast behind him pass. But to his surprise the patrol car pulled off the road behind him. He was sure he wasn't speeding. He was fairly sure he didn't have a tail light out. He couldn't figure out just what was going on. As he reached into his glove box for his registration, he looked in his rearview mirror and saw a female officer getting out of the driver's side... and Mayor McGeorge out of the passenger side. Both were coming up to his truck.

"Mr. Yerushaliim, would you step out of the truck, please," the officer said. He opened the door and got out.

"What's going on officer.... White (he looked at her ID badge). I don't think I was speeding."

"It's my fault for having you stopped, sir" said the mayor. "I know I'm the one who asked you to leave town and I'm sorry for that - especially now. I looked all over for you yesterday but didn't know where you'd gone or even where you'd come from. I put out an APB on you and this officer saw your truck leave town a while ago. She came and got me and brought me out here. It's my daughter. She somehow contracted meningitis and the doctors say she is spiraling downward and maybe has only a few more hours to live. Do you think you could come and see if you can help her. I don't know how you fixed Terry, but I saw him walking that afternoon, after meeting you, - walking as well as anyone. I don't know how you did it but will you come and try to work your magic on Susan? Please. She's my only daughter. I beg of you."

Officer Miller had been listening to all this. She had heard about Terry, too. Didn't really know if she believed it, but if the Mayor says he saw him walking around, it must be true. She wondered... She kind of snuck her hand out and touched Kris' shirtsleeve... and she felt something like a mild taser sting course through her body. And she knew - she knew she had just been healed of that menstrual problem she had been having since she was a teenager... Kris looked at her. She looks sheepishly away. Kris said, "Officer, your faith has healed you. Praise be to God." The mayor had no idea what was going on. Neither did Gale or Dale.

They left Chris' truck there on the shoulder of Highway 53 and got into the police car with the Mayor and Officer Miller. She put the siren on, flipped a U-Turn and headed back toward Sea Gull Harbor as fast as Kris had ever ridden in a car. When they arrived at the Mayor's house, the Mayor jumped out and opened Chris' door for him and ushered him quickly inside. But as soon as the front door opened, they knew something terrible had happened. The Mayor's wife came running to him. She died! Mitchell, she's gone..." and she started weeping as only a mother can when her child has died, as her husband held her and as he, himself wept without restraint.

Kris said, "I'm not so sure you're right. She's only sleeping. She's in some kind of coma. She'll be alright. All of you, out please - Mr. Mayor - Mrs. Mayor - you stay."

The doctor shook his head sadly and gave a smile that clearly said, "You poor fool..." and he left the room along with Susan's cousin - her best friend - and Mrs. McGeorge's parents.

The mayor and his wife watched through their tears as Kris went over to where Susan lay. He took her limp hand in his and he said in the gentlest voice you can imagine, "Susan - Susan - Susan, wake up. Open your eyes..." And amazingly, Susan's eyes fluttered a little bit, she opened them and looked at Kris and saw he was holding her hand, and she said, "Who are you? Why are you holding my hand? Mom, what's wrong? Dad?"

Well, you can imagine the emotion in that room at that moment. Susan looked a little confused, but the Mayor and Mrs. McGeorge were just overwhelmed with relief and joy and the release of grief and fear. Even Kris had tears running down his face. It may have been the happiest moment that old house had ever seen. The mayor rushed out into the living room where the others waited and, with tearful joy he said, "She's OK. She came out of it. Susan seems well!" Grandma and Grandpa rushed in to see for themselves, Susan's cousin did the same. The doctor looked mortified and stormed out of the house - KNOWING he hadn't been wrong - but apparently, somehow, was.

They invited Kris to stay for dinner, but he said he really needed to get back to Telhum before dark with is load, so Officer Miller drove him back to his truck. On the way, she asked him, "How did you do that? How did you make that little girl well? How did you make Terry walk? How did you send that electrical charge through me and heal me?"

Kris loved that kind of question but he was well aware that if he answered with total truth what he said would make no sense whatsoever. Miracles are so much more complicated than simple answers can contain - or, sometimes, even complicated answers... "It has to do with the most powerful connection within the human psyche," he began. "You see, there is far more of a connection between our bodies and our minds than most of us are willing to admit. And the connection even reaches into the soul and the heart and then, ultimately to God Himself. When you BELIEVED with your mind what the Mayor said, it quickly headed for your soul and your soul said, 'Sandy, YOU have a need. It will work for you, too.' Then you reached out in total, innocent faith, and touched me. You KNEW with your mind that your body would be healed. You BELIEVED with your soul that it was true. God picked up the powerful connection and made it happen.... I know that probably sounds like a lot of gobbledy-gook to you, but it is beyond our mind's ability to grasp how it all works... We all know that our minds have the ability to make our bodies sick. Worry causes ulcers. Anxiety causes high blood pressure. Anger, hostility and resentment cause our bodies to release those long-dormant cancer cells (I'm not saying that all ulcers or blood pressure issues or cancer come from our minds, but much of it does). Stress gives us headaches and neck and back aches, keeps us from sleeping well - sometimes heart attacks... The mind/body connection is pretty intense when it causes negative things, but those same connections can be used to cause amazing positive things to happen... When we are able to transform our minds from the negative to the positive, GOOD things happen in powerful ways like what happened to Terry and Susan and you. God SO honors our faith - our belief that He CAN work - that He DOES. Now, it's much more complicated than that, but that's more or less the layman's version. There's my truck now. Thanks so much for the lift. It's been great getting to know you a bit."

    Kris drove the eighty miles back to Telhum without further incident. Most of the way he hummed and smiled. It's no fun being expelled from a town, but leaving on a positive note AFTER being asked to leave made him feel rather good.

    Kris arrived back home at about eight. He unloaded the truck and headed for bed, exhausted after a full day and lots of emotion.

    In the morning his typical "Kris' Club" group gathered in his showroom. They were all there. He was a bit surprised to see that somehow Gale and Dale had known about the gathering and had joined the others. He asked them where they had spent the night and they said they had arrived yesterday afternoon and met Tony peering through the shop window, obviously trying to see if Kris was back yet. They struck up a conversation and Tony invited them to stay in the vacant mother-in-law apartment above his garage for as long as they'd like... free!

    "So how'd the trip go?" asked Sam. "Anything happen?"

    "No, not much," said Chris, even though it was apparent that Gale and Dale had already filled them all in on what had happened with Terry and the little girls and what they had heard just before heading out about the Mayor's daughter, Susan.

---

[1]This quote is from the book, "Hold Tight" by Harlan Coben, Penguin Group, 2008. p. 228

THEY WHO HAVE EARS
Matthew 10: 5-14

Everyone was gathered around the big round oak table in Kris' showroom within an hour of his getting up the morning after returning from Sea Gull Harbor. Kris knew that this day would be unlike any he had ever had in his life. He knew that some time that day - probably sooner than later - the press would arrive. Film crews would park their mobile units on his lawn, reporters would shove microphones in his face and everyone would shout questions at him. He wasn't looking forward to it, but he knew it was inevitable. You can't do what he had been doing for very long without word getting out and the newshounds jumping all over it. Kris had just returned from Sea Gull Harbor. When he left there was a cripple who could now walk, a little girl who used to have a heart murmur now without one, a little boy with asthma with clear lungs, a girl everyone thought dead alive, a police officer healed of a long-standing women's issue...

"Guys, I'm afraid I have to ask you to do something again. This favor is far bigger than the last one." [If you recall, shortly after Kris opened for business he had printed up 10,000 fliers announcing an open house "Grand Opening" at the furniture store and he had asked these friends, who were now meeting daily in his showroom to drink coffee, study the Bible, and listen to Kris' ideas - he had asked them to distribute the fliers. They had and the fliers had produced amazing results - in part because Kris had hand-written scripture references on each one and recipients found them, eerily, applying to themselves].

The twins - and the latest additions to the little group - in fact, they joined only about twelve hours ago - the night before - asked what he was talking about. Tony Snavely explained: "It was the darndest thing you ever saw. We passed out all these fliers all over the thumb area and people just swarmed the place. Kris knew they would so he managed to have enough food on hand for them all. I've still got some of the left-overs in my freezer. It kind of launched the business... and we all started meeting here, learning from this guy. He's really pretty sharp."

"Sharp's not the word," said Nat Tracy. "I've been a teacher for fourteen years and I've already learned more from Kris about life and the world than I ever knew - in just a couple of months!"

"OK, guys, enough with the accolades," interrupted Chris. "We don't have much time. Here's what I want you to do. I know that Gale and Dale told you what happened in Sea Gull Harbor. You know that the mayor's daughter, who had contracted meningitis was made well. You know that Terry Johnson, the handicapped guy, is walking. They told you about the women's children being healed. People are saying that I did those things and more. And while it is more complicated than simply that, they are right. God wanted those people healed for a specific purpose and that purpose is about to come to light. The purpose is so that I might have a platform to talk to people and tell them some of the things you and I have been talking about for the past few weeks.

"Here is what I want you to do. Tony, contact the post office this morning and tell them you need an immediate leave of absence for two weeks. Nat, school is out for the summer so you're all set. The rest of you have your own businesses. I want you to take the next two weeks off. I've got a mission for you."

This, of course, was a bit of a thunderbolt. They knew Kris was always rather intense internally but had always put on the calmest of demeanors. People saw him as a man wholly centered and at peace... And he was, of course, but he also had that intensity that comes when a person knows what they are about and where they are heading and they know they have a finite time to get there. Kris was most definitely a planner. He knew what he was going to do long before he did it. He knew what he was going to say before the words tumbled out of his mouth. To ask them to take such immediate action was out of character. Campbell was the first to speak, "Kris - I don't know what you've got in mind, but I've got a father who's on his death-bed. I can't leave town, if that's what you're thinking."

Jesse interjected, "I've got several cars over at the shop that are waiting repairs, Chris. I can't just take time off. My customers will be furious. Benny is a good mechanic but he's slow."

"Let the dead bury their own dead," Kris said to Campbell. "Your father isn't dead yet, Ken. My guess is that he won't be for another few years. He won't miss you for two weeks. Your sister and brother can watch him. And Jesse - come on... You know Benny has been waiting for you to be gone so he can test himself to see if he is the mechanic he thinks he is. He won't ever find out with you watching over his shoulder. Let him be the boss for two weeks."

Kris had never been quite so blunt with them and they weren't sure they liked it - Campbell especially. He felt some family obligation and Chris, who had always held family up so highly, seemed to be telling him now to forget those obligations... Nevertheless, he was the first to acquiesce. "OK. I'll bite. What do you want us to do for the next two weeks? THEN we'll decide if we'll do it."

"I want you to be me," Kris said. "I want you to do what you've seen me do. I want you to do what you've heard I've done. I want you to teach as I've taught you. I want each of you to go to the little towns - as many as you can get to in the next two weeks - and find people who have an obvious need. God will lead you to them or them to you - however that works. You will lay your hands on them and ask God to heal or strengthen or rescue or whatever it is they need. God already knows you're going to be asking and will guide those people to cross paths with you. Whatever you pray for will happen. This will gather a crowd - sometimes small, sometimes large - and you must tell them of God's power and love and forgiveness. Stay there as long as it seems reasonable, then move on. I warn you, though, that there will be some towns where people won't listen. Instead they will see what you are doing as some kind of magic or trickery - they won't believe their own eyes and they will be upset at what you have done or with what you say. Don't argue. Just apologize for bothering them and walk away. Move on to the next town on your list. I think it would be better if you partnered up. Some of what you experience will be pretty hard to take alone."

"Are you serious?" asks Nat. "We can't do that. We can't heal people. We'll make fools of ourselves. Kris, we've heard what you did in Sea Gull Harbor but we weren't even there. We, ourselves, have never seen these supposed healings you've been doing. How do you expect us to do them?"

Campbell jumped in, "I'm a fisherman, Chris. I don't talk in front of groups of people without breaking out in a cold sweat. I don't think I could do such a thing."

"Me, neither," said Michael. "I'm an accountant! Give me a back room and books filled with numbers and I'm in my element. I can't *HEAL* people. The very idea is preposterous. We're just ordinary people."

"Look. I know it's outside your comfort zone," said Kris. "That's why you'll each have a partner - to support one another. But you can do it. GOD will strengthen you. GOD will guide you. GOD will give you the words to say. Remember last month when I told you that God doesn't expect success - He expects faithfulness? THIS is where the rubber meets the road. You may fail. You may be laughed at. You may be run out of town. But you will have attempted to do something good and important. THAT is success. And don't worry about what you're going to say. Just be yourselves. It'll come.

Campbell - imagine you're talking to that hull full of fish - I've seen you do it - you talk to them like you love them. Think of the people you talk with as fish..."

"Now - you need to decide whether you'll do it or not. I'll love you either way. But you've all got to get out of here before this place becomes a bee hive... And if you decide you're going to do it, head out first thing this afternoon after telling your spouses what you're up to - no need to worry them any more than necessary. Tony, you divide up the region by zip codes and make assignments - in two weeks you can all cover a lot of territory if you keep moving - so plan on going out beyond Michigan if time permits... Go with God, my friends. Go with God..."

You can imagine all that is coursing through their minds as they get up to go. It all seems rather surreal. Kris had just asked them - with no warning - to go WAY outside their comfort zone and do something that makes almost no sense whatsoever. They began to think: *What, exactly, do we really know about this guy? Is he some kind of whacko who had taken them in? SHOULD they just drop everything and take off on some kind of missionary blitz?* None of them were comfortable with what Kris has asked them to do. None of them even knew if they could.

Gale and Dale were the newest members of the group. Gale spoke, "This is exactly why we came here. We KNEW Kris would do just this sort of thing. Haven't you felt it? Haven't you felt that he is something really special and that WE are special because He chose us - or allowed us - to tag along on whatever it is he is up to? Dale and I'd follow him the ends of the earth. Whatever the rest of you decide to do, we're going."

"Yeah, but you're a charismatic. The rest of us are Methodists and Congregationalists and Catholics. We don't do the 'feeling' thing so well," said Jesse. "We're not into that 'Holy Spirit' thing."

"But you guys saw his miracles, too, didn't you? Didn't you see 5000 people show up for the Grand Opening? Didn't you serve the food that never seemed to run out? Didn't you hear how he spoke over at the Methodist church and see how it affected people? Haven't you been awed by the way he talks to people during his workshops about God? Haven't you seen him pray?"

"You're right," Nat replies. "Kris is the most amazing thing to happen to this town in - like - forever. If he wants us to do this, then we should. I'm in. Michael, will you partner with me? Maybe together we can do this."

And they all agreed. They HAD to do it. They HAD to tell others about what God can do in their lives even though most of them already knew. Besides, if Kris was right and they really could, wouldn't it be totally awesome to heal people?

Just before lunch the camera crews rolled in just as Kris had expected, along with a dozen or so other reporters and news trucks. He had loved his life in Telhum. He knew that now it would never be the same. He could hear the young woman reporter standing in front of her camera man, "We're standing in front of the home and workshop of local furniture builder, Kristoff Yerushaliim. It has been reported that yesterday Mr. Yerushaliim did some rather amazing feats in Sea Gull Harbor. According to Mayor Mitchell McGeorge and others who were at the scene, Yerushaliim brought his daughter, Susan McGeorge, age 14, back from an attack of meningitis, supposedly AFTER her doctor had pronounced her dead. Dr. Lindholm was not available for comment. We're waiting now to see if Mr. Yerushaliim will speak with us and explain just what happened..."

While she was speaking, a couple of print reporters came up on Kris' porch and started knocking on the door. He took a deep breath and opened it as dozens of camera flashes made him feel like a movie star - or a criminal... He shielded his eyes with his hand as microphones were shoved toward his face and reporters started calling out their questions, "Mr. Yerushaliim - is it true? Did you heal the mayor's daughter?" "How did you do it?" "Do you think she was really dead?" "Has anything like this ever happened to you before?" "Why were you in Sea Gull Harbor?" "Are you a native of Telhum?" "Is this 'healing thing' something you can do any time or just on occasion?" Kris held up his hands to have them stop their questions so he could actually say something. As the crowd quieted down, one piped up, "SHOW US ONE OF YOUR TRICKS! LET US GET IT ON FILM!"

"Everyone wants to see me do something. But I'm not a trained pony. I don't perform on demand. What I've done or what people think I've done is of little importance to me. My purpose is to capture the world's attention so that they might listen to what I have to say. Yes, I've done some things that would be hard to explain even if you were to be an eye witness. I've done them so that you would come here today. I've done them so that I can, with your help, tell others. My message is this: God loves you. God loves you more than you can possibly imagine. I know that isn't something new to you. Everyone already knows that. In fact, I know that if I asked any one of you here this morning if you love God you'd say 'yes.' But here is the thing. There is so much more to being a Christian than loving God and God loving you. You must DO something if you love God.

"A man finds the perfect girl and he falls in love. She loves him too. He tells her and she tells him but if they never DO anything because of that love it means nothing. Their love is there but it is pretty meaningless. Rather, he buys her flowers and takes her to the theatre and schmooze's with her parents and plays with her little brother. If he didn't, she wouldn't be so sure his love is anything more than words (even though it is). After they get married, he helps clean the house and take care of the kids and takes her out to dinner and makes friends with her friends and their husbands. If he doesn't do any of those things she may still know she is loved because he says so, but what kind of love is that? The one who truly loves <u>always</u> DOES things to demonstrate it.

"You all call yourselves 'Christians.' You say you love God (and you really do - I would not deny that) but what do you DO other than SAY SO to show it to God? Does the Sunday School Superintendant at your church have to beg to find teachers? Does the minister have to guilt you into being on a committee? Do you set being in worship as a top priority in your family or do you attend when there is nothing better to do on a Sunday morning? What do you DO to show God love? What do you DO to keep that love alive? Every single day God DOES to show love to us. He brings the sunshine and the rain. He supplies our needs for food and shelter and clothing. He gives us health and wealth and freedom. He forgives our sins... Every day... The church in today's world has become a place where we are served rather than a place where we serve - it is a place to be entertained rather than a place of sacrificial giving and deep commitment. If every Christian stepped forward and would do just ONE thing to serve the church - take on one "job" ministers would be turning people down - there'd be too many people doing too much. If every Christian, in his or her LIFETIME would find someone in need of faith and bring that person in, churches all over the world would have to have building programs. Christians lament how empty their neighborhood streets are on a Sunday morning - their neighbors don't go to church - yet most have NEVER invited even one of them to get up and out and to go to worship God with them. To love is to DO things. So many say they love but don't DO.

"God's house is always just one generation from extinction. And here in Michigan there seems to be a malaise that keeps people in the pews satisfied with just being in the pews. We, as lovers of the creator, must DO something. It doesn't have to be huge. There are a lot of us. If each of us do something every day to show God we love Him, that will be enough."

Kris paused in his little sermon, "Mr. Yerushaliim, how did you do those amazing healings?" Kris shook his head and looked down in disappointment. They hadn't heard a word he had said. All they wanted was the pizzazz. They didn't care what he had to say... Well, maybe some of what he said would be reported in sound bites on the evening news. Maybe SOMEBODY would hear his message. Maybe his seven friends hitting all the towns in the area for the next couple of weeks would wake people up. He so wished that people would have a vision for what God can do in and through them if they would just get off their duffs and DO something...

The reporters started in with their questions again, "Sir, will you be going back to Sea Gull Harbor to see the mayor's daughter again?" "Do you have any plans for a 'healing tour?'" "How do you decide who will be healed and who not?" And Kris turned, without saying another word, and walked back into his house, gently closing the door.

That night, on the 6:00 news there was a report titled "The Healer of Sea Gull Harbor." Just before they showed a brief clip of Chris, the voice over said, "Kris Yerushaliim, a Christian Shaman who reportedly brought about some amazing healings in the lakeside village of Sea Gull Harbor spoke today on relationships and how important it is to take action when one is in love" and the sound comes up and Kris hears his own voice, "A man finds the perfect girl and he falls in love. She loves him too. He tells her and she tells him but if they never DO anything because of that love it means nothing. Their love is there but it is pretty meaningless."

Well, maybe the newspaper tomorrow will have a bit more of what he said... Maybe people will hear - maybe not.

SUNRISE OVER LAKE HURON
Matthew 13:1-13a

      I suppose it's possible that no one from the little town of Telhum had ever been on television before. In fact, except when violent storms came in from Lake Huron and did significant damage Telhum was seldom ever even mentioned on TV. So when Kris had television station mobile vans sitting on his front lawn and reporters from newspapers all over arriving in town and talking to anyone who would give them a few lines to quote, it made quite a stir. Millie's Bed and Breakfast, with vacancies nearly 300 nights of the year was booked solid for the next three weeks. After Kris appeared on the local channels, the networks picked up the story and, with some modification, made Kris a national curiosity overnight. He started getting calls from *The Today Show* and from *Good Morning America* - he started getting so many calls from everyone imaginable that he had to unplug his phone just to get some peace. Everyone wanted to interview him. But he turned them all down. He said something about how they would hear him speak through other channels - that they would hear it when the ever widening ripples of communication reached them on a personal level. He told them that sound bites and 7 minute interviews with Katie Couric wouldn't accomplish what he wanted to accomplish. But his stonewalling them, of course, made them even more anxious to get his story - to get to know what this guy was all about and where he was going with his unique gift of being able to heal people.

      Mayor McGeorge, from Sea Gull Harbor, was interviewed on Piers Morgan's CNN show. Sitting beside him were Terry Jackson, the man who was formerly in a wheelchair, Doctor Lindholm and Police Officer Sandy Miller. Piers was, as always, gracious, but clearly skeptical of all the hype. "Mr. Mayor, I must say your story is one that has captured the attention of the nation. Your daughter, Susan, came down with meningitis and died, you say. This KrisYerushaliim comes along and brings her back to life. Now, you've got to admit that story, as wondrous as it might be, will raise some eyebrows. Do you really believe she was dead and was, somehow, raised by this furniture maker who was in town simply to visit your town's sawmill?"

      "I wasn't actually at home when she died," Mayor McGeorge admitted, "but my wife was. My wife's parents were there and her cousin was there. They tell me there was no doubt. All I know is that she was pronounced dead by the doctor here and that today she is alive and well. SOME kind of miracle happened."

"Doctor Lindholm, you were on the scene. In fact, you were the one who pronounced her dead. How do you explain what happened?"

"Clearly she was not dead. I admit that I made a grievous error. I believe Susan was in a cataleptic state caused by some nervous system condition or some emotional trauma that I did not have the instrumentation to detect. In Catalepsy breathing is imperceptible for all practical purposes and the diagnosis of death is not uncommon. Most famously, novelist Edgar Allen Poe describes it in his book "The Premature Burial." In that story, the cataleptic was in the state so long that he was actually buried. Was Susan dead? Of course not. No one returns from that state."

"Terry Jackson," says Piers, "I understand you have a bit different take on Mr. Yerushaliim."

" I do. I was in an auto accident fifteen years ago and was paralyzed from the waist down. Kris touched me. He helped me get out of my wheelchair. He prayed to God and I was I could walk."

"Remarkable," said Morgan. "Officer Miller, you had an opportunity to talk to this man and you say you asked him how he did it. What did he tell you?"

"I didn't understand most of it. But he started off by pointing out how our negative thoughts and emotions cause physical problems and that 'the other side of the coin' I think he called it, works equally as powerfully. Our positive thoughts and emotions bring about healings - but he pointed out that there also had to be some kind of connection with God wanting it to happen... I don't really know how it all works. But I've seen death and I'm pretty sure Susan was dead."

The conversation went on for a while longer and Piers asked his video people to roll a section of the affiliate station's film of Kris on his front porch: "... I'm not a trained pony. I don't perform on demand. What I've done or what people think I've done is of little importance to me. My purpose is to capture the world's attention so that they might listen to what I have to say."

"I find that intriguing," says the host. "What did he mean by that? Was what he did simply a gimmick to get people's attention? Isn't that a bit deceptive? Viewers, send us an email or a tweet answering that question. 'DID the events at Sea Gull Harbor contain an element of hucksterism? Is this something we should condone or condemn? What IS the message that this healer from Michigan is so desperate to share - and why?' Tomorrow evening we'll talk to YOU, our viewers, about all of this..."

I don't know how many people watch CNN and the Piers Morgan show, but apparently enough that people started heading for Telhum - or maybe it was because the aired segments of Chris' speech hit YouTube and had received 900,000 hits. People poured in. They brought the sick and the crippled and the depressed and the hurting of every variety. The local newspaper sent out an emergency request to everyone in town and in all the neighboring towns asking them to register any spare rooms they would be willing to rent out (at an exorbitant rate of courswe) on a special website they had set up. And the reservations came pouring in. There wasn't a bed unspoken for for more than fifty miles around.

Kris didn't watch much TV - too time consuming and mind numbing. He had read somewhere that a study showed that four hours of TV viewing a day would shorten your life by a year. A clever commentator had pulled out a calculator and concluded that a year lost comes to about a half hour a day so concluded that watching four hours must shorten ones life by a half hour. Rather sobering when put in those terms.

So he didn't know what the buzz on the news was. All he knew was that, before he unplugged it, the phone was driving him crazy.

Kris had a sunrise calendar. Every morning he set his alarm clock early enough to get up and out and down to the lakeshore in time to watch the sun come up. He LOVED the birth of a new day. There was a long dock that belonged to the town of Telhum that he enjoyed walking on all the way to the end and sit quietly watching the world come to life - sparkling water all around him and as he looked out for as far as the eye could see.

No one knew he did this except his "club." He had invited them to join him but none ever had. Sunrise was sleep time, not nature gazing time. But that was OK with him, he enjoyed the solitude and the absorption into nature that he felt. He prayed best out there on that dock. There wasn't any time in life where God was nearer to him than when he was alone in nature. Somehow God seemed to hear his words without all the world's interferences... He imagined he could hear his Heavenly Father speak - *"I love you, Chris. May your spirit be at peace today. Do my will."*

But today something was different. A reporter from one of the small town newspapers had been staking out Chris' house to try to get some kind of exclusive so as to make a name for himself. He had promised that he would let some of the big guys know if Kris showed himself (all in an effort to curry favor and maybe get his toe in the door to bigger things), so when Kris came out of his house at 5:15 and headed toward the lake, John Sanders followed him. He then got on his cell phone and called his new buddies. They called their partners and all of them together inadvertently awoke the host families and the other guests and in an incredibly short time, dozens of people were heading, in the pre-dawn morning, for the lake. When they got there they saw Kris sitting out there at the end of the dock meditating and, most likely, praying.

It's almost impossible for any group of people to move noiselessly even when they are trying to but even more so in the stillness of dawn before even the birds begin their morning medleys. Kris turned and saw a small crowd gathering. People who live along a lake know that it is foolish for very many people to be on a dock all at once so nobody went out to where Kris was. They stayed on shore just looking at this unusual man sitting out there seeing them invade his solace. He wearily got up and walked to the base of the dock. "Sit down - all of you. Let's talk."

The people sat on the slightly damp sand on the beach and got comfortable. It amazed them how Kris could just talk normally and they could hear him so clearly. The lake and the hill leading down to the beach and the pre-dawn quiet made for some excellent acoustics. "I've been sitting here this morning thinking about God. What a wonderful place to do it. Look around. God is everywhere. But let me tell you what I've learned about God's Kingdom over the years. It's in the form of a story: *There once was a man who rented a certain farm. The man did all the work and the owner paid all the expenses. Then they would split the income from the property. It was a mutually beneficial arrangement and everyone was happy with it. This went on for years. But one day the man was clearing a fencerow and was digging out a stump - hard work - necessary work - the kind of work every farmer in the world does every day. His shovel hit something hard but it didn't seem to be a rock. He dug it up and discovered it was a metal box. He pried it open and inside found gold bullion from a century ago - pirate treasure, no doubt. It was a fortune! There may have been as much as three million dollars worth in there. But it wasn't his. So he reburied it, went home and crunched some numbers. He planned to buy that farm and capture that treasure for himself. He calculated what the farm was worth and then added half to the total. But he didn't have enough to make the purchase. So he put his house up for sale. He sold his farm equipment. He sold his car and his pickup truck and his wife's car. He advertised a "moving sale" and emptied his house of every stick of furniture. He counted his cash. It still wasn't enough. So he went to the bank and borrowed a substantial amount. Then he went to the farmer and asked if he could* buy his land. He negotiated hard but he knew that no matter what it would take for the farmer to sell, that is what he would pay. And, of course, everything is for sale if the price is right and he bought the farm.

"In the same vein but a different story: *There was a woman who loved to go to garage sales. She knew prices and she was an excellent negotiator. She also knew a lot about antiques and art. One day she found an original Wassily Kandinsky, "Composition V," at a sale. She couldn't believe her eyes. She knew the painting was worth about $100 million. What was it doing here? And with a price tag of $175! Unfortunately she didn't have $175 on her but there was no way she was going to let this get away. She went to her car and then brazenly approached some of the other garage salers with things she'd like to sell. She had her sunglasses, a digital tire pressure gauge, a sunshade, a GPS... But it wasn't enough and others were looking at the painting! She HAD to have it. "Hey, shoppers - I'll sign over the title to my car to the first person who will pay me $200 cash! It has no lie! It's free and clear! This offer is good for the next 60 seconds!" And, although everyone thought her crazy, a couple of people came rushing over to her with the cash and one very lucky garage saler drove away in a $23,000 car for $200. And she bought the Kandinsky.*

Another story: "*A man, one spring several years ago, decided to over-seed his lawn. He wanted to pump up his grass and make the whole thing look better. He was using one of those hand-held crank spreaders and walking back and forth across his lawn to sow the grass seed. He watered it twice every day for two weeks until the grass had a chance to germinate and take root. Some of the seed that he spread landed on his driveway and some on the sidewalk. Obviously it didn't grow. In fact, the birds feasted on it. Some of the seed fell on soil that was mostly clay and the grass had a hard time growing. It germinated but the little root tentacles couldn't break through the clay and it dried up as soon as he stopped watering. Some of the seed he spread got into the landscaping and the mature plants there kept the sun from getting to it so it didn't survive, but you know, most of that seed did exactly what it was supposed to. It fell onto the existing lawn, slipped between the blades of grass to the soil. It germinated, took root and grew. And that man had a beautiful lawn all summer long and the next one and the next and for years to come.*"

"Kris- what are you talking about? You're being a bit obtuse, aren't you? Tell us about your miracles. Tell us about how you did them and when and where you're planning to do the next one. We want to be there," one of the reporters called out.

Although Kris' friends hadn't been there at the beginning of this little exchange on the dock, they arrived at the shop that morning and when he wasn't there they knew where he must be so they went down to the lake just in time to hear the last of Chris' stories and the comments afterward. Later that day Jesse asked him, "Chris, what was that all about? What was the point of those little stories you were telling? Wouldn't it be better to just say what you mean? Wouldn't it be better if people actually KNEW what you were saying instead of having to guess at it?"

"Every person has to discover God's truth for themselves, Jesse. In so doing they take it to heart. If I - or you - were to just tell them something, they might believe it but it is irrelevant to them. That's how we learn - truly learn. We DISCOVER for ourselves. A child can learn that 3x6 is 18. He can learn that multiplication fact and all the others and accept them as being true. But every teacher knows that unless those abstract facts can become concrete in their thinking they can go no further. So she will give them six sets of three objects and have them count them. Voila. They get it! It latches in to their brains and it is there forever as fact.

"If people don't get what I am saying to them, then they are not ready to hear. They are not ready to discover. They are not ready to go deeper in their faith. They are not ready for God. Did you notice what the first question was? It was a guy wanting a show. He wasn't ready for truth. To him my stories were just stupid stories. They said nothing to him. So if I had just said it straight out it would be like throwing pearls into a pig sty. God and Godly things and ideas and concepts are too noble for that."

"I know just what you mean," says Nat. "Last week when we were out in the small towns around here, that is exactly what we experienced. I was telling people about God's love and some people kept coming back at me with 'Katrina' and 'Haiti' and 'Oak Creek' and '9-11' and 'Sandy Hook.' They said God can't love us if He allows those kinds of things to happen. I was tempted to get into a debate about how small our understanding of the things of God is but it seemed pointless."

"Yes. It would have been pointless. Those people were not ready to receive the love of God. They need to grow up until they can understand that they are unqualified to decide what God can and can't do...that it is us who are made in HIS image and not HE in ours. We have no authority to dictate how, when, where, and whether God acts.

What arrogance to say we won't believe in God if such and such happens. Our belief in God or non-belief changes nothing.

"Let me tell you one. See if you can figure it out. It's another farmer one... It, too is about God's Kingdom... This farmer sows his field with seed wheat. He is meticulous and makes sure his seed is clean and his planter is set for placing the wheat at the optimum depth given the prediction the weather people are making about rain this season. He fertilizes it and, if there is too long a stretch of dry weather, he irrigates it. But unbeknownst to him, one of his neighbors who has harbored a grudge for years, came in right after he planted his wheat and distributed about a bushel of thistle seed and a peck of Queen Ann's Lace seed such that when the wheat grew, so did the weeds. The farmers was incredulous at the number of weeds that were in his field when all started to grow and his sons offered to go in and pull them out before harvest because clean wheat brings a much higher price than wheat mixed with weed seed. But the farmer told them not to because if they did the wheat would take a beating as they traversed the field inadvertently trampling the wheat. Wait until after harvest. We'll get a blower and drop the wheat through it and the weed seeds, being lighter, will blow away and we'll collect and destroy them at that time."

Kris' friends looked puzzled as to what exactly that all meant. But they knew that to figure it out - this and so many other mysteries of God - would do them good and would make whatever the lesson is more powerful and useful in their lives.

THE END OF THE BEGINNING
John 16: 17-22

AP International. Telhum, Michigan, August 15
Today in the tiny eastern Michigan town of Telhum, Michigan, the body of a local holy man, Kristoff Yerusahaliim was discovered. His body was discovered on the outskirts of town by two unnamed women who were jogging along the country road. Yerushaliim's body was found among the boulders along that village's Lake Huron shoreline. Authorities say the man was apparently whipped and beaten severely and left to die. Under investigation is a radical religious group which had been critical of Yerushaliim's teachings.

Yerushaliim, according to locals, was a man with extraordinary talents who had reportedly healed people from serious illnesses over the course of the past several months. Professionally, he was the owner of the Yerushaliim Furniture Works and was known for the manufacture of fine furniture.

In an interview with a former member of the religious group under investigation, Mark Wollam said that the group is adamant about doctrinal purity and religious correctness and that Yerushaliim was a "burr under their saddle." Wollam said that Yerushaliim taught an unconditional love of God for all people. That doctrine, according to the radical group's thinking, "is contrary to all that is sacred" said Wollam. The religious group, known simply as "God's Own" is an activist group which has periodically protested at main line churches throughout Michigan in an attempt to urge people to understand and live by the strictures of religious belief.

Funeral services for Yerushaliim are pending arrangements being made and notification of family members.

Campbell and Jesse and Michael and Nat and Tony and Gale and Dale were gathered around the Oak table in Kris' showroom. They each had a key and they knew Kris wouldn't mind them being there. The sadness in the room was palpable. They didn't know much more than what they had read in the newspapers. Kris was alive and well one day and gone the next. He had kind of alluded to the fact that he had some enemies last week, but they hadn't taken him too seriously. Since when does one's religious beliefs bring trouble? This is America, isn't it? Isn't there freedom of speech and freedom of religion? Don't we have a right to share our opinions and beliefs? That part of their thinking was anger.

But hadn't Kris assigned them to go to neighboring towns and do exactly what he had been doing? Hadn't they done it? Were members of "God's Own" going to come after them next? That part was fear.

So mixed with their grief over losing Kris was a fear for their own safety and for that of their families. Not so long ago they were just five locals sharing coffee and shooting the breeze over at Daisy's Diner. It seemed like years ago. Before Kris came into their lives life was good - predictable - easy - safe - no complaints. None of them knew they wanted anything more than they already had. But then Kris came along. Kris had made their lives... *glorious*. He had given them purpose for living such that they had never had before and assigned them to DO things of lasting - eternal - personal importance. He had taught them the meaning of love and power and compassion and seeking and finding God's will. He had taught them how to pray in a way they never learned in church. He had fed them and loved them and was the most amazing friend they had ever had... And now, unintentionally but most certainly, he brought turmoil and fear into their lives - more than they had ever had in their small town lives. They still believed all he had said but they had never really counted the possible cost of believing. They remembered Kris making reference to a book by Dietrich Bonhoefer. His words still rang in their ears: "Cheap grace," he said, "Cheap grace is the grace we bestow on ourselves. Cheap grace is the preaching of forgiveness without requiring repentance, baptism without church discipline, Communion without confession.... Cheap grace is grace without discipleship, grace without the cross..." and the other side of the coin, "Costly grace is the gospel which must be sought again and again and again, the gift which must be asked for, the door at which a man must knock. Such grace is costly because it calls us to follow. It is costly because it costs a [person] his life, and it is grace because it gives a [person] the only true life. It is costly because it condemns sin, and grace because it justifies the sinner. Above all, it is costly because it cost God the life of his Son... and what has cost God much cannot be cheap for us. Above all, it is grace because God did not reckon his Son too dear a price to pay for our life, but delivered him up for us [to die]."

Now they thought of those words with infinitely more understanding. When Kris read those passages and taught about them it all sounded good but now... now it really meant something. "*What cost God dearly most surely can't be cheap for us.*" What a profound thought. As it cost Kris his life, our own lives may be required - and we must offer them as a reasonable price for eternity, for forgiveness, for peace, for the very security of our souls...

Some people go blank when they are in grief. Some people become philosophical. These seven were of the latter ilk. They couldn't help but to think of all the wondrous truths Kris had taught them and how now, at his death, all that theory becomes reality and comes down on them like a ton of bricks... Truth, when it meets our lives, changes those lives forever - and not, really, before then.

As they thought of all that Kris had said to them in the months they were together, they were astounded at how much was there. The central core, of course, was love. That is what it is all about when it comes to God. He created and he judged his creation good and when God says something is good He means he LOVES it it is so good... And then, wrapped around the love core is a layer of forgiveness.

Kris had pointed out that good never lasts long. The whole of creation is bent out of shape slightly such that evil taints even the best of us. Although none of the seven could imagine that Chris' goodness was tainted with anything. He was just SO good - maybe that is just how we always remember loved ones who have died... But wasn't he? Wasn't he, morally and socially and intellectually and in every way you can think of, good? Once he had said there is none good - that all of us need a purifying relationship with God in the hopes that His perfection would somehow rub off on us and we could resist sin. Kris said that the third layer of the God-system is commitment. It is a commitment to God and seeking His will in all we do and all we are. Then the next layer is a hybrid layer of love inter-mixed with forgiveness. Once we are committed to following God then our own lives change such that we love others and forgive them when they wrong us and we do it as often as God has forgiven us...

Well, as they thought about all Kris had said, the conversation got a bit heavy. It would take a while to absorb and understand all Kris had taught them. Especially now that it seemed to matter so much more than it did when he said those things. They tacitly agreed to put the heavy stuff aside for now - they'd talk more about it later. But they, of course, continued to talk about their lives with Kris.

They remembered their last time together:

"Guys, I've got to tell you something," he had said. "This isn't easy to say but you've got to know. I've got some enemies out there who want to stop me - us - from doing what we're doing. I'm afraid it's going to get ugly."

"What? Because you've been healing people and feeding crowds and raising Susan McGeorge from the dead? Who could be against that?" asked Jesse.

"Well, those things can be interpreted in a variety of ways. You've been around long enough to know that there have always been 'faith healers' around. Some of them pretty good but some of them nothing but phonies. They've ruined it for the true healers, I'm afraid. But it's more than that. My enemies aren't against my healings as much as they are against what I've been saying."

Nat jumped in, "What you're saying? You haven't been saying anything so radical. You've been saying that God loves each and every one of us no matter who we are - no matter what our race, color, creed. Isn't that what the church has been teaching for as long as it has existed?"

"Yes and no. The ministers have been preaching it but you've been to churches. The Methodists are all Methodists the Catholics are all Catholics, the Congregationalists are all Congregationalists. If it's a white church it is all white. If it is a black church it is all black. If it is Asian it is all Asian. Wealthy churches have all wealthy people. Middle class churches have only middle class people. Now don't get me wrong, people are most comfortable being with people like themselves. But the church should be different than general society. Christians ought to be totally and wholly integrated and loving it. Churches ought to be places where people can be radically different from one another and people will still love them and respect them and fellowship with them. They are there to love God TOGETHER. They are there to serve God TOGETHER. They are there to enjoy God's amazing family TOGETHER.

"That's where the rub comes. Some people don't buy it. They are so ego-centered that they believe God made some grievous mistakes. He INTENDED to make everyone like them but for some unknown reason didn't and therefore not all were included in the 'in the image of God' thing."

"You can't be serious," says Tony. "And even if some kooks believe that, so what?"

"They not only believe it, they are committed to it. They will stop at nothing to prove me wrong."

"Why should they care so much?" Tony interjects. "Nobody cares about that kind of thing."

"God does. And they do. It is up to me to prove that all I've said is true. I'm going to be away for a few days but when I get back, you'll know - and the world will know - that I am right. It is almost finished."

"Where you going?" asked siblings Gale and Dale simultaneously, as twins can sometimes do. "Do you want us to come along? How can we help?"

"Where I am going you can't go. It's something only I can do. But don't worry, I'll be back and good things will begin to happen. I've got this friend who will come and continue my instruction and work."

That was a rather strange thing for Kris to say, of course, but no one questioned him - just another of his parables, perhaps. They were probably supposed to figure it out for themselves. Was he bringing a buddy up from Inkster? So far as they knew THEY were his only friends - certainly his closest (they felt a bit jealous thinking that he had other friends they knew nothing about).

Now that they thought about it, it seemed a bit surreal...

"So, what do you think he meant?" asked Jesse. "Where was he going? When? Why couldn't we go? Who is this mysterious 'friend.' What's almost finished? I suppose that is mute now that he is gone. None of it matters anymore."

"I just don't get it" says Campbell. "Why would someone kill an innocent man - a man who had done good things and had such charisma that everyone liked him?"

"We'll never know" responded Tony. "people are certainly a mystery. I've no idea what makes them do what they do."

"So what are we supposed to do now?" asked Caseu. "Going back to my little cubby to do accounting seems somehow wrong. I don't think I could concentrate now, anyway."

Jesse says, "We don't have to go back to our lives just yet. Let's let ourselves just mourn for a while - at least until after the funeral. I know I've already asked Benny to cover the work at the shop for a few days. I just need time to figure out where I am right now and what Kris would want us to do."

"What Kris would want us to do?" says Campbell. "You've got to be kidding. Kris is dead. He doesn't CARE what we do. But I agree. Let's just hang tight. I'm a bit worried about those wackos. If they got Kris what's to prevent them from coming after us. He had us going all over the place doing exactly the same things he was doing. Why would they leave us alone?"

"That's all in the past," said Tony. "I'm not doing any of that stuff anymore. It WAS kind of cool doing those healings, but I've never really been comfortable talking about God to people. It's all so personal and private. I feel like I'm exposing myself and making them feel uncomfortable."

"Oh, come on, Tony. Don't be such a wuss," said Jesse. "What we did was the most exciting thing we've ever done in our lives and you know it. We asked God to lead us to people to whom we could minister and HE LED US! We spoke and people listened! Anything like that ever happen to you before? I think not. I don't suppose we can do it again. It was a rather unique experience but I'll tell you, if Kris walked through that door tomorrow and asked me to do it again I would, in a heart beat. Telling people about God's love changed lives! It was scary but it was one of the highlights of my life. Yours too, I'll bet."

Well, the discussion went on for quite some time that day. In fact, the guys didn't just spend their usual couple of hours there drinking coffee and eating sweet rolls. They spent the entire day there, talking and reminiscing and philosophizing. It was well after dark before they broke up and headed to their homes. They would meet again in the morning, as usual. They had decided to continue their gatherings until at least after the funeral. Then they'd probably have to re-frequent their old haunt - Daisy's Diner. Life is strange how it radically changes and then so quickly can lapse back into old patterns...

But what none of them knew was that what they had started with Kris was just the beginning of their new lives. What they had done would look like nothing compared to what they would yet do.

The next couple of days were somber days in Telhum. No one in town wanted to admit that Kris was gone. Their little town had seldom encountered such hatred and violence - certainly not directed at one who was about as non-violent and loving a person as you'd ever find. Kris hadn't really been with them all that long, yet he had captured their affection and devotion. They knew there would never be another Chris, but they could hope. They could try to live their lives in such a way that their children and grandchildren could sort of know Kris through them - to BE him to them in some tiny way. At least that's what they hoped...

The reporters left town en masse. Kris was a sensation in life. His brutal death was newsworthy, of course, but no one wanted to cover the funeral of some unknown flash-in-the-pan in this God-forsaken little town. After they were all gone, on the eve of Chris' death, church bells began to toll. The Catholics started it. The priest had been devastated by the violence in his community and hoped the church could help salve wounded spirits. The Methodist sexton joined in. Rev. Johanson insisted. Kris had made such an impact on his congregation when he spoke there. People were STILL coming to church after those Sundays when he filled the pulpit. The minister of the Congregational church had his bells ringing, too. He was so concerned for Telhum. He didn't know what would happen to this lovely little town now. This show of unity among the churches might help a little.

"Man of Sorrows!" what a name
For the Son of God, who came
Ruined sinners to reclaim.
Hallelujah! What a Savior!

Bearing shame and scoffing rude,
In my place condemned He stood;
Sealed my pardon with His blood.
Hallelujah! What a Savior!

Guilty, vile, and helpless we;
Spotless Lamb of God was He;
"Full atonement!" can it be?
Hallelujah! What a Savior!

Lifted up was He to die;
"It is finished!" was His cry;
Now in Heav'n exalted high.
Hallelujah! What a Savior!

When He comes, our glorious King,
All His ransomed home to bring,
Then anew His song we'll sing:
Hallelujah! What a Savior!

- Words to this song:Philip P. Bliss

THE FUNERAL
1 Corinthians 15: 12-22

"Listen, gentlemen... I know you were friends of the deceased and I know he was quite well-liked around town, but my hands are tied. They really are. If no family or friends are available or willing to take on the expense of a funeral, I'll embalm the body according to law and have him laid in a potter's grave out at St. Andrew's cemetery. That's all I can do. Without payment up front I cannot even allow a wake to take place here in the funeral parlor. Now, if you can come up with, say around $6500 (that's $800 for the cemetery plot, $550 to have it opened and closed, $2800 for the casket, $1900 for body preparation and service expenses, $235 for document fees)... we can give him a nice farewell."

"But Mr. Black, we don't have that kind of money. Are you sure you can't find any of K ris' relatives?" asks Jesse.

"Believe me, I've tried - and it's not even my job. That's the job for the Medical Examiner's Office. I'm not supposed to even be involved in that sort of thing. But I called down to Inkster to a colleague of mine since I understand that's where Mr. Yerushaliim was from. He told me that he did, in fact, handle the funerals for both of Mr. Yerushaliim's parents but that there was no other family on record as having taken part in any of it. I'm a friend of the Medical Examiner and he's tried whatever he could to find relatives, too. He even called the Greek embassy in Washington to try to track down the parents. They were immigrants from there, apparently. He was told that there are no Yerushaliim's anywhere in his records as even existing anywhere in Greece. He said 'Yerushaliim' is actually a Hebrew word - means 'Jerusalem.' But that's as far as anyone has gotten."

Jesse said, "We really can't let Kris go without a proper burial. Please, don't do anything for another day. We'll be back to make some decisions by tomorrow."

"I'll wait until then. But not ANY longer. I have obligations and there are laws about bodies being embalmed and buried within a reasonable amount of time. Health issues, you know."

They left the Funeral Home and went over to Daisy's Diner for a slice of her award-winning cherry pie and to discuss what to do. Dale and Gale, the twins, had an idea. "You guys are always talking about how Kris had you all go to all the neighboring towns and distribute those fliers for his Open House and how hundreds of people showed up."

"Thousands," interjected Campbell.

" How about if we do that sort of thing - only this time we pass out fliers asking for donations to bury Kris?" Jesse suggested.

"That's just wrong," said Michael, the accountant. "That was for an occasion. I'm not even sure asking for money like that is legal. Besides, suppose we don't get enough to do anything. What are we going to do with the money we do get? And if we did it and raised more than needed what do we do with the extra money? I see IRS violations written all over that plan."

"Maybe we can just let people in town know - we can put out those little canisters on business countertops you always see" said Tony.

"Too time consuming. It would be too little too late" said Michael. "But we COULD give the mayor down in Sea Gull Harbor a call and see what he can do. That's where all those amazing healings took place. There might be enough interest in honoring Kris down there to do the trick."

So they called Mayor McGeorge. He thought it a wonderful idea and said he would personally work to raise the full amount and have it to them by Friday noon (politicians have an amazing way of raising lots of money for whatever they really want to do). He got on the phone. He called Terry Jackson and Sandy Miller and the two women who had believed Kris could heal their kids. They and their loved ones promised a total of $4500 and said they'd bring it to the Mayor's office within the hour. The mayor himself came up with the remaining $2000 out of his own pocket. He knew that he had received something more precious than money when he got Susan back. He owed Krismore than a paltry $2000 for what he had done for him. Didn't they all? The least he could do was to honor him at his death.

When the mayor called back two hours later and told them he had the needed funds, Kris' friends were astounded - so quickly! How was that even possible? Apparently people who appreciated what Kris did for them could really come through. They all decided that they would put in what money they could themselves and they'd have a blow-out funeral like Telhum had never seen. They called Mr. Black and told him of the Mayor's success and Mr. Black told Jesse that he was a personal friend of the Mayor's and if he said he had the money he most certainly did. He would begin the preparations immediately, knowing the fees were on their way. He would be finished with the embalming by Friday afternoon and they could have Kris laying in state by Friday evening. Sam told him that would be perfect.

At this point they did, in fact, take Gale and Dale's suggestion. They printed up some fliers giving a brief bio of Kris along with a photocopy of the newspaper article about Kris' murder and details about the funeral. Kris would lay in state on Friday evening at the funeral home from 5:00 until 9:00 and then again (assuming a lot of people would want to pay their respects) on Saturday. The funeral would be at the Methodist church on Sunday afternoon at 2:00. Then they went from house to house all over Telhum and into the nearby towns and passed them all out - about 2500 of them.

And people came. At 5:00 on Friday there were dozens of people at the funeral home. By 7:00 many of the early visitors had gone home but were replaced by dozens more. There was a steady stream until the funeral home closed. Then, on Saturday, even more mourners showed up. It was, for Telhum, almost like one of those political funerals where people file by, waiting in long lines to touch the casket. No one knew how many actually came to pay their respects but Mr. Black said he had never seen anything like it. There were so many people on such short notice. But people didn't just file by. They stayed and talked with one another... They talked about Kris and how he had helped them or about something he had said that impacted their lives or how he had been so kind. A few talked about his religion and how special a relationship he had with God and his peculiar manner of praying. Some said he had literally changed their lives through his words and his wisdom. It seems a bit uncouth to say it, but Kris' wake was probably the biggest social event in Telhum since... since his open house.

Some of the visitors commented on how "natural" he looked laying there in the casket. Others reminded them that there is nothing natural-looking about death. True, Black had done a remarkable job on Kris' wounds and bruises, but still... Here was a man who seemed to be life itself now without life. There really is nothing natural about that.

Quite a number of the guests in those two days cautiously reached into the casket and touched Kris' hand or cheek or forehead. They were rewarded for their efforts by forever remembering that touch - how cold and hard and lifeless it was - nothing at all like the man they saw walking the streets of Telhum - chatting with everyone at his shop - teaching how to make a dovetail joint at his workshops - laughing... All who touched him wished they hadn't.

Mayor McGeorge and Sandy and Terry came up from Sea Gull Harbor to pay their respects. They would stay overnight at Millie's B&B for the funeral the following day. You could see the distress on their faces. Their loss was especially sharp because of their brief ultra-powerful encounter with Kris. They would never forget him - they'd never want to.

Sunday morning arrived all too soon. Not much sleep was had by anyone, yet the people who knew Kris best headed for Kris' store - to meet there at their usual 7AM coffee time. Usually they didn't meet on a Sunday, but today was an exception. They knew that today would, perhaps, be the last time they would be together like this. Nat got to the shop first so reached into his pocket for the key. Tony, Michael and Jesse were with him. Coming up the street they could see Dale and Gale. Campbell must have gone out fishing early. He'd be there shortly. Nat put his key into the door lock and started to enter when suddenly he stopped and took a step back. In almost comic fashion, Tony and Jesse and Michael, who had started forward, all collided into Nat. "What are you doing Nat. Stop goofing around." But then they saw what had startled Nat. Sitting there at the big round oak table, smiling at them, was Kris.

"Who are you and what are you doing here?" demanded Jesse. "Get out of here before we call the cops."

"Jesse, It's me, Kris. Nat - Michael - Tony - come on in. Sit down. I've poured you some vintage wine. And here is some of that pita bread you chide me about all the time. It's fresh and it's delicious."

Jesse and Nat and Michael and Tony all came in cautiously and pulled out chairs and sat down. None of them could take their eyes off this guy, whomever he was. None of them said a word. He LOOKED like Kris and his voice sounded like Kris' but there is no way...that was impossible. Every one of them had reached in and touched Kris in that casket. That body could not be revived. They could hear Dale and Gale coming up the walk. They anxiously awaited their reaction. Dale and Gale came in chatting and looked at the guys who all looked as though they had seen a ghost and then they spotted Kris. "Whoa! Dude! You're back! Awesome!" said Dale. Gale said, "Fantastic! How'd you do that, Kris? YOU WERE DEAD AS A DOOR-NAIL! This is the coolest thing I've ever seen! Guys, what's wrong?"

"This isn't Kris, you fools" Sam said. "This guy is pulling some kind of scam. He's a Kris look-a-like."

The guy who looked like Kris said, "Jesse - the rest of you - eat with me. Drink with me. Let's talk." And the Kris look-alike began to talk to them about God and truth and faith and life and eternity and as he talked they knew. This was NOT an imposter. This really was - as astoundingly impossible as it was, Kris. And tears began flowing freely down their cheeks, making their pita salty tasting, but they didn't care. All they knew was that the utterly impossible had happened IN THEIR LIVES and that they could never go back to not believing all that Kris said ever again. They would never doubt again. They could not waver from this day forward. They could only believe and trust and tell others of this most unexpected and unlikely outcome. Who would believe them? They scarcely believed it themselves - yet they knew it to be more true than anything else in their lives.

"Where's Campbell?" asked Kris.

"Probably went out fishing early. He'll be here soon," said Jesse

And just as Jesse said that, Campbell walked in. He looked around at all the red eyes and tear stained faces and then saw Kris. "Campbell, he's back!" said Tony. "Kris is alive! Can you believe it! Isn't it the most amazing thing you've ever seen?"

Campbell looked directly at the Chris-man for a moment before saying anything. "No. This man certainly looks like Kris - sort of - but not exactly. You all obviously believe he is Chris. But you and I both know that's not possible. You're fooling yourselves. He's fooling you. I won't believe it until I can examine his wounds and see for myself."

But he never did. Kris spoke, "Campbell..." and at that single word - his own name out of Kris' mouth, Campbell fell on his knees and began to weep and said, "My God - My God - Kris..." And Kris took him by the arm and lifted him up and gave him a bear-hug like this burly fisherman had never had even as he continued to sob. They all gathered around, holding one another, blubbering like babies.

Mark Black was quite certain he had closed the casket the night before. He distinctly remembered lowering the body with the crank, carefully arranging the funeral bedding and closing the lid. He remembered turning the lid crank to seal the casket. This wasn't one of those 'I know I did it - it's automatic' things. He clearly remembered looking down at Chris' body and wondering what this man was that so many people had come to pay their respects - that in 10 hours friends could raise enough money for the entire funeral bill. He had looked down at him, lowered him, closed the lid and cranked the latch quite deliberately. But there it was. The lid was open.
"*Maybe I'm losing it... 'Wait a minute,'* he thought, as he rushed over to the dead man's box. *'Oh, no. This can't be. The body's gone! Where'd the body go? What's going on? ... This can't be happening! Someone has stolen the body of this poor soul!'* And he rushed to the funeral home office and called the police. "Yes, officer, that's what I

said. Someone came in during the night and stole a body awaiting burial this afternoon. You've got to get over here right away and find whoever did this and get the body back before 2:00. You can't imagine what this could do to my business. ... No. I don't know who would take a body nor why. All I know is that it's gone and you HAVE to find it. Please come now!"

Pastor Johanson felt honored to be able to host the big event in his church. Kris' friends made it clear that THEY would put the funeral service together and that Mayor McGeorge and Terry Jackson from Sea Gull Harbor would be the main speakers and that he and the other clergy in town would be limited to a three minute slot each.

As you may recall, Kris was a regular attender at each of their churches, attending Sunday on a strange kind of Sunday morning worship marathon schedule. He wasn't quite sure what to say in his three minutes. What can a minster say of any significance in three minutes? Even though he was a minor player in the service, he was honored to have it happen here at St. Eremos Church. Judging from the number of people he had heard visited the funeral home yesterday there should be quite a turn-out. The sexton had put out all the extra chairs they had. He hoped they would be enough.

At 1:30 Johanson was getting a bit anxious. Guests were already starting to arrive and the body wasn't even there yet. And where were those men who insisted that they would be in charge? The Sea Gull Harbor mayor had already arrived. The Congregational minister was there. The Baptist minister was there. The Priest had just pulled up in the parking lot...

By 1:45 the church was already almost full. Still - nobody in charge - no body - nothing. Johanson had the acolytes light the candles. The organist began to play as people chatted or sat in silent meditation. A couple of his church members had taken it upon themselves to direct traffic in the parking lot - cars were lining the street waiting to get in.

By 1:55 Johanson was in a near panic. He was a young minister. He had done exactly three funerals in his entire career and he was sorely aware that those weren't very good. What was he going to do? The church was packed. People were standing because there were no more seats - there must have already been more than 400 people. Every square inch of the sanctuary was filled with human flesh. The fire marshal would have a fit if he were to see this. He should probably talk to one of the other ministers. Maybe they'd know what to do in a situation like this. They all had more experience than he did at this kind of thing, but how would that look? This was HIS church. But what would even *they* do? Black hadn't even delivered the body yet! You can't start the service and then, midway through have the body wheeled in... that's just so not cool.

At 2:00 Johanson rose from his chair on the chancel and came to the microphone. The organist played the final few bars of what she was playing and all grew quiet. He tapped on the microphone to make sure it was on. "Ladies and Gentlemen, I'm sorry to say that the funeral services for Kristoff Yerushaliim will be delayed. The funeral home hasn't brought the remains and the organizers of the memorial service seem to be waylaid. I'm sure we will get underway shortly. Please be patient. Please enjoy Mrs. Carroll on the organ as she plays some wonderful hymns of our faith. We will get underway shortly, I'm sure.

But before he sat down and before Mrs. Carroll had played the first note on the organ, the sanctuary doors burst open and in marched Jesse Johnson and right behind him came Tony Snavely and then Nat Tracy and Campbell Story and Michael St. James and Dale and Gale Dudley. They all gathered on the chancel and each had on the biggest smile you ever saw and everyone wondered what was going on. This was unlike any funeral any of them had ever been to. Johanson and the other ministers stood, almost spontaneously, clearly concerned at the inappropriateness of what they had just seen. Just then the doors burst open again and in marched.... Kris!

Pandemonium broke out. Women fainted. Old men's mouths dropped open. Children cheered. Everybody was talking and shouting and calling to Kris and he just smiled and waved and laughed and was eating it up.

He made his way to the front of the sanctuary. When he got to the chancel he hugged the seven and then he gave hearty handshakes to the ministers - pulling each of them in for a hug as well. People were cheering and weeping and astonishment was everywhere. It was, really, like nothing any of them - or any of us - have ever seen or experienced. The emotion - the power - the wonder - the undiluted joy - was overwhelming.

Kris held up his hands to quiet everyone. But he must have held up his hands half a dozen times over the course of several minutes before any semblance of order came about. And when the people quieted he spoke to them.

"You have now experienced the power of God. You will never forget it for as long as you live. You, gathered here, now believe in the impossible. You, gathered here, believe in God and God's love and magnificence. Truth is revealed to you in a way in which you cannot deny. You have been blessed today! But even more blessed will be your children and your cousins and your elderly parents and you grandkids who have not seen what you have seen but still believe because you have told them. And that is what you must do. You must tell them. You must tell your families and your neighbors and your friends. You must go beyond Telhum and tell anyone who will listen. Will they think you odd for believing in life after life? They may. But that changes nothing. You KNOW! There will be no funeral today. Mrs. Carroll, would you play my favorite hymn - it's on page 66 of the church hymnal - a rousing rendition, if you please - everyone - sing!" And that day, the hymn "To God Be the Glory" was sung like it had never been sung at Mt. Eremos before or since.

    Kris hung around town for another month and a half. He chatted with everyone he met. He seemed to always have this wonderful smile on his face that made everyone happy. During that time Telhum may have just been the happiest place in the nation - perhaps the most joyous place on earth. It was a town full of true believers.

    The news crews never came. People had called them, of course, but they weren't interested, they said, in 'flying saucer' kinds of stories - only facts, thank you. Then one day Kris was simply gone. No one knew where. Maybe back to Inkster. Maybe to other towns. But on the last day anyone saw him the sun shone a bit brighter, the sky was a bit bluer, and spirits were a bit higher.
    - Philip P. Bliss